Museums and Popular Culture

Contemporary Issues in Museum Culture
Series Editors: Susan M. Pearce and Elaine Heumann Gurian

Other volumes in the series

Museums and Popular Culture

KEVIN MOORE

CASSELL

London and Washington

Leicester University Press
A Cassell Imprint
Wellington House, 125 Strand, London WC2R 0BB, England
PO Box 605, Herndon, VA 20172

First published 1997

British Library Cataloguing in Publication Data
A catalogue record for this book is available from the British Library.

ISBN 0 7185 1435 1

Library of Congress Cataloging-in-Publication Data
Moore, Kevin, 1960 –
    Museums and popular culture/Kevin Moore
        p. cm. – (Contemporary issues in museum culture)
    Includes bibliographical references and index.
    ISBN 0-7185-1435-1 (hc)
    1. Museums – Great Britain – Philosophy. 2. Popular culture – Museums – Great Britain. 3. Museum exhibits – Great Britain. 4. Museums techniques – Great Britain. I Title. II Series. AM41. M66 1997
    069'. 0941 – dc20   96-43599
                                                                CIP

Typeset by Pantek Arts, Maidstone, Kent
Printed and bound in Great Britian by
Creative Print and Design Wales, Ebbw Vale, Gwent

Contents

Figures

Preface

This book began as a relatively straightforward analysis of the representation of popular culture in museums. The rationale was that museums were established as temples of high culture, in part to bring the reforming power of the 'highest and best' achievements of our 'civilization' to the 'masses'. In recent years this ideological role of the museum has been revealed and questioned. There has been a move to democratize museums, both in terms of how they interpret high culture and to broaden the subject matter to include the culture and history of all members of society. The rise of social history as a discipline in British museums in particular has enriched museums through the portrayal of everyday life. Yet the representation of popular culture within social history displays has tended, I will argue, to be limited, marginalized or subsumed within a rather bland portrayal of leisure activities. The history in social history museums tends to be rather 'cultureless'. Popular culture has been regarded as an appropriate subject matter for museums in the United States for a little longer, but even here there is little existing literature in this field, reflecting that such developments are relatively recent. A valuable exception is rather limited in its scope (Schroeder, 1981). This book therefore aims to be the first substantial review of what has been achieved so far, and to offer a theoretically informed approach to a fuller, more dynamic and creative portrayal of popular culture.

This approach was therefore premised on the assumption that popular culture was both a suitable and a necessary subject area for museums, that it was somehow socially valuable for museums to do this. This needs to be clearly established rather than simply assumed. Why should museums portray popular culture? In one sense this appears to be a relatively easy question to answer, given the democratizing impulse in museums over the past two decades. However, to justify this development simply on the grounds that public museums have a duty to reflect the history and culture of all members of society only begs further questions. How exactly does society benefit from this? Would it really matter if museums remained largely temples of high culture, or if popular culture remained marginalized within social history? Who would benefit from the changes proposed, and how?

Evaluation of the benefits of developing representations of popular culture in museums proved much more intractable. If the argument was that it would attract new audiences and give them an understanding of their own culture, this only begged the further question of how exactly they benefited from this. If museum staff were pressed on this, it is likely that this would reveal that the benefit is never directly considered, or simply assumed, that somehow museums are 'good' for people, which brings us back dangerously close to the nineteenth-century notion of their 'civilizing' impact. Further probing would be likely to produce the suggestions of educational value, entertainment and political or social awareness. Yet how are we so sure that museums are capable of achieving any or all of these through the representation of popular culture, or any other subject for that matter? Furthermore, I began to question whether or not it was possible that these objectives could be achieved more satisfactorily in other ways, by other organizations. Do people specifically need museums in order to benefit in some way from an understanding of popular culture, or, indeed, any other subject?

This line of thought had therefore brought me to a consideration of the fundamental purpose and value of museums. I increasingly felt that it was essential to find answers to this for my initial brief to remain worthwhile. Rather surprisingly, this proved difficult. The ability of museums to provide a wide range of benefits to society tends to be assumed by those who work in them. Writers and academics who have reflected on the role of museums in society have invaluably probed beneath the surface to reveal the unspoken ideological underpinnings, but fail to address the ultimate question of value, beginning with the premise that museums are valuable institutions, but in need of reform.

Before focusing on the specific area of the relationship between museums and popular culture, I have therefore felt it imperative in this book to begin by addressing the more fundamental questions posed. Only by doing this could I establish the context for considering the role of popular culture. The analysis reveals that the two questions are inextricably linked. If we cannot consider the value of representations of popular culture in museums without considering the purpose of museums, paradoxically it is only by adequately reflecting popular culture, I believe, that museums will gain a fully worthwhile purpose. But this is not a one-sided relationship, for if popular culture gives meaning to the museum, the museum is revealed as the best means by which to understand and interpret popular culture. A final paradox, however, is that in the way that museums need to change to achieve this, they may cease to be museums.

This is not deliberately cryptic, and my aim is to guide the reader through some at times complex issues with as much clarity as possible. The first chapter provides a fuller background to the development of the ideas and questions which lie at the heart of the book, from the notion of popular culture and its relation to museums to the questioning of fundamental purpose. Chapter 2 considers the ultimate value of the museum and evaluates the range of supposed benefits museums can bring to society. The third chapter specifically focuses on the social worth of the interpretation of material culture, the 'real thing', as the core of the value of the museum, concluding that this has yet to be fully developed. Chapter 4 aims to highlight how exactly this might be achieved. Having defined and emphasized the social value of the museum through the as yet unrealized possibilities in the interpretation of material culture, Chapter 5 then focuses on the analysis of museum representations of popular culture thus far, and the opportunities which exist for the future. Chapter 6 explores this by means of a focus on a single artefact of popular culture. The final chapter explores the final paradox that the most effective interpretations of material culture, including and perhaps especially those of popular culture, will be best made in ways which could spell the end of the museum as we know it.

The argument I develop is inevitably coloured by my background and experience in British museums. I would like to think, however, that the key elements of my argument have a resonance for museums in other countries and cultures. Where possible I have included examples from outside the United Kingdom, from North America in particular.

Though I am dealing with a highly visual subject, this volume contains no illustrations. The reason for this comes from a view that the quality of such illustrations, particularly of artefacts, is inevitably rather disappointing in a book, something which only reinforces the value of museums, through their ability to display the 'real thing'! I look forward to the possibility in the not too distant future of producing a version of this book in multimedia form, which would make the use of illustrative material more viable.

I would like to thank all those colleagues in the museum world whose ideas have been helpful in shaping this book. Particular thanks are due to the students and staff of the Department of Museum Studies, for discussions with them have provoked my thinking and given me a sense of purpose. My thanks to Susan Pearce, the series editor, for her guidance and assistance. Thanks go to my daughter Zoë for showing me how we learn about ourselves and our world through material culture. Finally, I would like to thank Nina, my partner, for her comments, which have influenced my argument considerably, and for her support and encouragement.

In memory of my Dad, Robert Edward Moore

1

Museums in an age of paradox

Introduction

Museums and popular culture? Initially this seems to be something of a contradiction. Museums, traditionally at least, have been temples of 'high' culture, a celebration of the extraordinary and the outstanding; whereas popular culture is 'low' culture, the ordinary, the everyday. Museums have acted as the institutions which have defined 'high' culture, and this has necessitated, to a large extent, the deliberate exclusion of the material culture of popular culture. Yet in a postmodern world, where the distinction between 'high' and 'low' culture has been challenged, museums, it is argued, stand revealed as artificial constructions, their fundamental purpose attacked, producing, it is argued, a 'crisis of representation' (Pearce, 1992, p. 241, and Chapter 11 *passim*).

This 'crisis' may be academically clear cut, but it has yet to become so in the day-to-day activities of most museums. There is a growing awareness of the difficulties in establishing and justifying a 'canon' of high culture, and a willingness to broaden the definition of this to reflect the artistic expressions of 'other' cultures. But those that hold the power in museums still tend to define their role as to inspire and educate through the finest expressions of our culture. As long as the definition of this is broadened to include, for example, the work of women artists, and more thoughtful approaches are made to the interpretation of collections to make them accessible to a wider audience, the traditional mission is seen as remaining valid. This has been challenged by a significant movement from within the profession over the past two decades seeking to 'democratize' museums. Opening access to a redefined canon of high culture is seen as only half of this process; equal stress has been placed on the need to redefine the subject matter of the museum to include the lives of the mass of the population, to reflect the ordinary as well as the extraordinary, popular culture alongside high culture. Why should museums necessarily be redefined in this way? Those who seek to do this are taking as much of an ideological position as the traditionalists. Whose ideas offer the best way forward for museums?

Definitions

First it is necessary to establish exactly what is meant by the term popular culture. Tony Bennett, a leading academic writer in the field, has commented that it is an 'infinitely elastic term. ... As soon as you try to put your hand on it, it evaporates' (quoted in Russell, 1990, p. 5). This might not seem very helpful, but if we consider the two elements, 'popular' in itself is difficult enough to define, and is clearly historically contingent (Shiach, 1989, pp. 19–34); and 'Culture is one of the two or three most complicated words in the English language' (Williams, 1988, p. 87). Bennett is not alone among respected writers in the field in eschewing any attempt to define the term accurately, primarily because of the political and historical contingency of what is 'popular', who are the 'people': 'The most that one can do is to point to a range of meanings, a range of different constructions of the relations between popular culture, "the popular" and "the people", which have different consequences for the way in which popular culture is conceived and constituted as a site for cultural intervention.' Popular culture cannot be pinned down because it is an ever-changing part of the political battleground for 'hegemony' (Bennett, 1986, p. 8). This, however, represents just one theoretical approach to popular culture among many. The problem of definition is exacerbated by the fact that popular culture has been explored from a wide range of academic disciplines and theoretical perspectives during the twentieth century. A useful review has concluded that each theoretical approach provides a definition of popular culture consistent with its own theoretical framework: 'popular culture is defined on the basis of the way it is explained and evaluated theoretically', whether this is, for example, mass culture, the Frankfurt School, Gramscian or Althusserian Marxism, feminism, cultural populism, structuralism or postmodernism (Strinati, 1995, p. xviii).

While this can be accepted to a degree, the same point could be made about any term, including 'museum'. What these theories all share is the notion that popular culture is defined not so much by what it is, but by what it is not. Popular culture is whatever is not defined as high culture. Where they differ is in how they perceive that culture to have been created. The multiplicity of approaches to the study of popular culture can be characterized, in simple terms, as adopting one of two fundamental positions. It is viewed either as a mass culture imposed by a culture industry to maintain the power of a ruling elite, or alternatively as a genuine, creative cultural expression from below, a form of consumer subversion in opposition to the dominant ideology (Strinati, 1995, p. xviii).

What is interesting for museums is that many writers on the subject, from whichever academic discipline and theoretical standpoint, who attempt to establish a working (and still essentially contingent) definition, often choose to do so in terms of material culture. Strinati, for example, comments that 'popular culture can be defined descriptively as covering a specific set of artefacts', with the rider that 'Different societies, different groups within societies, and societies and groups in different historical periods can all have their own popular culture' (Strinati, 1995, pp. xvii–xviii; see also Hebdige, 1988, p. 47; Bigsby, 1976, p. vii). Comparatively more academic work on popular culture takes material culture as its focus than in perhaps most other topics within the arts and social sciences, which in general share the wider neglect of material culture as a source in academic research (Pearce, 1992, p. 21).

Plotting popular culture

Although the inevitable contingency in any definition is accepted, this has still to provide a working definition. Which aspects of material culture can be defined as popular culture? The plot of the structure of value developed by Pearce, and used extensively with variations throughout her lengthy discussion of the politics of collecting, seems to offer a solution (Pearce, 1995, p. 291 and Chapters 17–22 *passim*). With the axes masterback piece–artefact, and authentic–non-authentic, spurious, it gives four categories of material, as shown in Figure 1.1. Pearce argues that 'The four quadrants which these two axes create structure most of our (European) ideas of material value' (Pearce, 1995, p. 291). Pearce demonstrates that these values are, however, relative, and change through time, so that objects and collections can be seen to move from one quadrant to another, either upwards or downwards. Furthermore, while at the top of the plot lies the museum, at the bottom lies the rubbish tip, into which many objects fall, either to be destroyed or occasionally to be rescued and revalued. This plot can define the material culture of which popular culture consists. The vertical axis authentic–non-authentic, spurious can be equated to 'high culture'–'popular culture'. The horizontal axis divides popular culture into two kinds of material culture, 'spurious masterpieces'

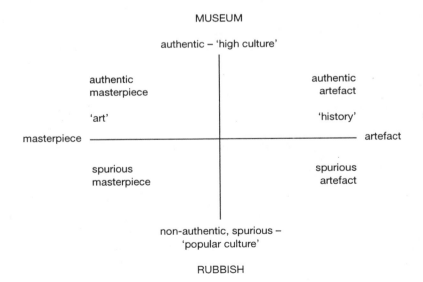

Figure 1.1 *Plotting 'high' and popular culture*
Source: Pearce (1995, p. 291).

and 'spurious artefacts', which can be equated to the division in the theories of popular culture between those which see it as an imposed mass culture (spurious artefacts) and those which see it as a creative cultural expression from below (spurious masterpieces).

The plot not only provides clarity in definition, but also explains graphically why popular culture has been traditionally ignored by museums. If museums exist simply to reflect high culture, even if this involves bringing this to a mass audience, then broadly speaking popular culture is invalid. Material has a place in the museum as high culture, either as an authentic masterpiece (art) or as an authentic artefact (science, history, archaeology etc.). The material culture of popular culture, what we might term 'popular material culture', is considered non-authentic, belonging below the horizontal axis, and not among the 'proper' museum material above. There are two possible minor exceptions to this. If popular culture is viewed as a creative cultural expression from below, in time a few aspects of this culture might be viewed as worthy of being added, on aesthetic grounds, to the canon of high culture, no longer spurious but now redefined as authentic masterpieces, and thus deemed worthy of a place in the museum. Alternatively, if popular culture is viewed as an imposed mass culture, again a few items might eventually be considered worthy of a place in the museum, as a result of the aesthetic quality of their design, which would involve revaluation from spurious artefact to authentic masterpiece.

That the purpose of museums is to reflect high culture alone has been challenged above all by the rise to prominence of social history as a discipline over the past two decades. Social historians, through their concern for 'history from below', have ventured below the horizontal axis of the plot, and revalued a great deal of material culture as historically significant and therefore 'authentic'. However, as we shall see, even social historians have tended to regard many aspects of popular culture as somehow still too 'spurious' to feature prominently in their work. The general picture remains therefore, as discussed in detail in Chapter 5, that representations of popular culture in museums are still in their infancy, and there is still a great deal of resistance.

Why should museums change?

A significant shift in purpose for museums is still therefore required if popular culture is to be taken seriously as a topic in its own right, and not merely a few exceptional aspects included in the museum if their artistic or historical significance can be 'authenticated'. How can this be justified? Why fundamentally should museums more fully reflect popular culture? One might argue that public museums exist for the whole of society, and therefore museums should reflect the history and culture of all. The use of the term popular culture implies that its opposite, high culture, is unpopular, not relating to or appealing to the mass of the population, who fund public museums. Below the horizontal axis of the plot are the mass of objects that the majority of the population use and value in their everyday lives. Seeking to argue that some of this material is either aesthetically or historically significant, and is therefore 'worthy' of museum representation, may be valid up to a point, but it raises all kinds of issues: in the first instance, who decides, and on what criteria? Postmodernists would question whether it is really necessary or even any longer possible to make such judgements. What to one person is art, to another is kitsch, and vice versa. Regardless of this, it is perhaps unnecessary to argue whether popular culture is worthy of its place in the museum as 'art' or 'history'. Given that it is the culture of the majority, it is arguably worth exploring in the museum in its own right. Such material does not need to be 'authenticated', raised above the horizontal axis by the museum, in order to be considered valid subject matter. The subject matter of museums should arguably be material culture and its significance in people's lives in its fullest diversity, not just those fragments which curators deem to be authentic. Instead of imposing a judgement as to what is art and history, and therefore what is not, museums could enable their audience to explore all kinds of material culture, and be provoked into considering for themselves such fundamental questions as: 'Is it art? Is it history? Do such judgements matter? How far is popular culture created or imposed?'

Why necessarily should such an argument hold sway? Who should make such a fundamental decision about the future role of museums? If through the democratizing impulse it is argued that this should be the public, have they been asked whether they would like to see this happen, or demonstrated the desire for this? Even if this was the case, should public opinion today be able to bring about a fundamental shift in the purpose of museums, which carry out their mission 'in perpetuity'? The relation between museums and popular culture thus appears to hinge on more fundamental questions as to the purpose of museums. It cannot be adequately answered until these are addressed. What are museums for? Who should decide this? Why do we need museums at all? And who are 'we'?

It is remarkable how little such fundamental questions have been considered. It is assumed by those working in them that museums are valuable. As a result, much of the effort and resources expended in museums is potentially wasted. Without a consideration of ultimate purpose and value, much museum work seems to me entirely self-fulfilling, only making sense through the ground rules and practices laid down by museums themselves. This is particularly true in the UK, given the strong British cultural and intellectual tradition of empiricism, which militates against a consideration of deeper philosophical issues.

How I got here: reflections on my own experience

It is partly my own experience in museum work over the years which has led me to the view that without a consideration of such issues, museums potentially serve a purpose which is self-defined and therefore of value only in its own terms. A brief consideration of this personal experience will also enable you to identify some of my inevitable personal prejudices and subjectivities. Any book is inevitably a deeply personal work. An awareness of this will, I feel, help you to get as much as possible out of the debates and arguments I seek to explore and develop, and to develop your own thinking beyond mine. In doing this I am influenced by the example of Eric Sotto (1994).

One of the major changes in museums over the past decade or so has been the development of social history, as a subject, in the UK and North America at least. A younger generation of graduates of the new social history in the universities have entered museums, attracted by the possibility of developing people's history outside of an elite academic environment. My background is as a social (and more especially) labour historian as both an undergraduate and postgraduate, influenced above all by E. P. Thompson's landmark *The Making of the English Working Class* (Thompson, 1963), which rescued working people from the 'condescension of posterity' to be seen as the makers of their own history. Before I became employed in museums in 1985, I regarded them as elite institutions that had shown little or no interest in working-class history. Yet I did have a strong belief that the material culture of labour history was worthy of preservation, and became involved in a labour history group in Liverpool, which sought to establish a small volunteer-administered collection, given the apparent lack of interest in the subject by the local museums service. However, in 1985 one of the last acts of the soon to be abolished Merseyside County Council, partly through the lobbying of the labour history group, was to establish a Merseyside Museum of Labour History, under the aegis of Merseyside County Museums. I was eager to be involved in this project, and was lucky enough to be employed as one of three research assistants working with the curator. The museum was successfully established from scratch in just six months – a highly rewarding if hectic introduction to museum work.

When the museum opened in March 1986, the contracts of the three researchers ended, but two of us gained employment on a new project which aimed to record the disappearing social history of the dockland areas of Merseyside (the other researcher went on to the University of Leicester museum studies course). I worked on this community-based project, which was initiated by a sociologist and an economic historian at the University of Liverpool, for over three years. Though the project involved exhibitions at local museums, I had a sense of unease that the other aspects of our work – popular local publications, oral history reunion events, a theatrical performance – all somehow seemed more successful. Yet I now wished to develop a career in museums, from a belief that museums had a duty to reflect the history of ordinary people, not least because they paid for museums through their taxes.

To that end I successfully applied for a place on the postgraduate museum studies course at the University of Leicester, in order, I hoped, to gain a firmer grasp of both the philosophy and practice of museum work

– and to be taken seriously when applying for jobs. The course was my passport to the profession, and did teach me a great deal about museums. I was left, however, with a slight sense of unease that fundamental questions about the purpose and value of museums were not explored. The course began with the assumption that museums were valuable to society – as long as they adopted a far more community-oriented approach. While this was in line with my own philosophy as a labour historian, I was still left with doubts as to whether people's history, and by inference popular culture, needed museums, even if museums seemed to need people's history.

In my first job as a 'proper' museum professional I was too busy most of the time to think about deeper philosophical issues. The early 1990s was a difficult time in most local authority museums in Britain, as the poll tax and cuts in public expenditure began to bite. As an historian of ordinary people I naturally chose to work in just about the grimmest northern working-class town I could find. The council, like many others, had no real notion of why it ran a museum at all, and much of my time was spent trying to get 'bums on seats' – that is, visitors through the doors – to avert the ultimate threat of closure. Inevitably doubts I had as to the need for museums came back. What could I identify as the role of this museum, given that it did not appear to have been clearly formalized? This is not to say that the work my colleagues and myself did was of no value – I am particularly proud of an arts project for people with learning difficulties that we undertook in partnership with the local arts centre (Moore, 1993) – but beyond a vaguely community-oriented approach, the work lacked focus. Further, much if not most of it could have been done elsewhere and by others, such as community arts workers or community historians. The museum and its collection increasingly came to seem like a millstone which prevented me from developing the projects I really wished to! The museum's collection seemed an irrelevance – all I needed was an office with the community arts team and a budget. The multiplicity of demands in the management of the museum and development of community projects meant that I began to head towards burn-out. I began to feel like a headless chicken, roaming around without rhyme or reason, trying to become proactive rather than reactive, but increasingly unsure of what to be proactive about.

I began to feel that perhaps this was all down to my lack of adequate management training. The biggest weakness of the University of Leicester museum studies course was that the management element seemed more geared to the 1960s than the 1990s. When a post of lecturer in museum management in the Department of Museum Studies at Leicester was advertised, I applied for it partly from a belief that this would give me the opportunity to teach myself about effective museum management! And indeed, over the past four years, learning alongside the students to a great extent, I have gained a good deal of knowledge that would have been invaluable to me in my previous position. I have learned the value of mis-

sion statements, strategic plans and performance management, which to
some extent offer answers to the questions of the purpose, role and value
of museums respectively. The mission statement succinctly states the purpose of an organization; a strategic plan outlines what it aims to do;
performance management provides some way of measuring the value of
what has been done (Moore, 1994, pp. 7–9). However, this knowledge in
itself still does not answer the more fundamental questions. These management concepts are self-fulfilling, in the sense that they make sense of a
museum's purpose, role and value in their own terms, but not if any of
these are intrinsically inappropriate. A museum could demonstrably fulfil
its mission and plan, as indicated by its performance measures; but what
if the mission and plan implicitly were of little or no value? They could
include a desire fully to reflect popular culture, but on what grounds
would this ultimately be justified? There is clearly a stage beyond these
management concepts that needs to be considered.

Any answers?

My experience as a curator had led me to question the value of museums
in fundamental terms, and my experience as a lecturer in museum studies
in the field of management had provided only superficial answers. This
coincided with the moment at which my research into museums and popular culture had become stuck on the same basic questions. A literature
search confirmed that such basic philosophical questions have rarely if ever
been considered. The lack of serious academic attention before the 1970s
was not a surprise, in that museum studies largely only developed as a discipline from this decade onwards. Much, if not most, of the literature in
museum studies in turn has been concerned with the practical rather than
the philosophical, the how rather than the why. In the 1980s a theoretically informed critique of museums began to develop, involving both
museologists and academics from other disciplines. These critiques drew
upon a wide variety of approaches, depending on the favourite political
philosophy or philosopher of the author, in part a reflection of wider academic fashions. A strong early strand of critique was post-Marxist, in turn
splintered into a range of individual influences: for example, Althusser
(Meltzer, 1981), Gramsci (Bennett, 1988), E. P. Thompson (West, 1988),
Foucault (Hooper-Greenhill, 1992). This has now been further usefully
broadened to include the influence of structuralist and post-structuralist
(Pearce, 1992) and feminist (Porter, 1988, 1991) approaches, with a particularly strong emphasis on museums and multiculturalism (Karp and
Lavine, 1991; Karp *et al.*, 1992; Kaplin, 1994).

   What these at first apparently heterogeneous works have shared is a
critique of the museum as an ideological construct, a battleground
between competing ideologies, but largely controlled by the dominant
elite. It is this common core that has led such authors to be placed
together, whether willingly or not, under the banner of the 'new museol-

ogy' (see Stam, 1993; Harrison, 1993, for helpful reviews of the by now quite substantial literature). However, much of this 'new museology' has had little impact on the day-to-day work of museums, for a number of reasons: the strong empirical tradition in museum work; because much of this literature is only available in relatively obscure journals; the sometimes impenetrable prose used; and the lack of understanding of the realities of museum work, among those writing from other disciplines, rather than from within museum studies.

Only since the early 1990s has such thinking reached a wider audience than students on museum studies courses, through articles in the more mainstream museum press. Susan Pearce's presidential address for the UK Museums Association conference in 1993 highlighted the postmodern challenge of the new museology: 'The hierarchy of intellectual and aesthetic values that make up the tradition of western high culture is being challenged by a kind of "cultural relativism" in which all things are seen as equal and no firm footing of value or understanding can be established', and proffered that 'This requires a critically reflexive approach to museums and what they can do, and a struggle towards honesty in thought and expression which admits to problems and tries to strip the mystery away from solutions' (Pearce, 1993, pp. 25–7). In the USA, Chapin and Klein in *Museum News* similarly popularized this postmodern museology, arguing that 'These are rough times for the museum world. The security blanket of modernism has virtually unravelled. Diverse constituencies demand a voice, calling for multiculturalism. Budgets are threatened. Even what constitutes "museum" is subject to shifting, fuzzy boundaries. ... Museums inculcate values of the dominant culture. ... Museums create social myths. ... Museums are the repositories of social guilt.' The article concluded: 'Rather than serving to perpetuate dominance, how can museums help us learn to deconstruct and resist dominance?' (Chapin and Klein, 1992, pp. 60–1, 76).

This summarizes a fundamental weakness of this new museology, in that it has offered a convincing critique, but as yet not much of a substantial analysis of a way forward. As Stam has commented,

> In the political sense, the potential mission of museums according to The New Museology is enlarged, even glorified, to include the fostering of social justice. But at the same time, the potential social role of museums seems diminished by the negative tone of New Museology rhetoric. Attempts to define new missions seem riddled by doubts about the possibility of knowing in any meaningful sense, or of communicating effectively, or of presenting a message that is untainted by class or personal interests. (Stam, 1993, p. 275)

Even if the more academic new museology was available to museum staff, it is difficult to see how far it could offer a clear direction. But perhaps it has served its purpose; it has made the critique, and it is now up to those museum workers who agree with this philosophy to develop an appropriate museum practice. There are signs that this is beginning to happen.

This is not the job of academics but of practitioners.

Valuable though this 'new museology' may become in democratizing museum practice, it does not directly seek to address the more fundamental questions that I have posed. Even if it becomes possible to develop a politically correct (in the non-pejorative sense!) museum, is this necessarily desirable? Might not the political analysis of the flawed ideological nature of museums suggest that it would be better to get rid of museums altogether, as outdated vestiges of imperialism, as fundamentally too flawed and beyond redemption? Maybe museums simply cannot 'help us learn to deconstruct and resist dominance'. According to Karp, 'We could argue that the museum is a uniquely Western institution, that exotic objects displayed in museums are only there because of the history of Western imperialism and colonial appropriation, and that the only story such objects can tell us is the history of their status as trophies of imperial conquest' (Karp, 1991, p. 16), though he immediately draws back from what he regards as a 'pessimistic position'. But what then is it about the museum as an institution which means that it is worth democratizing and reforming, including to reflect popular culture in all its forms? This fundamental question remains.

Weil has posed the question as to whether the museum is 'truly a worthwhile institution': 'To those who work in them, it appears all but self-evident that, notwithstanding their temporary shortcomings, museums do make an important contribution to society.' But he then ducks the question: 'Without disputing the museum's claim to worthiness, what these questions will address instead is its relative worthiness. ... Are you really worth what you cost, or merely worthwhile?' (Weil, 1995, pp. 33, 34, 38). Sola writes equally provocatively and wittily about philosophical issues, but again even in his more stimulating pieces, does not directly question ultimate value (Sola, 1992a). Watkins has asked 'Are museums still necessary?', but again essentially this does not seek to establish the ultimate value of museums. It is a defence of a more traditional notion of the function of museums, against what he perceives as a loss of identity, through a drift into new and often inappropriate areas of work: 'Museums are still necessary only when they function as true museums' (Watkins, 1994, p. 25). This is an important debate, which we will return to in Chapter 2, but does not offer a direct answer to the fundamental questions.

Shaw has sought to do this, by considering whether museums are obsolete, on four grounds. The first is that museums were invented in historical circumstances very different to our own, so whether they are of value today cannot simply be assumed: 'had museums not been created when they were, would anyone bother to invent them today?' (Shaw, 1985, pp. 1–4). Second, there are now a wide range of alternative media to explore the past, other than the museum exhibition. Museums do not have a unique role, 'Unless, of course, one returns to the old idea of "real things" having an almost magic effect on those exposed to them. I suspect that there *is* something in this, but it is rather esoteric territory, and is not the way that museums justify their existence.' Third, Shaw argued that society does not seem to place a particularly high value on museums: 'Why are museums *still* so poorly funded? Why do they make contact with so small a sector of the population, why do they still have such a poor public image, or why have they never developed a philosophy of what they do?' Finally, he considered whether it could be that 'there are other organisations better fitted to meet the needs which museums purport to serve? ... other organisations are taking on the roles, techniques and themes which public museums have considered to be their exclusive preserve', whether private collectors, local history groups, preservation societies or heritage centres.

Some of this reflects the concerns of the time, the mid-1980s, when museums felt under threat from the rise of the 'heritage industry'. Since then museums have improved their public profile, in part by taking on board many of the features of the competing heritage centres. However, the questions remain highly pertinent, and we shall return to many of the issues raised. Shaw, however, failed to offer any answers: 'Are we perpetrating some terrible con by not letting on that they are obsolete? Or could it be that there is a need for museums, a need which no other medium can meet? I hope so.'

In order to make sense of the relationship between museums and popular culture, it therefore became clear that in this book I would first have to address the fundamental questions of the purpose and value of museums. It is necessary to establish why museums are worth having at all, before it is possible to consider whether the representation of popular culture is a key part of this. Yet here lies a paradox, in that it may be that museums can only adequately justify their value to society if they do represent popular culture. What follows is an attempt to unravel this paradox.

This is not simply an academic exercise. I arrived at these questions and this paradox as a result of contradictions and uncertainties in my own practical museum experience. Hence this book aims not merely to provide an answer to the broader philosophical questions – 'Do we need museums?', 'Why do we need them?' – but also to tackle the practical results of such an analysis: 'What kind of museums do we therefore need?' I am seeking not only to interpret museums, but also to change them. I see no point in an academic discussion of the role of museums without seeing this through to a consideration of how museum practice could concretely be improved. As I am now no longer a museum practitioner, but a museologist, I can only do this by influencing museum workers. This book therefore attempts to bridge the gap between the theoretical works of academic museologists and other academic writers on museums, and the other, highly practical strand of museum literature, from a belief that both are diminished by separation from the other. Works on museum practice without a theoretical foundation are of limited value, because they fail to answer the ultimate 'why' questions: 'Why should we do it this way?' Equally, the value of the works of a theoretical nature has been limited because they do not adequately attempt to address the implications for museum practice. I subscribe to the view that there is nothing as practical as a good theory. This book is aimed to be academically rigorous, but not purely academic. The audience I am writing for is anyone with an interest in museums, but specifically those working in them. The success of my efforts in writing this book depends on whether the ideas within it influence, provoke or challenge the thinking and ultimately the practice of museum staff.

2

Museums don't matter?

There is a serious crisis of institutional identity and a crisis of concept. ... The truth is, we do not know any more what a museum institution is.   *(Sola, 1992a, pp. 102, 106)*

Introduction

Do we need museums, and if so, why? What and who are museums for? We cannot answer such questions unless we know exactly what a museum is. Surprisingly, perhaps, we lack a single internationally accepted definition of a museum, with significant variations between those of the International Council of Museums (ICOM), the Museums Association (MA) of the United Kingdom and the American Association of Museums (AAM) (see figure 2.1, derived from Ambrose and Paine, 1993, p. 8). The AAM definition, for example, is both broader in terms of the institutions it covers and more detailed interms of the functions and purposes.

Figure 2.1 Definitions of 'museum'

Museums Association, United Kingdom (MA)
A museum is an institution which collects, documents, preserves, exhibits and interprets material evidence and associated information for the public benefit.

International Council of Museums (ICOM)
A non-profit-making, permanent institution, in the service of society and its development, and open to the public, which acquires, conserves, researches, communicates and exhibits, for the purpose of study, education and enjoyment, material evidence of man and his environment.

American Association of Museums (AAM)
A non-profit permanent, established institution, not existing primarily for the purpose of conducting temporary exhibitions, exempt from federal and state income taxes, open to the public and administered in the public interest, for the purpose of conserving and preserving, studying, interpreting, assembling, and exhibiting to the public for its instruction and enjoyment objects and specimens of educational and cultural value, including artistic, scientific (whether animate or inaminate), historical and technological material. Museums thus defined shall include botanical gardens, zoological parks, aquaria, planetaria, historical societies, and historic houses and sites which meet the requirements set forth in the proceeding sentence.

Some have commented that it is too restrictive to attempt to reduce museums to a single definition of function and purpose. Weil has contended that 'differences of scale, discipline, audience, history, ideology, format, financing, context and purpose – must far exceed whatever elements they have in common ... we have too often chosen to ignore the very rich ways in which museums differ and to focus instead on their thin margin of overlap' (Weil, 1990, p. xiv), and that 'museums are not like a set of Russian dolls nested one inside another and all alike except for their scale' (Weil, 1990, p. 31). Kavanagh similarly comments on how museums vary significantly in differing cultural and political contexts (Kavanagh, 1994, p. 3). Even if this is accepted, if we are to call all such institutions museums, there has to be an ultimate core which they all share, or they are not all museums. The definitions of ICOM, the AAM and the MA share a common core, which is arguably best encapsulated by that of the MA: 'A museum is an institution which collects, documents, preserves, exhibits and interprets material evidence and associated information for the public benefit.'

A definition is not the same as a statement of purpose or 'mission statement'. In the absence of this, 'there is only an uneasy consensus on the underlying purpose of museums' (Middleton, 1990, p. 13). A mission statement for museums as a sector would be invaluable, for it would address the key questions I have posed: what is unique about what museums do, why exactly it is worth doing this and who benefits from this. This would be as difficult an exercise as establishing a common definition has proved to be, but is an essential undertaking. This has been attempted for the independent museum sector in the UK, but the resulting statement appears to offer little or no improvement upon the MA's definition (Middleton, 1990, p. 14). To a degree the MA's definition contains the elements of a mission statement, as it identifies the unique role of the museum, and defines those who benefit as the public in general; but it fails to consider why ultimately this is worth doing. In framing a mission statement, non-profit organizations are encouraged to consider the notion of 'organized abandonment'. If what your organization offers is no longer of value, or is provided in a better way by someone else, the organization should either take an entirely new direction, or decide to abandon its mission and disband itself (Wolf, 1990, p. 19). How do museums stand up to such a test? This chapter seeks to answer this by developing a mission statement for museums, in part by deconstructing the MA definition of museums.

Which public?

Who are museums for? This might at first glance appear an unnecessary question to ask. We tend to assume that museums are for everyone, yet it is only public museums which seek to serve all of society: private, university, regimental and independent museums, for example, are perfectly at liberty to identify a particular market. If the majority of museums, as public institutions, aim to attract as wide an audience as possible, how far do they succeed? Although there have been a number of national studies to quantify this, interpreting the results is fraught with difficulties. The statistics can be twisted to support almost any position. Those keen to play up the significance of museums can point to an *estimated* 110 million visits per year in the UK (Davies, 1994a). Yet research has also suggested that around 20 per cent of the population in the UK never visit museums at all, only about 50 per cent visit at least one museum or gallery in a year and a mere 2 per cent visit 11 or more times (Merriman, 1989, 1991). All this begs the question of what would be a level of success for museums to achieve in this respect. Is it reasonable to expect even public museums to attract everyone in society on a regular basis, however this is defined? Should we not accept that some people will never be interested in visiting museums? This does not necessarily mean that such people think that public funds should not be used to support museums.

If public museums cannot be expected to appeal to everyone in equal measure, any more than other public institutions, they do have a duty to serve all sections of society, in terms of equal opportunities. A major survey concluded that 'Demographic profiles of visitors to museums do not reflect profiles of the general population. The sort of people who are more likely to visit them are the better-educated and the better-off, and those who are less likely to do so are the less well-off, particularly the retired and the unemployed' (Merriman, 1989, p. 156). A recent interpretation of a range of survey material has indicated that visitors and users are drawn from a wider social spectrum than this suggests (Davies, 1994a), but the statistics still show that museums do not appeal equally to all social classes. Art galleries considered in isolation appear to attract an even more socially elite audience (Schuster, 1995). Ethnicity, elderly age and disability have also been revealed as significant factors in non-visitation (Hooper-Greenhill, 1994, Chapter 3). There is no doubt that, for whatever reason, public museums are as yet not adequately fulfilling their mission to serve all sections of society equally.

Why have the public never been directly asked whether they wish to have museums at all? What benefits do the public see themselves as receiving from museums? Do they wish to receive these benefits? Even if they do, how far do they perceive that they can receive these benefits elsewhere? How satisfied are the public with museums? Given the choice, would the public prefer that their taxes are spent on public museums or something else? What would attract those that currently do not visit to come to museums? If museums reflected popular culture more fully, would this attract more visitors? Museums have generally acted on the assumption that there is no need to ask such fundamental questions, perhaps from a fear that it might be disturbing or even dangerous to do so. The marketing research that has been undertaken into the penultimate of these questions has drawn a rather depressing picture of the image of museums among non-visitors and even many visitors (Fisher, 1990;

London Museums Consultative Committee, 1991). Other research has drawn far less negative conclusions about public attitudes to museums, but disturbingly for history curators, suggested that only 7 per cent of the public regarded visiting a museum as the most enjoyable way of finding out about local history (Merriman, 1991, p. 120).

What public benefit?

What benefits do museums seek to provide to the public? There has been little discussion of this in any depth. The MA definition and its accompanying explanatory notes do not elaborate upon 'public benefit', beyond a recognition that museums are 'the servants of society'; the ICOM definition gives 'study, education and enjoyment'; and the AAM 'instruction and enjoyment'. Ambrose has commented that 'museums provide cultural and social, economic and political benefits to their communities which support them ... what museums do goes a long way beyond a simple functional description' (Ambrose, 1993, p. 8). Similarly, a report by the Museums and Galleries Commission (MGC) in the UK, *Museums Matter*, which sought to make the case for museums, contended that 'By explaining history, and the rationale behind the physical and scientific world, museums help millions of people to understand life better and enjoy it more ... the museum is an important focus, a centre for the community, a reflection of civic pride and a sign of self-respect, a place for refreshment and enjoyment, a place of potential delight' (MGC, 1992, p. 9). Museums are thus claimed to provide a very wide range of benefits to the public, but in not very precise terms. Weil has argued that 'We need to be able to define the purposes for which a museum deals with its public in far finer and more precise ways than we thus far have' (Weil, 1990, p. 64).

The range of benefits claimed to be provided by museums can be broadly categorized as falling under one of four headings: scientific and technological, economic, social or political. The following analysis considers each in turn, to evaluate the relative significance of each.

'Museum collections are important sources of knowledge and information, the proper study of which by staff and researchers contributes greatly to advancement in both arts and the sciences. They also provide support in the practical application of a range of other activities, e.g. environmental health, planning services, medical and forensic research' (MA, 1991, p. 7). While this is undoubtedly an important contribution to society, stressing the public benefit of museums in this sense does not make for a strong argument: 'if museums were to be presented essentially as centres for scholarship, the competing claims of universities and research centres might be difficult to overcome' (Weil, 1990, pp. 28–9). This is a subsidiary benefit that museums provide, rather than the core of their purpose.

In recent years a great deal of emphasis has been placed on the positive economic impact of museums, in creating jobs, attracting tourists and day-trippers, and playing a part in bringing further investment to economically deprived areas (Audit Commission, 1991, p. 13; Ambrose and Paine, 1993, pp. 10–11). The research of Myerscough has been particularly significant in fostering economic arguments for supporting the arts generally, including museums. Myerscough argues that jobs are created not just in museums and arts organizations themselves: this also results in a boost to ancillary service industries, particularly shops, restaurants and hotels. He concludes that 'The arts are a cost-effective means of job creation. The arts were a cheaper way to create extra jobs than other forms of public sector revenue spending' (Myerscough, 1988, p. 149), in that the subsidy of public money per job was lower. This report has been used by some local authorities to help justify increased expenditure in museums and the arts.

However, Myerscough's conclusions have been seriously challenged by two economists, who have made a detailed study of the economic impact of one museum in particular: the North of England Open Air Museum at Beamish (hereafter Beamish) (Johnson and Thomas, 1991, 1992). Their detailed analysis led them to conclude that the museum had created 156 jobs in direct employment, and about 100 additional jobs in associated activities, and others created indirectly as a result of the museum, giving a gross employment figure of 256. However, they argued that account had to be taken of jobs lost elsewhere as a result of tourist and leisure expenditure at Beamish being diverted from other attractions and businesses in the north-east. Calculating 'diverted jobs' is complex and cannot be entirely accurate, but they conclude that in the region this figure is 195 jobs, giving net employment for Beamish as 256 – 195 or just 61 jobs. If a larger geographical area than the north-east of England was taken, then the diverted jobs figure would be even higher (Johnson and Thomas, 1991, pp. 113–16).

Johnson and Thomas proceed to criticize Myerscough's optimistic findings, arguing that it is 'crucial to note that the Myerscough study seems to ignore the diversion issue, yet an elaborate case for more support for the arts is built', but clearly many jobs created in one place are lost in another: 'employment ... is unlikely to be the major consideration in justifying the operations of museums'. They are also sceptical about whether museums are well placed to provide wider economic benefits: 'if subsidies for museums and the arts are viewed as a method of stimulating economic activity and employment in an area then the cost-effectiveness of such spending must be compared with other methods of achieving the same goals. It is quite possible that public assistance to shopping centres, sports facilities or rock concerts might produce larger returns' (Johnson and Thomas, 1991, pp. 117–19).

Weil has similarly argued that using the economic argument as the key benefit provided by museums, as some have done, may actually be dangerous: 'Consider ... the museum improvident enough to base its case for public support on an economic study that quantifies its value to the community in terms of tourism, jobs and purchasing power. What will justify the continuing public investment in such an institution when some other entity (a sports team, a theme park, a rock concert amphitheater) can demonstrate that – for a similar public investment – an even greater economic impact might be achieved?' (Weil, 1995, p. 36).

If the economic benefits argument is ultimately unhelpful, surely we are on stronger ground with the social? Bold claims are made for the social benefits of the museum – for example, 'In a very real sense museums enhance the quality of people's lives' (Ambrose and Paine, 1993, p. 9) – but rarely, if ever, is any evidence provided to prove this or identify it more precisely. The social benefits can be further broken down into: community identity, education, and leisure and entertainment.

'Museums have a key task to play in providing an understanding of identity and a sense of belonging to a place or community. In the face of immense and often painful cultural change in many countries, museums can provide a valuable sense of connection with the past and present, and serve as a springboard for the future' (Ambrose and Paine, 1993, p. 3). Much has been made of the community role of museums in recent years, to the point where it has become a cliché to use the phrase community-oriented service, and indeed use of this fashionable term has often concealed a lack of any significant change in the museum's relationship with the community. 'Community' is a much over-used and ill-defined concept by museums (Tucker, 1993, p. 7). Where museums have attempted to work with the community to develop a local identity, it is difficult to prove their success: 'The most difficult factor in evaluating such an approach is how to measure success. It is not quantifiable in terms of numbers of visitors or income generated, but rather in the feel of the museum' (Bott, 1990, p. 28–30). In any case other institutions – community centres, religious centres and particularly successful local football teams – can equally be said to play a key role in developing local identity and pride. This benefit of museums should not be overplayed, as it is far from unique. Where a sense of community identity is identified as needing to be developed by a local council, why should a museum be the first thing that springs to mind? There is also the danger that fostering a strong local identity, through a museum or any other agency, could create an 'us' and 'them' hostility against the rest of the world. Some communities perhaps need to lose a little of their closed identity! This is reflected in the MA's view of the social role of museums: 'Museums foster a sense of identity with, and pride in, the community. They also help to develop cross-cultural understanding and appreciation of other people's customs and history' (MA, 1991, p. 7). This latter purpose of museums is also one of the three key strands of the influential American Association of Museums report, *Excellence and Equity* (AAM, 1992). While museums have not had a strong track record in the past, a significant number are now taking up the challenge both to serve a multicultural audience and to educate around these issues. The *Excellence and Equity* report sees this as a key element of the educational purpose of museums.

'Through the provision of both formal and informal learning resources, museums fulfil a vital educational role which meets the needs of all ages and which caters for all levels of attainment' (MA, 1991, p. 7). Great emphasis has been placed in recent years on the educational value of the museum, to the point of almost stressing education as the key function. Much excellent education work of social value is carried out in museums, but paradoxically the expansion of education carries a danger: 'some museums have begun to stress general educational objectives as the principal outcome for which they ought to be valued. By doing so, they may ultimately leave themselves vulnerable to the claims of more traditional educational institutions that these latter could, with only a little inexpensive tinkering, deliver a comparable value at a fraction of the cost' (Weil, 1995, p. 36).

A rather traditional variant on the educational benefits is the ability of museums to provide 'inspiration': 'Museums and galleries offer people a chance to encounter and be moved by the great works of human imagination and creativity in the arts and sciences' (MA, 1991, p. 7). This stresses what museums uniquely have to offer, but assumes that they have this effect, and that this is something that the public desire.

While museum staff eagerly press the community identity and educational benefits, market research suggests that although the public are aware at least of the latter, as strong in their motivation to visit are the leisure and entertainment aspects. Museum visiting tends to be a social activity, 'combining looking at something interesting while enjoying the company of people whom we enjoy being with' (Davies, 1994a, pp. 65–6). Yet if museums are therefore clearly part of the leisure and entertainment industry, this again carries dangers. For if museums seek to compete directly with other forms of leisure activities on these grounds alone they risk being caught in a race they cannot win. Museums cannot compete head-to-head with Disneyland. If museums overstress entertainment they run the risk of losing their public subsidies; and would the public be willing to pay theme park prices for a museum? (see Dickenson, 1994, p. 112).

Clearly museums do provide social benefits, but as much in the sense of a leisure activity, as in educational or community roles, and perhaps more so than most museum staff appreciate. There are also dangers in over-emphasizing any of the three sources of benefit outlined.

The emphasis on museums playing a key social role in community development and multicultural awareness has been successfully promoted, largely by younger members of the museum profession, in the USA and the UK in particular, to the point where it has become enshrined, as we have seen, in key documents of the AAM and MA. This, however, has not been without its critics, who accuse the proponents of such developments of stepping over from a social into a political role. The editors of the journal *Museum Management and Curatorship* are particularly critical of the changes encompassed by *Excellence and Equity*: 'museums have entered the political arena as agents of community development and social change', but this political agenda is unwanted and unhelpful: 'politically motivated sociologists have hijacked the museums ... Excellence and Equity will actually undermine the existing pluralism represented by a wide diversity of small, independent institutions with differing agendas, and ... will tend to replace them with amorphous multicultural entities which are hag-ridden by political correctness', which 'can corrupt society as efficiently as any of the dogmas of the Marxist-Leninist states' (Editorial, 1994, pp. 125–8). Many would dismiss this as reactionary and unhelpful. Yet it is quite clear that the authors are right to state that to promote community development and social change through multicultural awareness and education is a political stance. It might be the one that many people in museums now espouse, but it is none the less a political one.

This debate highlights the fact that all museums are implicitly political institutions, that objective neutrality is impossible – not just in the more blatant examples of the propaganda museums of the former Eastern bloc, but also through the more subtle ideology implicit in the museums of the Western capitalist nations. Those who argue for change are aware of this lack of neutrality: 'museums have never been nor can they be neutral spaces, they can become public arenas, settings for examining civil society, in which the histories and creations of particular groups are represented for debate and reflection' (Karp and Lavine, 1993, p. 84), but equally this reflects a further political choice. The editors of *Museum Management and Curatorship* concur that neutrality is 'largely illusory', but ask what was wrong with the previous scenario, where 'the very differences within the museum community ensured that somewhere within it, most viewpoints could be accommodated and fostered. Individual museums might be narrow in their outlooks, but overall their variety, combined with the invitation to found new museums with new agendas, provided the mechanism needed to accommodate the constantly changing museum needs of the community' (Editorial, 1994, p. 125). Implicitly, however, this is also a political choice, a call for a return to a more mainstream Western liberal notion of museum development, as opposed to a more radical agenda.

Museums therefore cannot escape politics; even if they claim to eschew a political stance, they inherently have one in supporting the status quo (Pearce, 1992, Chapter 11, for a detailed discussion). Museums have not become political; the issue has been revealed because a more radical political outlook is increasingly voiced in museums. By examining issues such as racism and sexism museums are not becoming political, but widening and developing the political issues that museums engage with, issues which for too long museums have ignored. And clearly there are many important social and political issues museums are only just beginning to address: 'We live in a dangerous time of anomie, a time of severe environmental deterioration, of grinding poverty with class and ethnic violence erupting across the globe. There is no shortage of worthy social issues for us to participate in' (Sullivan, 1993, p. 70).

However, two important questions in particular arise from this. First, which political stance should museums take on such issues, if we accept that they have no choice but to engage with them? Young curators seek to push forward a radical agenda, but how viable is this if it is not shared, by either the community the museum serves, or, perhaps even more importantly, the governing body which funds the museum? If, for example, you are a Labour-voting curator working for a Conservative-dominated council, elected by local people, then surely the politics of the museum must reflect your paymasters: both the politicians and the taxpayers. The radicalization of museums in the USA in recent years may have usefully raised key issues and challenged myths and stereotypes, but because it is out of step with government and funders and broad public opinion, it has left museums open to charges of 'arrogance, elitism and political correctness'. 'The past few years have seen the museum profession buffeted by unfavourable public attention and media coverage, governmental scrutiny, funding uncertainties, and a politically charged enquiry into the role of museums in American society' (Bunch, 1995, p. 33).

Are museums an appropriate political battleground? And if we accept that they are, those of a radical perspective must accept that there will be many defeats, at a time of rising reaction in the USA in particular. Or do we fall back on the liberal notion that museums should aim to be neutral, offering a range of political perspectives to allow visitors to make a choice?

These are difficult but important questions, which lie outside the scope of this study to resolve; the key point for this argument is that it is not easy to see how a museum can convey benefits to the public through an engagement in political issues. How far can any museum have a political impact, and how on earth could this be measured? The impact a museum can make in the lives of disadvantaged people has, I would argue, tended to be exaggerated. What evidence is there to suggest that those living in a deprived inner-city area see a museum as offering any kind of solution to their problems? Museums would surely come way down the list of desired improvements to any disadvantaged area. People may visit, use and enjoy the museum, but given a choice between a museum, a new school wing or a hospital ward, what would they be likely to choose?

Yet some politically radical curators seem to believe that their work can make a significant contribution to improving the lives of disadvantaged people. While it may make some contribution, there is no doubt that other work is far more directly valuable in bringing about social improvement. Museum work is not a form of social work! As Tucker has commented, to assume that community museum projects 'really make a difference to their subjects is a delusion, and moreover, an insult to real social workers, police officers, teachers and housing officers who strive to make a material contribution to the quality of people's lives, often at no little danger to themselves' (Tucker, 1993, p. 7). Moreover, there is a danger that left-leaning museum staff are being used to fulfil a right-wing government agenda, without realizing this. Museums in the UK are successfully bidding for funding for projects in deprived inner-city areas:

These rather dubious central government funded initiatives are in the main cosmetic, the aim of which is to provide 'bread and circuses' to some of the people who are unfortunate enough to live in areas of economic deprivation. Sending a handful of earnest, liberal-minded middle-class museum curators out into [the inner cities] is a hell of a lot cheaper than spending real money on jobs and infrastructure. There's nothing like a nice display, prepared and organised for and by working-class people and mounted in a high profile museum to give the impression that things are getting better.

(Tucker, 1993, pp. 6–7)

Museum projects of this kind, far from improving the lives of the disadvantaged, may just be papering over the cracks, actually helping to mask deprivation. Indeed, they have sometimes been seen as such, patronizing and unnecessary, by some in the community. One radical black group in the 1970s described neighbourhood museum projects as 'more white-oppressive culture doing an imperialist thing' (Robbins, 1971, p. 67). A further point is that resources attracted to such museum projects are lost from housing, education or employment schemes. Museums cannot be apolitical, and they can help to enable their users to understand the world in a political sense, but they are not useful vehicles for directly bringing about political or social change. If you want to change the world, become a politician, not a curator ... or maybe not.

Museums can provide some technological, economic, social and political benefits, but these have tended to be exaggerated. The profile of museums by the 1960s had become poor, and they did need to improve their status and image by becoming more socially relevant. But in the process the benefits of museums have been oversold, and promises made that cannot be delivered. The danger of this is that funders and the public will see that the benefits that museums claim to provide can be delivered more cost-effectively and directly by other agencies. Museums have begun to compete in a wide range of fields – for example, economic development, tourism, heritage, leisure, entertainment, education, community work – but, as Hatton terms it, 'are museums trying, by force of financial necessity to compete in the wrong race(s)?' (Hatton, 1994, p. 143), are they entering races with competitors they simply cannot win?

Furthermore, in pushing (or being pushed by funders) to compete in one or more of these races, museums are often ceasing to be museums. Museums which stress research become more like universities; museums in the tourism race become visitor centres; museums in the heritage and/or entertainment race become Disney-style rides; museums in the education race become children's hands-on science centres; museums in the community race become community centres. There is no intrinsic problem with this, if these new organizations provide public benefits, provided it is recognized that they are no longer museums as such, or are at least an extreme hybrid form. One should simply accept that to survive in these races museums have to become what they are competing with – and hence they do not survive as museums.

Defending museums *as* museums

If we believe in their value, then we must defend museums as publicly beneficial institutions *as* museums: 'If museums cannot assert their importance *as* museums, then museums may not be perceived as important at all' (Weil, 1995, p. 36). Too much as a profession we seem to have lost confidence in the very specific benefits of museums. Museums do not just provide benefits to the public; they provide them through a very specific mechanism: 'collecting, documenting, preserving, exhibiting and interpreting material evidence and associated information'. If this mechanism is no longer seen as valuable, if we no longer believe that we can provide educational or other benefits through these activities in relation to material culture, then the museum is dead.

What lies at the heart of this lack of confidence in the museum as a museum among many younger curators (particularly, as we shall see, social historians) is a lack of faith in the value of material culture. This is explored more fully in Chapter 3, where it is challenged head-on, and the value of material culture in museum work is reasserted, but not in the problematic traditional manner. Ambrose, in his guide to establishing new museums, argues that those who are interested in interpreting the cultural or natural history of a place or area too often jump to the conclusion that the development of a museum is the only way to meet such an aim. He stresses that it might be, but it may well not be: 'Quite often an alternative approach can be more appropriate and more cost-effective', and he gives a number of examples, including 'a series of leaflets, a pictorial history book ... a video, an educational resource pack ... a festival. ... A museum may not be the relevant medium for your purposes at all!' (Ambrose, 1993, pp. 8–9). These are laudable alternatives to museums: the paradoxical problem is that in many museums, these are too often the methods which are now used. The very essence of a museum is being denied. For museums are not museums if they are not centrally about material culture.

Ideas from strategic management and marketing are helpful. Hatton has considered the concept of 'critical resources': 'Only very few resources are critical in the sense that they can differentiate you from the competition. The resource has to be unique' (Wernerfelt, quoted in Hatton, 1994, p. 141). What unique resource do museums have, that no one else has? This needs to be identified, so that museums can be sure that they are competing in the right 'race'; that is, one they can 'win' or survive and prosper in, for 'You cannot expect superior performance in a fair race against equals. Instead, you need to look for races where you have an advantage' (Wernerfelt, quoted in Hatton, 1994, p. 143).

So what exactly is the 'critical resource' of museums? This has never been adequately defined. At first glance it would appear to be the collections of material culture and associated information they hold, 'The objects museums hold in trust for the public are ... what distinguishes them from other cultural institutions' (AAM, 1984, p. 35). Weil has argued that the growing number of museums that have moved away from a strict focus on material culture, 'so-called single subject museums – story-centred rather than object-centred ... relying on ... "theatrical constructs" instead of ... a "giant cabinet of curiosities approach"', run the risk of being seen as 'uncompetitive':

> The experiential outcome at which these museums aim may eventually (as soon, perhaps, as the widespread advent of virtual reality) be accomplishable by other ... less costly means. The museum that casts its aspirations in such nontraditional terms cannot complain of 'apples and oranges' when it finds itself unexpectedly measured against organizations of other kinds that can provide a comparable value at a far lower cost.   Weil, 1995, pp. 36–7)

Thus in denying material culture as the 'critical resource', such museums have drifted into races they cannot successfully compete in.

In defining the critical resource in these terms, it is necessary to clarify exactly what is meant by 'material evidence'. In the MA definition, '"Material" indicates something that is tangible, while "evidence" guarantees its authenticity as the "real thing".' 'Evidence' therefore begs the question as to evidence of what. The material that is of value to the museum depends on what it regards as 'authentic', which relates to the plot developed by Pearce, discussed in Chapter 1. 'Material', as something which is tangible, can be defined as something that has substance, is capable of being touched. What limits are placed on material beyond this? I have used the terms material evidence and material culture interchangeably. Material culture has been taken by some to mean everything that has been affected by humankind, including the landscape, plant and animal species, even the manipulation of flesh and air which produces song and speech, so that 'the whole of cultural expression ... falls within the realm of material culture' (Pearce, 1992, pp. 4–5, 1995, pp. 13–14).

The AAM definition reflects this much broader definition to an extent, defining the material of interest as 'objects and specimens of educational and cultural value, including artistic, scientific (whether animate or inanimate), historical and technological material'. As a result, 'museum' is a much wider term in the USA, including botanical gardens, zoological parks, aquaria and historic sites. Elsewhere, material evidence or material culture is taken to mean 'objects', 'those discrete lumps capable of being moved from one place to another' (Pearce, 1992, p. 5). In Chapter 7 we will consider whether the broader US definition is valuable, in avoiding an artificial distinction between different kinds of material culture, between museums as understood in the UK and other organizations in the field. But the analysis up to that point will remain concerned with material culture, and thus museums, as defined by the MA and ICOM.

It is not the holding of collections of material evidence alone which is the 'critical resource' of museums, given the popularity of collecting in society; nor the ownership of incomparable collections of high culture, given the quality of many private collections. The 'critical resource' of the museum, I would argue, is the expertise in collecting, documenting, preserving, exhibiting and interpreting material evidence: 'Museum collections are a mere physical substance of the wisdom for which they stand' (Sola, 1991, p. 131). As vital a part of the package, therefore, as the material evidence, is the 'associated information', 'the knowledge which prevents a museum object being merely a curio, and also includes all records relating to its past history, acquisition and subsequent usage' (explanatory notes of MA definition, quoted in Ambrose and Paine, 1993, p. 8). Yet museums seem to have lost sight of or confidence in this critical resource, increasingly unsure of the value that can be derived from material evidence. What this reflects is that too much of the material evidence in museums does not have adequate associated information. For much of the collections this reflects curatorial practice in the past. But even in contemporary practice, the feeling remains that the associated information gathered is still too limited. Partly this is a reflection of museums trying to collect too many objects with too few resources.

If museums were to regain confidence in their 'critical resource', and re-enter the race they define themselves and therefore can 'win', this is not enough. This 'critical resource' is museums' key 'feature', but this needs to be put across to the public as the key 'benefit', to use basic marketing concepts. The key 'benefit' is the 'USP' – the 'unique selling proposition' – what museums offer to the customer or user that no one else can. Hatton questions how far museums have stressed this to the public: 'Does the public (or for that matter, the museum profession itself), fully understand and appreciate the differences between those potential competitors and the unique services museums claim to offer? ... Perhaps museums have failed to inform the public sufficiently for them to see there is a difference?' (Hatton, 1994, p. 142).

Museums have gone further than this, by confusing the public that their competitors are the same as themselves. In doing this museums are conniving in their own defeat. Watkins gives the example of the science education centres for children, which contain little or no material culture, but which the museum world in both the USA and the UK has validated through accreditation and registration. If such centres are allowed to become museums, what does it any longer mean to be a museum, in the eyes of the public? 'By blurring our understanding of what museums really are, we open the field up to the assaults of the business world' (Watkins, 1994, pp. 28–9).

Museums are faced with two choices: either to accept that the USP of museums is no longer viable, and adopt another (and in the process cease to be museums); or to reinvigorate the existing USP through a new self-confident approach, which makes it clear to the public how exactly they can benefit from what museums very specifically do.

Some may feel that this is far too constrictive a role for the museum, as we shall see, but in pursuing other roles, museums cease to be museums. This is fine – as long as it is recognized – but also presupposes that the traditional role of museums is invalid or outdated, something I will argue strongly against in Chapter 3. We need to identify and stress to the public the benefit of museums, not choose our public benefit first, and then alter the museum to suit, to a point where it is no longer a museum.

So how do the public benefit exactly from the collection, documentation, preservation, exhibition and interpretation of material evidence? The discussion of 'public benefit' earlier in the chapter looked at generalities which were not clearly linked to, and derived from, these functions. So how can we proceed? One approach is to consider the value of each function, before we consider the overall 'package'.

What benefits are derived from collecting, documenting, preserving, exhibiting and interpreting such material evidence? Some have suggested other terms to encompass these basic museum functions. For example, Davies has proposed that museums are concerned with guardianship (collecting, care and interpretation) and access (communication and education) for a social purpose (Davies, 1994b). Weil, influenced by van Mensch, has focused on preservation (presupposing collection), study and communication (combining exhibition and interpretation), again strongly stressed as being for a social purpose (Weil, 1990, pp. 57–65).

Davies and Weil are right to stress the social purpose, and the degree to which museums have endangered themselves by failing to stress this sufficiently in the past, yet they both fail to explore further what exactly that social benefit is. Their suggestions as to the functions (aside from changing exhibition and interpretation into communication) appear unnecessary. There seems no intrinsic problem in the functions outline in the MA definition – the problem with them is that they have not been sufficiently connected to a social purpose – 'collecting, preserving, documenting and communicating material evidence and associated information' has not been adequately linked to 'public benefit'. Let us now consider each of these functions in turn to assess their value to the overall USP.

Collecting is not unique to museums. Research suggests that about 30 per cent of the population in the UK and the USA see themselves as collectors (Pearce, 1995, p. vii). Nor can museums claim to have carried out this activity particularly effectively. Much of the material in museum collections is not regarded as valuable any longer – at least in today's terms. Nor have museums adequately grasped the issue of contemporary collecting. Major 'gaps' in the way collections represent society both in the past and today have been identified. Collections to some extent have of society (Pearce, 1992, pp. 120–2). A further issue, first identified over twenty years ago, is how far museums can continue to build up collections – particularly in the light of cost factors (Washburn, 1968). Despite the spread of the use of collecting policies, collecting remains a largely untheorized and ill-considered area of museum work. For this reason, it is the subject of a major forthcoming volume (Knell and Moore, 1997). While documentation of the collections is clearly a vital function, it is one which again museums have not carried out with particular efficiency or effectiveness in the past. And despite the great emphasis in recent years in clearing documentation backlogs, through accreditation or registration, much material due to past practice will remain with only limited 'associated information'. The Museums for a New Century report of the AAM described the preservation of collections as a 'chronic, unquantified problem' (AAM, 1984, p. 40). Again, while standards have been raised over the past decade, this remains an issue of serious concern in many museums, particularly in view of funding constraints. Communication in its widest sense has perhaps been the one area of museum work which has witnessed the most marked transformation in recent years. However, some areas of concern have emerged, despite the general picture of improvement, particularly, as will be discussed in Chapter 3, in terms of the marginalization of material culture in exhibitions.

For each of these functions then, often rather poor performance in the past, at least if judged by today's standards, has given way to steady improvement, but much remains to be done in each field. Problems in the carrying out of these functions have curtailed the ability to provide specific 'public benefit' through each of these means. But why have and do museums experience problems in carrying out what are, after all, basic functions? Partly this is not so much a result of a lack of professional skills, standards or training, but a management problem – trying to do too much with too little resources, the jam has been spread too thinly. There has been a lack of focus, resulting in far too general and unattainable goals being set. In turn this is a reflection of failing to define adequately, as we have seen, 'public benefit', the ultimate goal. As almost any activity can be said to achieve some 'public benefit', there has been too much of an 'anything goes' approach. It was simply assumed that each of these functions would somehow contribute to the public benefit.

What exactly does each individual function contribute to the 'public benefit'? Collecting in itself is merely accumulation. It is only a necessary step towards a more significant function. If museums did not document these artefacts, we would have no 'associated information', and would know little or nothing about them; but again, documentation leads to a further function, and does not have a direct benefit to the public in itself. So what of preservation? Again, this is clearly only a means to an end, not the end itself: preservation for what?

Collection, documentation and preservation thus serve some greater purpose. That purpose is to enable material culture to be used in a communication process by and with the public, both in the present and in the future. Communication through material culture thus lies at the heart of what museums are about – the other functions are secondary. Gee, in questioning some fundamentals of museum organization, has suggested that the 'competitive edge' of museums (therefore the USP) is 'real things excitingly interpreted' (Gee, 1993, p. 8). In more detail, Jenkinson valuably argues that 'most importantly' a museum is 'a place that is working to provide a lively and unintimidating, and at times challenging and contentious, context in which contemporary and historical cultural expressions can be

created, represented, explored and criticised by increasingly diverse publics
that engage with this process in a broad range of ways from pure specta-
torship to direct participation' (Jenkinson, 1994, p. 53).

Yet this still begs the question: what does this exciting interpretation
and democratized communication achieve – how exactly do the public
benefit from this? This communication in museums is clearly not simply
about entertainment, though hopefully this is part of the package. What
we are inevitably moving towards is that museums are about education,
in its very broadest, least didactic sense. One might suggest that their mission is to provide opportunities for people to learn about themselves and
their world, indeed their universe, in an entertaining and stimulating
manner, through an understanding and appreciation of material culture.

The *Excellence and Equity* report argues that 'The missions of museums ...
should state unequivocally that there is an educational purpose in every
museum activity' (AAM, 1992, p. 3). I think we need to go much further
than this: education, or perhaps more correctly learning, is the purpose of
every museum activity. This is not to deny that museums cannot provide
benefits in terms of leisure, entertainment, tourism, community identity
etc. It is to argue that the ultimate USP, the unique ability of museums, is
as a centre for 'learning' through material culture. It is salutary and interesting to note that after this lengthy discussion of purpose, I have
returned to something close to a definition of museums offered in 1895
by G. Browne Goode, then the Assistant Secretary of the Smithsonian,
which still seems more valuable (if we were to update the language a
little, particularly the term 'man'), than those in contemporary usage: 'A
Museum is an institution for the preservation of those objects which best
illustrate the phenomena of nature and the works of man, and the utilisa-
tion of these for the increase of knowledge and for the culture and
enlightenment of the people' (Goode, 1994, p. 42).

This might be seen as far from radical. There are many in museums
who would question what would be seen as such a traditional definition,
particularly through its central emphasis on material culture, as will be
discussed in Chapter 3. I will seek to defend the traditional notion of the
benefits museums provide, but together with a radical new approach to
how this is done, in terms of both the form of communication through
material culture, and the definition of which material culture best illus-
trates 'the works' of humankind.

The past for the future, or the present?

One final part of the MA definition remains to be deconstructed, the
notion that a museum is an 'institution', 'which implies a formalised
establishment which has a "long term purpose"'. Anderson has commented that

> The concept of a museum as 'an institution' is proving hopelessly restrictive when in
> real life the boundary between 'museum' and 'not museum' is crumbling before our
> eyes. ... If the 'museum' is not an institution containing objects but instead the context

for interaction between artefacts and people, then we must be aware that this interaction is now taking place outside the institution, not just in printed books and in the street but in many media. The gallery is becoming a smaller part of the totality of the wider museum ... by the year 2000 museum collections may become world-wide commercial property capable of being disassembled and reassembled at will in virtual museums in some virtual reality.   (Anderson, 1992, p. 160)

One might argue that the virtual might never be able to compete on equal terms with engagement with the 'real thing', but this is an intriguing argument. If museums are about the 'interaction between artefacts and people', as a learning experience, do we need formal institutions to achieve this? Institutions and organizations in the business world and elsewhere are changing very rapidly, and the 'virtual corporation' is already with us. The implications of this will be considered further in Chapter 7.

Finally, what of the notion of the 'long-term purpose' implicit in the museum as an institution? As Kavanagh has noted, 'There are no guarantees as to the future of museums. The majority of the national museums and a good proportion of the main local authority and university museums in the UK were founded in the second half of the nineteenth century; the substantial proportion of independent museums have been founded since 1960' (Kavanagh, 1994, p. 11). Individual museum closures demonstrate the impossibility of guaranteeing a future. Furthermore, we cannot say whether future generations will want or need museums at all. The relatively short history of museums is testament to the fact that they do not fulfil some timeless human need: museums are contingent to their times. 'Museums were established as a pragmatic solution to a particular set of practical problems, and may prove to be a peculiarly 19th and 20th century solution to these problems' (Anderson, 1992, p. 160). The needs they meet may disappear, or alternatively be met by some other means. Some have identified a growing scepticism with museum claims to be of value by serving a future need, which relates to the postmodern critique of museums by the 'new museology':

This fundamental preservation function of museums was an assumed public good and governmentally fundable in past generations, when pride in the past and confidence in the future were unchallenged assumptions. In this more nihilistic age of instant gratification, nuclear and environmental threat, and economic malaise, such confidence in the future is being challenged everywhere. In this more cynical age, where it is the norm to deconstruct the historic and artistic past and challenge all the paradigms and values that informed the founding of our institutions, it is hard to build any public or professional consensus on what, if anything, has lasting value and ought to be preserved for the future.   (Sullivan, 1993, p. 54)

Weil notes that in a similar crisis for the museum as an institution in the USA in 1971–2, in offering a defence, he was aware that 'The past was in bad odor, and there was considerable talk that it should perhaps be overturned. The only thing left to "sell" was the utility of museums to the present ... all of the virtuous and wonderful things that museums could be doing for everybody right now, at this moment, immediately, and no wait-ing!!!' In this, Weil argues, 'the priorities were inverted ... collecting and preserving are and must remain the foundation for all of the museum's other activities. The custodial role is central', in order to 'preserve the options of the future' (Weil, 1983, pp. 52–3). Lowenthal has similarly argued that 'alarmingly, populist "presentism" risks disenfranchising the greatest majority – the future' (Lowenthal, 1992, p. 27).

But how far is this argument sustainable? What proportion of resources can we justify putting towards a future need that has not even yet been identified? Sola argues that many museums, under the guise of meeting future needs, have become entirely self-fulfilling: 'the main feature of the nature of museum institutions ... is a mission of continuation: whatever they contain or speak of, their task is to continue ... striving for the eternity of the institution ... when the real job is quality of living, tolerance, dignity of diversities etc.' (Sola, 1992b, p. 396). In looking too far to serve the future, museums neglect a present, which might bring about their destruc-tion. Where is the future of a museum caught up in war? In any case, serving the future is an impossibility, even if we could see into it: 'The big lie of our museums is incurable unless they cease to claim eternity, immortality or infinity. They should know better than anybody else how inconstant and unstable everything physical is.' How desirable is it to attempt to fight nature in this way: 'If the right to die is guaranteed to people, should not objects have the same privilege? ... Many museums already look like inten-sive care hospital departments' (Sola, 1992a, p. 104).

From this the museum emerges as a device for denying death, meeting an existential need for museum staff in particular: 'this will remain when I am gone'. This serves *their* psychological needs, rather than those of future generations. In contrast, Sola argues, 'The future of museums has to contend with the phenomenon of death, as it is part of our life-cycle. By doing so, it will be possible to break with the exhausting obligation to keep the physical evidence alive. ... This also comprises the death of museums and similar institutions, ideally through their fulfillment' (Sola, 1992b, p. 400). Should not museums and their collections, like ourselves, have a life and then a death; should not there come a point where their function is complete? In trying to achieve immortality through museums, do we not distort and diminish their current role?

Museums cannot claim to serve the future because that future may well not exist. They can only serve the present. If it is a widespread public wish that we create 'a pharaoh's grave' of artefacts for the future in our museums, if museums somehow meet a common existential impulse to immortality through physical remains, only then does concern for the future seem justified – on the grounds of the present. But if we collectively decide that we do not care about the future, does this matter? If in using museum collections now, for genuine benefit, this rules out their future use, is this not justified? Does it depend on how beneficial this is in the present? Or to put it another way, what benefits in the present are we pre-pared to sacrifice for the good of future generations?

'I read once that it takes 75,000 trees to produce one issue of the Sunday New York Times – and it's well worth every trembling leaf. So what if our grandchildren have no oxygen to breathe? Fuck 'em' (Bryson, 1990, p. 23). While we can safely assume that future generations would like some oxygen to breathe, it does perhaps take a peculiar kind of arrogance to assume we know what they will want from us. How do we know that they will be grateful for all, some or even any of the material culture we have so graciously preserved for their benefit? After all, we are not entirely delighted with what we have inherited from our forebears.

If it is an assumption that museums are about the future, it is also an assumption that they are necessarily concerned with the past. There is no mention in the MA or ICOM definitions that the museum is necessarily concerned with historical material; the AAM definition mentions historical evidence, but along with a range of others. You may consider this sophistry, as any material is instantly historical, but it is a useful reminder that there is a tendency for museums to become obsessed with the past, at the expense of the present.

These are awkward, deliberately provocative arguments, but they need to be posed. There needs to be a delicate balance between the past, the present and the future; at the moment museums seem to have tipped this too far in favour of preserving the past for the future, by-passing the present. For what is the value of museums if they do not have an impact on the world now? If museums do not tackle the key issues that face us – war, poverty, ethnic tension and the like - then there may be no future for museums or ourselves. This is not to say that museums can radically change the world – but they can and must have some impact, to be of any benefit here and now.

If I seem to be contradicting myself, in stating a *political* role for museums, having played this down earlier in this chapter, it is from a view that museums are inevitably political institutions, that political issues can be addressed through material culture even if museums do not tend do this as yet, as we shall see in Chapter 3, and that museums are as valid a place for the discussion of political ideas as any other. Indeed, museums, by dealing with the material world, are perhaps the *best* place to consider some of the key 'political' issues of our time. For what is poverty but an unequal distribution of material culture? What is environmentalism but a concern to preserve material culture? The development of capitalism since the industrial revolution has produced an explosion in consumerism on an unprecedented scale. As Madonna has told us, 'We are living in a material world.'

3

Back to basics?

The problem with things is that they are dumb. ... And if by some ventriloquism they seem to speak, they lie.
(Crew and Sims, 1991, p. 159)

Far from being silent, the number of voices which speak through and for 'dumb things' are legion.   *(Hebdige, 1988, p. 80)*

The object is inexhaustible.   *(Pearce, 1992, p. 219)*

Introduction

How far can we learn from material culture – and what can we learn? Increasingly, as we shall see, the role of material culture in the museum is being challenged or downgraded. Yet we live in a material world, and define our lives and our identities through material culture: 'Objects hang before the eyes of the imagination, continuously re-presenting ourselves to ourselves, and telling the stories of our lives in ways which would be impossible otherwise'. Studies of how significant objects are to our self-image suggest that objects 'act as reminders and confirmers of our identities, and probably our idea of our identity resides more in ... objects than it does in any idea of ourselves as individuals' (Pearce, 1992, pp. 47, 55). This seems equally true of communities or even nations; what else could explain the 'culturocidal' war in the former Yugoslavia, in which cultural monuments, including museums, were deliberately targeted? Material culture is central to our lives: why does it appear to be increasingly less central to much museum practice?

Formalists and analysts: two problems

In the Victorian era, there were no doubts as to the centrality of objects and their ability to teach; and what they were seen to teach were the moral values of the ruling classes. Ettema has termed this the 'formalist' perspective, because it focuses on the form of objects:

> Museum artefacts seemed to actually contain abstract moral qualities that would be self-evident in their appearance. The physical nature of artefacts was merely a reflection of their spiritual nature. By exhibiting the best products of human civilisation, museums would communicate those vital qualities to the public. Since the important lessons were in the objects themselves, no further explanations were really necessary. Thus, the formalist perspective in museums resulted from a belief in the reforming power of artefacts.   (Ettema, 1987, p. 66)

Bound up with this were notions of social control; as Sir Henry Cole commented in 1857 about what was to become the Victoria and Albert Museum, 'public museums may furnish a powerful antidote to the gin palace' (quoted in Goodwin, 1990, p. 28).

The formalist perspective long held sway in museums, and still has much support today, in traditional but influential circles. Sir David Wilson, formerly director of the British Museum, has commented: 'It is the objects which are important: they must speak for themselves' (Wilson, 1985, pp. 57–8). The explicit agenda of social control through the reforming moral power of objects has gone, but the formalist perspective remains strong:

> As the old social imperatives fell away, however, curators continued their research for purely antiquarian reasons. The more sophisticated and successful their antiquarian researches became, the more the formalist perspective appeared to be self-justifying. Thus, education in history museums is no longer defined as moral uplift communicated through objects. It now consists in simply learning about the objects themselves. In the absence of a well-defined social purpose, the medium has, indeed, become the message. ... Thus history comes to be the story of material progress. ... In short, museums teach materialism. (Ettema, 1987, p. 72).

Increasingly, however, this refined formalist perspective is being challenged as 'biased and irrelevant to modern social needs, merely celebrating the "great white men" of history and their technological and artistic creations' (Ettema, 1987, p. 64). Museums are revealed as political institutions, reflecting outdated dominant social values: 'Museums represent the discredited past but give no guidance for the future' (Jenkinson, 1989, p. 145). The emphasis has been switched from the celebration of the achievements of 'great white men' to the history and culture of society as a whole, but with a particular emphasis on disadvantaged groups. This has been culturally specific, taking different forms in different countries, and developing at distinct times. In the USA, the strength of radical politics among women and the black community had an impact on museums in the 1970s, whereas in Britain the issues of gender and, even more so, ethnicity remained relatively ignored until the late 1980s. Conversely, an emphasis on working-class history developed in Britain from the early 1980s, reflecting the historical strength of the labour and trade union movement. In Scotland, this had developed even earlier (Moore, 1994b). In the USA, this was much slower to develop (Rubinstein, 1990). In contrast, Dutch museums had begun to tackle a wider range of more controversial subjects relating to disadvantage in society, including sexuality, from the late 1960s (van Lakerveld, 1994).

It would be interesting to study the cultural relativism of these developments, and also the sociology in terms of what kinds of people were coming into museums to make these changes, and why they chose to work in museums. Clearly, this owes much to the democratization of higher education since the 1960s, and the political radicalization of generations of graduates into the 1980s. Chiefly these developments have taken place under the banner of social history, graduates from this burgeoning academic discipline forming the catalyst for change in museums over the past twenty years or so. This movement has radically and valuably broadened the subjects museums are willing to tackle; brought about significant improvements in interpretation through a desire to reach and communicate with all in society; and sought to demystify and democratize the whole process of museum work. Museums have benefited immeasurably from this in terms of new subjects, ideas and audiences. Despite the political and funding obstacles of more recent years, this 'movement' is still pressing forward into new and previously taboo subject areas, such as sex, politics and religion. At the same time, more traditional 'formalist' museums have come under stringent analysis and criticism from curators, museologists and other academics for marginalizing the history and culture of women, ethnic minorities, the working class and other disadvantaged groups.

Social history in museums has had a profound impact, particularly in Britain and North America. Criticism of such highly welcome developments might therefore appear churlish or even unfair. There are some problems, in terms of the subjects tackled, audiences targeted and reached, and the process of democratization. But the key problem is in terms of the role of material culture in this approach. Ettema terms this new social history approach the 'analyst' perspective, which in part reflects the fact that it has become applicable to not just social history in museums, but also other disciplines. In making explicit the difference between this and the formalist approach, Ettema highlights the problem which emerges in terms of the role of material culture in the analyst perspective: 'the insurgent analytical perspective attempts to teach not just what happened, but how and why it happened. It necessarily emphasises abstract explanations for the concrete events of history ... collections are tools for teaching a more general history that focuses on the dynamics of past societies. ... Objects are the props, not the message.' The danger is that 'museum programs become increasingly abstract and their planners devalue the role of museum collections. Some museum professionals complain that analytical policies ignore at great peril the very things that make museums distinctive' (Ettema, 1987, pp. 63–4).

Is this fair criticism? And even if so, does it really matter? What theoretical position do the analysts have for the role of material culture? Museum social historians have rightly criticized the formalist perspective for lacking any coherent theory on the role of objects. This empirical, common-sense approach assumed that learning about objects was valuable. Jenkinson has written of the 'poverty of theory' in museums (Jenkinson, 1989). Yet it is arguable how far the social history/analyst approach offers a coherent theoretical perspective, not least in terms of the position of material culture. As Kavanagh, the foremost commentator on the rise of social history in British museums has commented, 'If social history in "museums" has evolved, it has been the evolution of a term, and of late an identity, rather than a definable and recognisable discipline, with tried and tested theories and methods' (Kavanagh, 1993a, p. 13), and that 'the absence of a firm and challenging intellectual foundation to history museum practice has to be noted' (Kavanagh, 1990, p. 61). Partly this lack of a firm theoretical basis is put down to the newness of the discipline in museum terms (Fleming, 1993, p. 1); but if the analyst perspective wishes to replace the formalist convincingly, it must offer greater theoretical consistency.

From the mid-1980s some valuable attempts have been made to do this. Davies noted that 'the sanctity of the object in our history museums is under attack', but from the analyst perspective concurred that objects had decreasing value for the new social history in museums, because they failed to provide answers to the questions posed, which could be answered much more readily by other forms of evidence: 'In the twentieth century the sources at the historian's call have multiplied. Photographs, film and tape now provide a vital extra dimension to historical analysis of recent times. At the same time the primary importance of objects retreats further and further from the mainstream in modern history. In this period artefacts have no value as evidence', and therefore should be 'collected principally for assisting with the presentation of a history derived from other sources'. Objects were merely useful for modern social history in that they could 'illustrate' interpretations, although they also 'have an inspirational or stimulating quality which may lead people to ask questions on a subject which they may not have hitherto considered' (Davies, 1985, pp. 28–9). Similarly, Jenkinson argued that material culture could not answer many of the questions posed by the museum social historian: 'in the field of social history objects only represent part of the story, and we therefore have to consider other, more effective ways of representing both the past and the present. ... Objects have only limited value for social historians.' In their place, like Davies, he proposed that museums should replace or supplement them with experience: 'It is people's experience, revealed in oral history and reminiscence, in film, video and photography, in writing, in performance, in painting and so on, that is the essential feature of an effective, relevant and responsive social history in museums' (Jenkinson, 1989, p. 145). These sentiments have found reflection in the thoughts of leading curators in the USA. Spencer Crew (currently director of the National Museum of American History) and James Sims argued in a conference paper given in 1988 that 'Traditional approaches to exhibition, which put the artefact at the centre of the presentation, limit the issues available for discussion. Concepts that stretch beyond the available artifacts, but are important points of consideration, are precluded in this traditional model' (Crew and Sims, 1991, p. 168).

Far from being concerned that material culture was increasingly marginalized by the social history approach, many curators welcomed this. There were, however, some dissenting voices, or at least those who expressed caution at this retreat from the central importance of material culture. Fleming warned that 'a museum with no objects and plenty of social historical discourse is not a museum, and visitors are not being stimulated, their imaginations are not being moved by real contact, physical contact with the past' (Fleming, 1987, p. 4). Kavanagh noted that social historians, in questioning the value of objects as evidence, had 'inadvertently questioned the relevance of the discipline to the museum' (Kavanagh, 1993a, p. 21); 'History provision without objects would be and usually is something else. ... Objects make museums, well ... museums' (Kavanagh, 1993b, p. 61). Kavanagh produced a trenchant defence of the importance of objects as evidence, drawing on material culture studies from the United States and ethnographic approaches from Sweden (Kavanagh, 1989). Yet this paper appears to have been largely ignored. The views of Davies and Jenkinson, representing an extreme view of the downgrading of the role of the object, have not become orthodoxy among social historians, but the general consensus has been in this direction: 'objects now had to exist alongside other *equally important* media as legitimate voices in the museum' (Whittaker, 1994, p. 3, emphasis added).

A major handbook of social history practice has been published in the UK, in which several authors, including the editors, have highlighted the debate about the role of material culture, but have done little more than identify that the problem has not been satisfactorily addressed: 'there are unresolved problems about fusing the study of social history with material evidence and its interpretation' (Fleming, 1993, p. 1); 'Artefact studies in social history are critically important. ... As curators we must believe that artefacts have a value in aiding an understanding of the past and are not solely three-dimensional illustrations of themes or narratives' (Rhodes, 1993, p. 101). Davies, formerly the most stringent critic of the role of material culture, commented that 'Surprisingly little attention has been given to the methodology of artefact studies, and this still remains an uncomfortable weakness with many social historians' (Davies, 1993, p. 9).

The debate around these issues has not been confined to social history curators in the UK. It has a wider resonance, in terms of a broader analyst challenge to the formalist perspective. Weil considered whether the 'proper business' of the museum was 'ideas' or 'things'. This represents a witty and provocative dissection of the formalist perspective, but not a clear alternative, in concluding that 'we must never forget that ideas – and not just things alone – also lie at the heart of the museum enterprise' (Weil, 1990, p. 48). A major conference at the Smithsonian Institution in 1988, 'The Poetics and Politics of Representation', was split along formalist and analyst lines: 'The participants tended to think of exhibitions as conforming to one of two models: either a vehicle for the display of objects or a space telling a story. This in itself conformed to the great divide between participants from art museums and participants from cultural-history museums that was found among the paper presenters and in the audience as well' (Karp, 1991, pp. 12–13).

This unresolved debate inevitably flared up again, first among social history curators in the UK. Tucker contended that 'our reason for existence –

material culture – is becoming more and more marginalised, rather than remaining the stimulus for the exhibitions we create. ... Whilst recognising the importance of oral history and photography, we must remember the central place of material culture in our activities' (Tucker, 1993, pp. 6–7). White responded in favour of 'the advantages of an enquiry-based historical approach in which the collecting of objects can play an integral part. While objects are arguably central to the function of the museum, they are not the only medium at its disposal ... the social history curator's primary concerns should be with people, past and present', while conceding that 'it may well be that we need to go back to our objects, such as they are, and find new ways of "reading" them' (White, 1993, p. 3). It seems astonishing that a curator could suggest that objects are only *arguably* central to the function of museums. The virulence of this debate led to the main annual conference of social history curators focusing on considering 'whether objects provide the best ways of communicating in museums – can objects in displays really provide a worthwhile or meaningful experience for our visitors? ... Do we need them at all?' (Harland, 1993, p. 6).

These polemical articles and the conference which ensued thus merely restated the problem, rather than providing a clear way forward. Moore and Tucker (1994) represented a conscious attempt to popularize Ettema's analysis of the formalist and analyst perspectives, and emphasize the need to move forward from both, by drawing upon advances in material culture theory. This has stimulated further debate (Johnstone, 1994; Davies, 1994c; Ross, 1994), and most notably Suggitt (1994a), who also uses Ettema's framework for analysis. Again, this is not a parochial debate. Simultaneously in the USA a very similar discussion centred on the role of material culture has developed, not confined to social history (Watkins, 1994; Resnicow, 1994; Roberts, 1994). Valuable though these debates on both sides of the Atlantic have been in highlighting the unresolved nature of this issue, they have lacked theoretical depth. The critique of both formalist and analyst displays is echoed in the development of the practice in exhibitions at the Canadian Museum of Civilization (CMC):

> A traditional museum method for creating exhibitions has been artifact-driven: the best artifacts are identified and a story built around them. ... This allows a museum's treasures to be displayed, but risks the omission of important themes if no treasures relate to them. ...
> CMC's past exhibits were created on the basis of an alternate, story-line driven approach, didactic in nature and emphasising cognitive learning. The story to tell was decided upon first, then the collections searched for good artifacts to illustrate the story. The narrative of this type of exhibition hangs together quite well, but sometimes the artifacts seem merely supplementary to the textual story, and their usage contrived. ... CMC now recognises the failings in its exhibitions of this type.
> (MacDonald and Alsford, 1989, pp. 72–3)

The specific approach developed at the CMC to overcome these weaknesses will be discussed in detail in Chapter 7.

So where does this leave us? Museums still have formalists, who, despite the critiques of Ettema, Weil and others, see no fundamental problem with the approach. Increasingly, however, the analytical perspective is gaining sway, but it does downgrade the 'primacy' of objects, placing them alongside other evidence of equal value. Analysts admit to only a slight concern about their ability to interpret material evidence. Then there are those who, following Ettema, wish to develop a new approach, using the burgeoning material culture theory (Moore and Tucker, 1994; Suggitt, 1994a). A deeper theoretical perspective is required, to move the debate beyond the simple and artificial binaries of:

> objects : people
> things : ideas
> formalist : analyst

We have not moved beyond a debate first identified by Weil 25 years ago, when at a time of social and political turbulence, the AAM conference 'polarized about the reiterated insistence that museums must become "people-oriented rather than object-oriented"'(Weil, 1983, p. 18). Johnstone (1994, p. 3) offers an uneasy compromise, where formalist and analyst approaches are both utilized: 'the average curator strives to seek a balance between work led by ideas and interpretations, and work led by the objects in or out of the collections'. Similarly, the SHCG conference on this theme concluded that the way the profession would continue would be through a mix of both object and issue-led work (Nisbet, 1994, pp. 6–9). Crew and Sims in the USA reached the same inadequate conclusion: 'Thoughtfully presented historical ideas should not play a secondary role to objects in molding the focus of exhibitions ... Either one can serve as the centerpiece and primary interpretive device of an exhibition' (Crew and Sims, 1991, p. 169). Yet this clearly is not a solution in itself: 'the underlying issue here is the balance between objects and people in the work of social history curators, and that is a debate that won't go away' (Tucker, 1994, p. 4).

If the object is dead, the exhibition is dead

Those in the analyst perspective who argue that ideas, as much as objects, can drive exhibitions still have to address Ettema's trenchant critique of their displays, which is worth quoting at length. The proof is in the pudding, in the sense that the strengths, but more particularly the weaknesses of this approach are revealed in displays:

> The objects themselves do not appear as solutions to the problems of history. ... This presents those who maintain the analytical perspective with a rather difficult problem. If museums are, by definition, dedicated to teaching history with artifact collections, it would seem that any approach that makes objects a secondary concern is inappropriate to the medium of museum exhibition. After all, it is their collections that make museums different from all other educational institutions. Yet the analysts' purpose is to convey abstractions about the past, and most abstractions are more easily conveyed verbally than visually. In interpretive exhibitions, the ideas and information end up in labels that are far too long for the attention span of most visitors. Objects seem

to take second place, becoming illustrations for the labels rather than significant elements in the learning process. ... Social history exhibits, runs the common complaint, are merely 'books on walls'. (Ettema, 1987, pp. 76–7).

Much recent social history exhibition practice in the US and Britain can be criticized in this way. This accusation that displays can become merely 'books on walls' has been echoed by others (Corn, 1989, pp. 244–6, 254; Moore and Tucker, 1994; Trustram, 1992, p. 26). Fleming has warned that 'Objects in a museum can become like extras in a film ... adjuncts to the plot. ... Displays should *derive* from material culture, not overwhelm it' (Fleming, 1987, pp. 3–4). Such views have been echoed by Ames in a major study of current practice in social history exhibitions in the USA:

Playing to strengths ... means recognising both the potential and limitations of collections. In the current push to bring academic history into museums, some unjustified praise has been heaped on exhibitions that have been little more than books on walls or cases of written documents. These may be exhibitions of historical materials but they are not, to my way of thinking, the kind of exhibitions history museums ought to be doing. (Ames, 1992, p. 318).

If curators focus on documentary sources, or oral history, or video, and not material culture, they are denying the very essence, what is distinct about museum exhibitions: 'The most important and unique characteristic of a museum exhibition is that it facilitates an encounter between visitor and three-dimensional object' (Belcher, 1991, p. 38). In rightly criticizing formalism, but rejecting material culture, the analysts are, as the saying goes, throwing out the baby with the bath water.

This means accepting that certain subjects unfortunately cannot be tackled through exhibitions, 'recognising that not all historic tales or all historic moments or all historic issues are equally accessible through material culture. What material culture of the past tells us about best is culture of the past. We need to accept the fact that some historical tales cannot be effectively conveyed by material culture. To plan an exhibition about such a tale is to set oneself a very difficult course' (Ames, 1992, p. 319). Simultaneously, Tucker in Britain was arguing that this 'should lead us to question the practicality of many of our projects, in that we are forced to face the fact that what seemed like a "good idea" is doomed to failure by the lack of material culture, a situation that no amount of designers and clever reconstructions can cure' (Tucker, 1993, p. 6). Indeed, one response to overcome the problem of the dullness of such exhibitions has been to have a high designer input, trying to find exciting new ways to display object-poor, text-rich displays. But Corn concurs with Tucker, in commenting on social history displays in the USA: 'Increasingly exhibitions seem to achieve their effects through a density of interpretive artefacts – through their theatrical staging, as it were – rather than through the display of historical things ... the interpretation in effect itself became the exhibit; original objects ... marginal to a visitor's experience' (Corn, 1989, p. 254).

Responses to this critique have highlighted that curators have become aware of the danger of 'books on walls', have reduced the amount of text, though this inevitably limits the analysis, and have included more three-dimensional material in displays (Ross, 1993; White, 1993). Certainly recent social history exhibitions in Britain have become more object-rich, and this is to be welcomed. But the fundamental problem remains that the objects are secondary, illustrations to a narrative and analysis driven by historical concepts and ideas. The exhibition is still a book on the wall – it merely has more illustrations in it.

A second defence is that to ignore certain subject areas, such as working-class history, 'because we will never have the material relics on which to base a display is to perpetuate the elitist approach to cultural representation which has dogged museums until very recently' (White, 1993, p. 3). This view, widely held among social history curators, can be criticized on three grounds. First, it does not overcome the argument shared by Ettema, Corn, Ames and Tucker that exhibitions on such themes will still prove unsatisfactory. It is not as if the exhibition is the only way of explaining and interpreting this history in the public domain. Others may be better qualified to tackle such themes in a wide range of other media, for 'Social history curatorship is only one among many approaches to the past, and not an all-embracing discipline' (Moore and Tucker, 1994, p. 22). Some social historians have recognized that the nature of collectable or pre-existing museum holdings of material culture must limit the themes tackled: 'Within the vast field of labour history we are looking for themes which can be illustrated through objects' (Trustram, 1990, p. 7). Yet the objects here are still seen as *illustrations*, not the focus.

Second, those who suggest that only tackling subjects for which material remains will 'perpetuate the elitist approach' of museums, by failing to represent disadvantaged groups, are in any case mistaken. Material culture is in fact the most *democratic* form of historical evidence. Written sources are inevitably skewed to the higher social classes, and the more remote the historical period, the more evident this is. Material culture gives the only direct route into the lives of ordinary people in many cases; it is all that they have left behind. The problem is that curators often lack the skills to 'read' such material evidence. For example, Deetz has demonstrated how much greater an insight into the lives of slaves in the USA can be gained from archaeological evidence than from written sources (Deetz, 1977, pp. 138–54). This important study also reveals a great deal of the lives of Anglo-Americans in the seventeenth and eighteenth centuries through an examination of a range of everyday objects (Deetz, 1977).

Third, it is an assumption that ordinary people have necessarily left behind less material evidence than the higher social classes. The fact that it is not currently in museum collections does not mean that it does not exist, if ultimately as archaeological evidence, as Deetz has demonstrated. Curators also need to reconsider the existing material in collections. Most of the collections currently in museums, if they were owned by the higher social classes, were *made* by the working classes. Decorative arts collections, for example, are the products of artisans, of ordinary craftsmen and women. Fine art collections contain a great deal of material produced by artists living in poverty. Such collections in museums only 'perpetuate the elitist approach' because they are interpreted by ownership rather than manufacture or creation, in the formalist perspective. Much of the material needed to explore the lives of ordinary people is already at hand; what is lacking is the curatorial ability or imagination to do so.

Despite the possibilities that do therefore exist, curators currently only tend to see a choice between 'ineffective communication' in the formalist perspective and 'inadequate content' in the analyst perspective (Ettema, 1987, p. 77). Some curators and museologists are critical of analyst exhibitions; many, particularly social historians, believe they are still the best approach. And certainly they do move forward in some respects from the formalist perspective – but at what cost?

Evaluating exhibitions

Part of the problem in analysing exhibitions is the lack of critical practice in museums, which has been highlighted: 'Considering the enormous amounts of time, energy and money museums invest in exhibitions – not to mention the millions of people who visit them – these primary vehicles of public programming are not regularly reviewed in ways that have consequence and from which exhibit planners can learn' (Kulik and Sims, 1989, p. 52; see also Kavanagh, 1990, p. 61). As a result curators tend not to learn from each other's past successes and mistakes, and constantly 'reinvent the wheel'. It also leads to a climate where developing new approaches is therefore exaggerated, in order for an exhibition to make its mark, rather than encouraging displays which sensibly and comfortably draw upon and develop successful techniques and approaches used by others. As one social history curator has commented, 'Often, the only criterion of "merit" for museum work seems to be curatorial "intuition" or "newness". Almost every new museum exhibition makes claims to "innovation" or "the breaking of new ground", but this in itself is no guarantee of improvement in practice, for "innovation", any more than "tradition", cannot be used as a quantitative measurement for anything' (Frostick, 1992, pp. 45–6). Curators seem unwilling to criticize each other's work, partly from a fear of receiving criticism in return, but more through a feeling of a need for mutual support. By criticizing each other's work and revealing flaws, the fear is that ammunition will be given to those, perhaps in political power, who might seek to cut funding. Yet this is unhelpful, because it does not enable museums to develop the best defence, an improvement in exhibitions and services, which can be greatly facilitated by a climate of constructive criticism. There has been some useful criticism in the past, but it has tended only to be an analysis of a curator's own project. A critical practice is slowly beginning to develop, but this has been hampered, particularly in Britain, by an overdefensive reaction by some curators to criticism of their work by others, which tends to personalize and obscure what could be a constructive debate.

Exhibitions have attracted little critical debate from outside the profession. In Britain the media focus only on high-profile art exhibitions in London, and it is difficult for other museums to attract coverage and criticism, even where they would welcome this. There is a growing literature of academic criticism of exhibitions, but as this tends to be by art or social historians, with little or no museum background, it tends to show insufficient awareness of what can and cannot be achieved through the exhibition form, rather than in an academic text (see, for example, Bennett, 1988; West, 1988; and also several of the contributors to Leon and Rosenzweig, 1989).

Critical attention from the media, academics and others is of value and should be welcomed and sought. But we also need to develop a museological set of criteria for evaluating exhibitions which recognize that these are a very distinct form of communication. Schlereth has produced a set of guidelines for history museum exhibition reviews, which are a useful starting point, but not a prescriptive list of questions to follow, and also guidelines to encourage reviews in the *Journal of American History* (Schlereth, 1980, 1989c). Beyond this level of critique, however, we need to develop a museological theory of exhibitions, which, being derived from current practice, would provide a framework of assessment and a means to develop models of good practice. What are the common threads of exhibitions of excellence? Only this can take us beyond subjective responses. As Frostick has argued, 'it is important that examples of successes and failures in social history curatorship are made widely available and synthesised into the broader theoretical framework within which curators operate' (Frostick, 1992, p. 45).

Several useful means to classify and analyse exhibitions have been put forward, not least that by Ettema. These all bear at least some relation to each other, as is indicated in Figure 3.1. Agren and Carlsson have provided a useful means of categorizing forms of exhibition, rising in five stages from the least developed to the most advanced. The first form is 'mass', a clutter of objects displayed together, usually unlabelled. The second form is a 'label' exhibition, where objects are ordered in seriated ranks with basic labels. The third is a 'thematic' display, where material is divided under differing subject headings. The fourth is 'narrative' where the exhibition form communicates a point of view, or narrates an experience, usually employing fieldwork, active collecting and the actual words of local people, and the use of diverse media. This evolves at a more advanced level into the 'total' form, which uses the fullest range of interpretive styles and techniques, including drama and educational programmes, and contains the elements of choice and involvement for the visitor, to allow active exploration of the subject. Achieving the 'total' form is not simply a question of using diverse techniques, which can be merely confusing, unless it reflects a firm grasp of

Agren and Carlsson	Kavanagh	Pearce	Ettema
Mass	Descriptive	Treasure/ Relic	Formalist
Label	Descriptive	Treasure/ Relic	Formalist
Thematic	Descriptive	Resurrection	Formalist
Thematic -	Descriptive/ Analytical		Analyst
Narrative	Narrative	Illustrated narrative	Analyst
Total	Narrative/ Descriptive/ Analytical		Symbolic synthesis

Figure 3.1 *Models of exhibition analysis*

the complexities of the subject (Kavanagh, 1990, pp. 132–5). This relates to Ettema's approach, in that mass and label are both variations of formalist displays, and thematic and narrative tend to be analyst. The total form appears to go beyond both formalist and analytical perspectives. This model is valuable, but not without problems, primarily that it is more descriptive than prescriptive. It is fairly easy to see how one can avoid the pitfalls of the mass and label approaches, which are still found in some displays, and move towards the narrative form, through active fieldwork and community involvement. However, it is much less clear how one attains the total form without simply overwhelming the visitor with a bewildering diversity of techniques. Agren and Carlsson's model suggests what exhibitions are falling short of, but not why.

Kavanagh has considered that history exhibitions might also be analysed in terms of the form of historiography they use, corresponding to the three principal traditions of history writing: narrative, descriptive and analytical (Kavanagh, 1990, pp. 131–2). Narrative is found in traditional local history galleries, taking the visitor from most often the Romans to the present day (or 1945!). The problem with this approach is that objects tend to be merely illustrations, punctuating the narrative where relevant, and are not the focus, and therefore analyst in Ettema's terms. Descriptive history in museums is found in a primitive sense in both mass and label displays, and more especially in complete reconstructions of environments. While they effectively recreate a moment in time, they do not tend to analyse why things were the way they were or why they have changed, tending therefore to be formalist. Kavanagh argues that analytical history is less often found, being harder to achieve effectively in the exhibition form, though in some senses it equates to thematic (Kavanagh, 1990, pp. 131–2). The danger is that text is used rather than

artefacts to provide the analysis, negating the possibilities of the exhibition form – again, the analyst perspective. Kavanagh's approach is useful
for analysing history exhibitions in particular, but not necessarily helpful
in evaluating their success or otherwise. While exhibitions which do not
offer analysis may lack substance or depth, the most effective displays
might contain elements of all three historiographic styles.

Pearce has developed a fourfold analysis of exhibitions, again with reference (but not exclusively) to history. First, exhibitions can simply
present objects or collections as relics of the past, particularly where they
are associated with illustrious historical characters or events (Pearce,
1992, pp. 197–202). In Ettema's terms this is formalist; in Agren and
Carlsson's scheme, this might be either mass (e.g. collections displayed in
a historic house) or label if relics in a museum. Second, Pearce identifies
exhibitions as 'art and treasure', 'displayed in splendid remoteness from
the daily round, icons of a spiritual life which is celebrated and exalted in
all its elevation ... we know that we are expected to gaze in awe and
admiration at the wealth offered to view.' This is the traditional formalist
art gallery display, again likely to be simply mass in a historic house, or
label in the art gallery. Pearce's third category is the 'illustrated narrative',
exhibitions where objects are subordinated to the narrative, presented primarily in terms of classic written historiography; the objects are shorn of
their potential multiplicity of meanings so that they can be integrated – as
supporting cast – into that chosen narrative. The objects 'are merely
mildly illustrative'; the exhibitions, in marginalizing material culture, produce a 'painfully familiar artefactual deadness' (Pearce, 1992, pp. 205–6).
This closely mirrors Ettema's critique of the analyst perspective. Finally,
there is what Pearce terms 'the resurrection of the body': reconstructions
involving a large range of artefacts and installations, with 'the intention
of simulation, of the re-creation of the past within a closed environment
where disbelief should be suspended. ... The exhibitions, however hon-
ourable their intentions may (or may not) be, offer only an ersatz mix of
shallow nostalgia and visible spectacle, a product to be consumed like any
other. ... The artefacts do not re-create but are reassembled, the original
authors are absent, and the voyeuristic viewers ... take their place in the
queue' (Pearce, 1992, pp. 207–8). Many reconstructions can be criticized
quite rightly in this way, and are clearly a variation on formalist in
Ettema's terms, simply involving the arrangement of objects in homes or
working environments, with little or no additional interpretation. In
Agren and Carlsson's terms, they would therefore be 'mass'. However,
well researched reconstructions clearly rise above this, certainly to the
level of thematic, exploring a theme at a particular moment in time.
Moreover, it will be argued in Chapter 7 that the best examples of this
approach actually point towards a way forward from the weaknesses of
both formalist and analyst perspectives. Pearce is critical of all four
approaches (see also Pearce, 1992, pp. 208–9), but does not specifically
offer a notion of an exhibition form to transcend the weaknesses of the

four she identifies. But the entire volume from which this analysis is derived is a source of ideas for such a transcendence, as will be discussed in detail in Chapter 4.

Finally, Ettema's analysis of formalist and analyst has already been demonstrated to have validity in analysing current exhibition practice. Ettema also seeks to find a way forward, combining the strengths of both the formalist and analytical perspectives:

> Instead of choosing between objects and ideas, we should learn to synthesise them. If we can understand the power that objects have over people, we can harness that energy and use it to communicate our historical ideas. We need a new understanding of objects that replaces both the formalist belief in their transforming cultural power and the analytical attitude of artifact as a cultural byproduct.
>
> (Ettema, 1987, pp. 77–8)

This dialectical advance Ettema terms a 'symbolic synthesis', which recognizes that 'objects are symbols used in human communication ... one that is primarily visual and nonverbal'. The key for the museum is therefore to reveal this social function of objects, and drawing on the work of Carson, Ettema argues that the proper study of museums is not the history of material things (formalism) but 'the history of materialism. How have we come to be a society so dependent on the production and ownership of objects? ... how people use objects to define and control relationships with other people ... As bastions of modern materialism, museums have an excellent opportunity to study the history of modern materialism.' Against the view that this closes certain themes from museum enquiry, because the material does not survive, Ettema gives the example of slavery, arguing that 'objects, however few, were still important symbols in the lives of the slaves'. He argues that 'Nearly an infinite number of goods-based approaches to social issues such as this exists; the problem for museums lies not in choosing the topic, but in addressing its material dimensions.' This is not an unwelcome narrowing of the subject matter tackled by museums, as some would argue: 'Teaching the history of materialism ... does not so much limit the scope of history museums as it focuses their attention on the issues they can best address' (Ettema, 1987, pp. 79–84).

This is a useful contribution, calling for a renewed focus on what I have identified as the USP of museums. It has found some support from those seeking a way forward from the formalist and analyst perspectives (Moore and Tucker, 1994; Suggitt, 1994a). But it does not fully provide a theoretical perspective from which to develop this. How exactly do we decode the social function of artefacts? It is a starting point, a call to arms, rather than the chart of a clear way forward. It is from this starting point that the next chapter will proceed to explore what is possible within the territory which Ettema astutely identifies.

Exhibitions are not for curators or museologists but for the public. How do the public view the different types of displays? Part of the problem has been that until the past decade or so, there has been little in the way of systematic evaluation of the responses of visitors to exhibitions.

This is now a burgeoning area of work, a very welcome development. Ironically, however, social history curators have probably been the slowest in taking up such evaluation. This is surprising, given their concern to democratize museums and involve the community as widely as possible. Even some major recent permanent social history exhibitions in Britain have had no element of visitor evaluation built into them. Evaluation of analyst (and formalist) exhibitions all too often consists of nothing more than a comments book for visitors. As a result we can say very little about the public's reaction to the move from formalist to analyst displays. Proponents of the latter will point to significantly increased visitor figures. Yet this only demonstrates their popularity over formalist displays of limited and unappealing subject matter. Equally, one could argue that the phenomenal success of the 'People's Shows' exhibitions in Britain in the 1990s – displays of the public's own collections in museums, discussed in detail in Chapter 5 – demonstrates that if the right objects are on display, then a formalist approach can be extremely successful. It is ironic that Walsall Museum Service led the way in developing the People's Shows, under the leadership of Peter Jenkinson, who in the late 1980s was the most trenchant critic of the importance of the object (Jenkinson, 1989). Similarly, displays which in Pearce's terms are 'resurrection of the body' are extremely popular, again where interpretation may be minimal. Ettema argues that despite the laudable efforts of the analysts, formalists can argue that people go to museums to see objects: 'It certainly is disconcerting for historians when the public rushes past didactic displays, missing the point by fixating on some precious and curious object' (Ettema, 1987, p. 77). Similarly, Tucker contends that 'It is a delusion to believe visitors ... are won over to museums by the book-on-the-wall approach ... what keeps new generations of people coming into museums is the magic of real things' (Tucker, 1994, p. 4). It is possible that many people prefer the formalist to the analyst approach, if this is the only choice they are given.

The lack of evaluation of exhibitions means that there is insufficient evidence to dispute or support such views. Two recent qualitative pieces of non-visitor research, while not directly addressing the issue of the role of objects, indirectly provide some limited evidence which is uncomfortable for the analysts in particular. A survey of non-visitors in London found that their preferred exhibitions were those which involved hands-on contact with objects, and also 'resurrections', such as the street scenes at York Castle Museum (London Museums Consultative Committee, 1991, pp. 40–2). Yet these are particularly derided by analyst social historians, who seem bemused and dismissive of this popularity: 'although such "total reconstructions" are clearly popular with the public there must be major reservations about their suitability for communicating ideas about major causes and effects within society' (Marsh, 1984, p. 3). A survey for the new museum service in Croydon again highlighted the desire for hands-on displays with objects, and not just for children. Older people 'have lived through recent history and their memories are already halfway there, breathing life into the artefacts. They experience intense emotion when they can touch and handle genuine objects from the past'. Again, a suggested version of complete reconstructions (resurrections) was popular: 'Surprisingly, old photographs of streets and people fail to make much impression. ... The idea is to recreate a scene ... on video exactly as it would have been using the objects, costumes and locations of the time. Once having oriented the visitor by film, he should then be invited to touch and use the actual objects that were demonstrated in the film' (Fisher, 1990, pp. 33, 35).

Further research on the relationship between people and objects, and specifically objects in museum displays, is required. The evidence that exists suggests that objects do have a power for people, but that this is too often negated by both the formalist and analyst approaches, which both fail to communicate with the material culture at their disposal, but for diametrically opposed reasons.

Historians or curators?

The inherent weakness of the analyst approach can be demonstrated by analysing the process of producing exhibitions from this perspective. Several social history curators have written interesting reflections on their approach. Wilkinson has described the process of putting together an exhibition for Hull museums in 1989, 'That's Entertainment: Popular Culture in Hull'. This was a highly laudable attempt to break into a previously ignored subject area, but the analyst approach tends to marginalize material culture from the outset:

> Our intention is to present exhibitions on themes in social history and the starting point for these is not the collections but the historical ideas. Social history collections contain a varied assortment of objects reflecting more the changing tastes and interests of previous curators than the ordinary life of the population. Because of their irrational and unrepresentative nature they cannot be the source of ideas for an exhibition. We begin as historians researching the subject matter and determining ideas. Once this academic work has been carried out we can turn to the collections to consider how objects can be used ... how they could be incorporated. Lack of objects, however, was not a reason to exclude subjects ... which I felt were important.
>
> (Wilkinson, 1989a)

Wilkinson is rightly critical of the weaknesses of the existing collections, but it does not logically automatically follow from this that 'historical ideas' rather than some other forms of material culture, not currently in the collections, should be the starting point. Immediately the approach is as 'historians determining ideas' through 'academic work', rather than curators interpreting people's material culture. Objects as a result are marginal – they are 'incorporated' where possible. Subjects are tackled even where there is no available material culture. Unsurprisingly, therefore, 'The biggest problem we had in presenting this exhibition was the lack of 3-dimensional objects for display.' The exhibition was clearly a success in the sense that the subject matter proved popular, but 'some nagging doubts remain. The amount of information we were able to include was very limited ... the final text was condensed to such a degree that ideas became generalised and simplified' (Wilkinson, 1989a).

This is inevitable in an analyst exhibition, which is attempting to put across complex historical ideas through an inappropriate medium – a display. One cannot help feeling that the excellent publication which accompanied the exhibition (Wilkinson, 1989b) was perhaps a more appropriate means to explore the subject. And this subject matter was more object-rich than others. A review of the preceding temporary social history exhibition at Hull, School Days: An Exhibition on Schools and Schooling in Hull, commented that 'Objects are used where appropriate, though the two-dimensional inevitably dominates.' 'The exhibition is accompanied by an excellent publication ... one might be forgiven for assuming that the exhibition is really there to promote the book' (Davies, 1988, p. 5). This is not, however, simply a question of arguing, as was discussed earlier, that some subjects are inappropriate, because insufficient material evidence survives, whether inside or outside the museum. It is a deeper question of attempting to use inappropriate social history techniques in a museum. Curators are attempting to 'tell stories' or discuss 'issues' of social history through exhibitions, but displays are not an appropriate way to do this effectively, compared with, for example, publications.

Oral history has been taken up with alacrity by social history curators in recent years, who see it as perhaps the best source to democratize the past. Having worked primarily as an oral historian for three years, I am well placed to appreciate its undoubted value in this sense, although this is of course limited to within living memory. Oral history rather than material culture has become the driving force behind many museum projects, but this is highly problematic. It leads curators to choose topics for exhibitions for which the material culture is purely secondary. For example, a curator working on an exhibition on a trade union leader found that 'we were trying to do a political exhibition with objects, such as banners, which bore only marginal relevance to the events we were describing. The extracts [of oral history] therefore became like objects, in that they were historical testament in themselves ... direct quotations are probably as important as the objects themselves which may be marginal to the event you are trying to interpret' (Mansfield, 1986, p. 52). Exhibitions led by oral history inevitably result in analyst books on walls. This is not to deny that this is not an important piece of history, but it would clearly be much better presented as a book, or radio or television programme, rather than an exhibition. Is it therefore appropriate work for a museum curator? Would it not be better to leave such projects to others whose brief it is to do such work?

This does not mean that oral history techniques are not highly appropriate to curatorial work. They can be absolutely invaluable in assisting in our mission, to explore people's relationship with material culture. A model of this kind of approach is McDaniel's study of the homes and material culture of black families, and how the houses were lived in and the objects used (McDaniel, 1982), an approach which to a degree informed the People's Story social history display in Edinburgh, opened in 1989 (Clark, 1988; Beevers *et al.*, 1988).

One of the most praised permanent social history exhibitions in Britain in recent years has been 'The Story of Hull and Its People'. Frostick, in a valuable discussion of the display she produced, comments that 'A great deal of time was spent deliberating the logistics of an exhibition about seven hundred years of almost 300,000 people's lives in 180 square metres of space. ... Theoretically of course the task is impossible' (Frostick, 1992, p. 51). Why, therefore, attempt what is impossible within an exhibition, but much more possible for the publication which accompanies the display? Displays simply cannot satisfactorily convey such histories adequately – it is no wonder curators become frustrated in attempting to do so. Again, the excellent publication which accompanied the exhibition was much more impressive (Frostick, 1990).

Similarly, an exhibition called 'Great City!', which opened in 1993, on the history of Newcastle upon Tyne since 1914, reveals similar problems. Ross comments that 'We started out like good little urban historians, asking standard urban history questions. Why is Newcastle the way it is? How have the structures of the past shaped Newcastle in the present? What was it like to live in Newcastle in the past? How have the experiences of the people contributed to the character and development of the city? ... being social historians at heart, people were central' (Ross, 1994, p. 43). But 'we' are not urban historians, 'we' are curators. The questions are inappropriate, they automatically marginalize people's material culture. As a result the exhibition is structured around text rather than objects: 'This basic structure was made physical through the panel text' (Ross, 1994, p. 43). The only way in which substantial elements of material culture get into the exhibition is through 'The People's Cases', a variant on the People's Shows, which 'enable people to contribute objects to Great City as well as memories, the things that illustrate their own families' lives' (Ross, 1994, p. 44). As a result this exhibition is far richer in objects than most social history displays, but objects are still largely marginal illustrations, except for the People's Cases, which are an unintegrated formalist element.

Museums are about the relationship between people and material culture; this is their USP. Frostick, however, comments that 'Our essential service, to the widest possible community, is to provide people with a sense of their own history' (Frostick, 1992, p. 49). This is a very much wider brief, and there are many people other than museum curators who are involved in this. One must surely add to Frostick's statement 'through an exploration of their relationship with material culture'. The fact that only 7 per cent of people in a major survey identified visiting a museum as the most enjoyable way to find out about local history (Merriman,

1991, p. 120) might not be such a bad statistic, and more a reflection of just how many alternative approaches to the past that there are. Similarly, Fleming argues that the task of museums is 'making sense of modern urban life. ... Social history curators have to learn the skills and techniques of the social scientist, which is a world away from learning about different types of police truncheons, the design of the kitchen cabinet, or being able to tell the difference between mahogany and teak' (Fleming, 1992, p. 37). Again, this is to turn social history curatorship into something completely inappropriate to museums. Urban historians are urban historians, social scientists are social scientists, and curators are curators, first and foremost. The second part of Fleming's quote is a parody of formalist curatorship. Yet much more is possible in the interpretation of material culture than what the formalists suggest, as will be discussed in Chapter 4. To the craftsmen and women who worked in mahogany or teak, or the workers who felled the trees in the rain forest; to the ordinary person who chose and purchased and used a particular kitchen cabinet; or to the policeman who had a particular truncheon to convey a particular status – such differences clearly were important. Material things and the (often minute) differences between them were and are important to people. Social science and urban history might provide some useful insights, but they are no substitute for the study of material culture and its meaning in people's lives as the heart of museum curatorship.

The rise of social history in museums, while it has contributed a great deal in terms of attempting to ensure that museums serve all their publics, has brought problems. Indeed, one can argue that history is in fact an inappropriate discipline in a museum, because it marginalizes material culture. Social historians are trained as undergraduates and postgraduates to use documentary sources, and perhaps oral history, but rarely if ever material culture. Academic social historians have ignored material culture in the past, particularly in Britain. There is some evidence that this is beginning to change, but academics disagree on the strength of this interest. Porter argues that 'social, cultural and economic historians have become fascinated with the history of material culture and the meaning of things' (Porter, 1992, p. 5), whereas Ormrod more recently has argued that 'historiographical trends have turned the majority of economic and social historians away from archaeological evidence, in the broadest sense ... a minority are moving in the reverse direction. The movement is insufficiently large and too recent to have produced any notable changes in courses and degree structures' (Ormrod, 1994, p. 12; see also Davies, 1993, p. 5). Paradoxically, while social history academics still largely ignore material culture, history provision in museums in Britain is now dominated by social historians trained by such academics. In North America there is a slightly stronger tradition of material culture studies in academia, but social history there too is now the dominant paradigm in history in museums.

Only if they attend postgraduate museum studies courses do social historians gain any understanding of material culture theory, but it is 'perhaps unreasonable to expect such training in itself to deconstruct entirely the document-centred academic approach that conditions social historians' (Moore and Tucker, 1994, p. 22). Kavanagh has gone as far as to argue that the term history 'may be unsatisfactory for the definition of the museum's discipline' (Kavanagh, 1990, p. 55), and that it may be that regional ethnography on the Swedish model might be a better term and academic approach. Elsewhere I have demonstrated the problems for specifically labour history in museums, which have resulted from allowing the museum approach to the subject to be dictated by the academic subject (Moore, 1994, pp. 155–62). Social history in museums is based on an academic approach which ignores material culture, as opposed, for example, to either archaeology or art. Why should history in the museum be so different? As Brown comments, 'Materials have a strength and a power all their own; consequently, as students of material culture we must constantly remind ourselves that our methods are not and will never be the same as those used by historians' (Brown, 1993, p. 142).

Unable to interpret material culture effectively, because unable to ask the right questions of it, social history curators have defined a new role, but one which makes them public historians, and not specifically museum curators (see Frostick, 1992; White, 1993; Ross, 1994). Museum curators should be public historians, but of a particular kind, specializing in the interpretation of material evidence. There is nothing intrinsically wrong with public history, but if museums are redefined in this way they cease to be museums, and become something much broader and more diffuse. Suggitt has argued that 'The museum canon ought to be broad enough to allow different types of projects, aimed at different audiences. Some may be object rich, some not. Diversity should be expected, after all, libraries have room for Jane Austen and Charles Dickens, as well as Catherine Cookson and Jeffrey Archer' (Suggitt, 1994a, p. 5). This is not a fair analogy. We do not find some libraries with books, and some without! Similarly, museum projects will differ in the material culture they explore, but they should all be derived from material culture, and its meaning for people.

Some argue that such decisions might be out of the curator's hands: 'Local politicians may require a museum to respond to issues, such as community bonding or environmental education, which are high on their political agenda, regardless of whether or not the 'primacy of the object' is compromised' (Davies, 1994c, p. 22). I would agree that museums have to follow this political agenda, but that such authorities need to be informed as to what museums can and cannot do, that they can address such issues through material culture, and the value of exploring material culture to do so be emphasized. If museums cannot be argued for as museums, then we may as well abandon them.

4

Stones can speak and objects sing

'What clue could you have as to his identity?'
'Only as much as we can deduce.'
'From his hat?'
'Precisely.'
'But you are joking. What can you gather from this old battered felt?'
'Here is my lens. You know my methods ...'
'I can see nothing,' said I, handing it back to my friend.
'On the contrary, Watson, you can see everything. You fail, however, to reason from what you see.'
                          (A. Conan Doyle, 1981, p. 146)

Too seldom do we use the artifacts that make up our environment to understand the past. Too seldom do we try to read objects as we read books – to understand the people and times that created them, used them, and discarded them. In part this is because it is not easy to read history from things. They are illegible to those who know how to read only writing. They are mute to those who listen only for pronouncements from the past. But they do speak; they can be read. But how?   (Lubar and Kingery, 1993, p. viii)

Stones can be made to speak – and the most ordinary of objects sing – by creative museum staff.
            (Editorial, Museums Journal, *September 1994, p. 7)*

Introduction

Objects are only dumb if we do not know how to 'let them speak'; they only lie if we wilfully misinterpret them. In any case, both of these charges could equally be made against documentary sources. If we cannot read, documentary sources are dumb! We also have to interpret them with care, to establish as far as possible their true meanings. On the contrary, objects are not dumb but inexhaustible, capable of an infinite range of readings and re-readings. But how can objects be 'read'?

It is only in the past three decades or so that serious academic attention has turned towards this. In 1957 one American historian commented that if the artefacts of man's past serve only as illustrations, then they might as well be reduced to ... pictures. One could save building space and custodial care by taking stereopticon views of the objects in museums, tabulating the dimensions and other data on computer cards, filing the pictures and the cards, and discarding the junk to antique dealers or depositing it on the city dump. ... There is, however, another alternative – the alternative of meeting the intellectual challenge of the artefact. ... By what critical method can they be examined? ... It is the essence of anti-intellectualism to say that these walls cannot talk. Of course they can talk. It is only that we cannot talk to them, cannot ask them questions, and cannot understand their answers. But until artefacts can be subjected to internal criticism and made to bear their witness, the task of historical methodology is unfinished.   (Hesseltine, 1989, pp. 99–100)

Pearce has offered an interesting explanation of why material culture until recently remained academically relatively neglected, in that modern Western thought places a low value on the material world and its products, paralleling Christian morality, although paradoxically capitalism places an inordinately high value on the material. Furthermore, because objects are independent of words, cannot adequately be described in words, we must see them and perhaps touch them to understand them, whereas academic study is 'dominated by linguistic modes of communication which find it difficult to appreciate the significance of material culture' (Pearce, 1992, pp. 17–23).

The academic study of material culture has flourished in recent years. There is now a multiplicity of approaches and studies, drawing scholars from a wide range of background disciplines. The field is now so large, and theories and approaches are so diverse, that it is difficult for those in museums to keep up with the scholarship. Yet despite this burgeoning field of study, curators have been slow to develop such ideas within their work. This has been especially marked in history, where the document-centred approach of traditional historiography has meant that, as a result, the analyst approach, which marginalizes material culture, has predominated. This is even the case in North America, where academic material culture studies have been at their strongest: 'Intellectually, North American history museums have only begun to explore the explanatory power of the artefact' (Schlereth, 1989b, p. 303). As a result, objects remain largely dumb, because their interpretation is so minimal. Equally, art curators have been loathe to take up new approaches to material culture, and remain largely trapped in the formalist perspective, where objects 'speak for themselves', but without adequate interpretation these objects may well 'lie'.

In both cases, art and history, this has much to do with management and organizational issues; it is difficult to bring about a radical change of approach in any organization, not least a museum. But this is only a partial explanation. It also reflects the fact that few curators engage with material culture theory in their undergraduate studies, though this is beginning to change in the USA and Canada, if not significantly in the UK. Art historians largely only consider the aesthetic aspects and do not grapple with the wider range of approaches to material culture. Social historians, in Britain at least, as we have noted, largely ignore material culture altogether.

Academics who study material culture are not necessarily concerned with museum representations, though Schlereth has notably and valuably sought to popularize their studies and insights for a museum audience (Schlereth, 1989b). Museologists therefore have a key role to play in introducing curators to such thinking. Museological training on both sides of the Atlantic is now beginning to do this, with material culture studies forming a key part of such courses. Indeed, in Britain it is noticeable that those who have been most negative about the role of material culture received their training on the highly influential University of Leicester museum studies course, before the introduction of a material culture component. Pearce's work (Pearce, 1992) is of particular importance, providing a thorough grounding in the intricacies and nuances of a variety of approaches to material culture theory, and offering a trenchant and convincing critique of the weaknesses of current museum practice in the light of this. Pearce also offers important new thinking in the field, as a significant material culture theorist, as well as a museologist interpreting material culture theory (see, in particular, Pearce, 1995).

This academic museological training in material culture is beginning to have an impact on museums in Britain. Indeed, it was instrumental in fuelling the recent debates around the role of material culture, by influencing a younger generation of social history curators, including myself. Yet this impact has not been as significant as one would wish. Partly this is because the study of material culture forms little or no part of the undergraduate studies of many of those enrolling on postgraduate museum studies courses. It is also because the implications for museum practice are not directly explored. While the closing chapter of *Museums, Objects and Collections*, 'Projects and prospects', offers some valuable thoughts as to future possibilities, it does not in detail discuss what these might be (Pearce, 1992, Chapter 12). This may have been beyond the scope of the study, and omitted from a desire not to be prescriptive, but to leave museum workers open to explore ideas from among those introduced. Yet a gap remains between theory and practice. Curators may appreciate new ways of looking at material culture, but still fail to see how these can be translated into practice, particularly as their implications are radically to challenge the formalist and analyst perspectives.

The theory needs to address the practical situation of curators more closely, the implications of theoretical developments need to be spelled out more clearly and directly. The landmark study by Pearce needs to be followed through into a much more practical guide as to how such ideas and approaches to material culture can be adapted in real museum projects and exhibitions. This is my intention in this chapter.

How can we read objects?

What can curators learn from the material culturalists? Schlereth is an expert guide through the complexities of this burgeoning, multidisciplinary academic field. He has outlined nine key approaches to American material culture studies (see Figure 4.1) (Schlereth, 1989a). These have been slightly rearranged from Schlereth's original listing, for reasons that will become clear. The art history paradigm equates to the formalist perspective in museums. Schlereth comments: 'Called "object fetishism" by its critics, "object primacy" by its advocates, this approach to material culture study remains content to "let the object speak for itself"' (Schlereth, 1989a, p. 40). However, Schlereth demonstrates that it would be unfair to conclude that no new methodological challenges or innovations had been made in this field in recent years, or that there was not something of value in this approach. Social history in Schlereth's terms is self-explanatory, from the discussion in the previous chapter, equating to the analyst perspective. The cultural history approach seeks the 'reconstruction of the origins and development of local and regional cultures in time and place' (Schlereth, 1989a, p. 46), finding visible expression in museums in outdoor historic village recreations in particular. The functionalist approach holds that 'culture is primarily a means of adaptation to environment, with technology being the primary adaptive mechanism' (Schlereth, 1989a, p. 53). The environmentalist perspective, derived from cultural landscape studies, particularly in terms of the diffusion of artefacts, can be considered to some extent a branch of functionalism. The structuralist view, drawing on semiotic theory, considers objects as signs and symbols. The symbolist approach appears to be an earlier variant of this, lacking the deeper theoretical perspective of the former. The national character focus seeks to use artefacts to explain the collective *Weltanschauung* of an entire nation. It seems to be a peculiarly American focus, drawing on functionalism and perhaps more so symbolism, but lacking a coherent theoretical basis. The behaviourist concept is concerned with focusing on the relationship of the individual to material culture, particularly its maker.

Schlereth notes that all of these approaches have had an impact in museums in the USA, but to widely differing degrees. The impact of art history and social history is obvious, as is cultural history through the proliferation of 'living history' outdoor museum villages and other site reconstructions. Functionalism is still powerful in archaeology museums, behaviourism in folk displays. The others have also had some significant museum impact, except structuralism, which 'has yet to inform a major history exhibition' (Schlereth, 1989b, p. 303). A key point to note from this is that while museums in the USA at least have to some extent benefited from this diversity of approaches (except perhaps structuralism), museums in Britain have been far less influenced, tending towards, at least in the arts subjects, art history or social history (formalist or analyst), with a smaller element of cultural history. The now dominant social history approach in history museums is one of only nine different perspectives which could be drawn upon.

Pearce has similarly considered the theoretical perspectives to material culture, and as a museologist, has placed a greater emphasis than Schlereth on how they currently or in future could have an impact in museums. In the core of *Museums, Objects and Collections* (Pearce, 1992, Chapters 7 to 10), Pearce focuses on functionalism, structuralism, history and behaviourism. As we saw in Chapter 3, Pearce divides the approaches to history into four: treasure, relics, illustrative narrative and resurrection. The relation between Schlereth's and Pearce's work is indicated in Figure 4.1.

Schlereth	Pearce
Art History	History: Treasure or Relics
Social History	History: Illustrated Narrative
Cultural History	History: Resurrection
Functionalist	Functionalist
Environmentalist	Subset of Functionalist
Structuralist	Structuralist
Symbolist	Relates to Structuralist
National Character	Relates to Structuralist
Behaviourist	Behaviourist

Figure 4.1 *Classification of theoretical approaches to material culture by Schlereth (1989a) and their relationship with museum representations identified by Pearce (Pearce, 1992)*

Schlereth argues that all the approaches are of value, but is not primarily concerned with their appropriateness to museum work. Pearce, on the other hand, in considering this directly, is, as we have seen, highly critical of the history approach. She argues that functionalism is of some value, and that structuralism can offer enormously helpful insights. However, she also argues that functionalism and structuralism, with their focus on society as a whole, neglect the individual and the cause of social change, and argues therefore that these must be linked to a behaviourist approach, which considers the relationship of the individual to the material world, and the historical dimension of this, bringing together the social and individual approaches, through a process called structuration (Pearce, 1992, Chapter 10).

The relative value to museums of these different approaches to material culture identified by Pearce and Schlereth will be considered below. Useful though it may be for a curator to be aware of such a variety of possible approaches, it does not take us as far as a full analysis of all the aspects of a particular piece of material culture. All of these are potentially helpful ways to consider the interpretation of the social significance of an object, but it would be valuable to have a clear framework for artefact analysis to which these approaches could be drawn as appropriate. Imagine you have a particular object in front of you: where will you begin in your analysis and interpretation?

Using artefact analysis in exhibitions

Several writers have produced thought-provoking schemes or models of artefact analysis (see Pearce, 1992, pp. 265–73), but the most valuable appears to be that of Pearce (1986). This does not appear to have had the impact it deserves in museum practice. One reason is perhaps that many curators do not see the value in 'dissecting' one object in this way, regarding it as too time-consuming, and unhelpful for display. Pearce has published two pieces which attempt to demonstrate the usefulness of this model by looking at particular objects, an infantry officer's jacket worn at the battle of Waterloo (Pearce, 1990) and a teapot (Pearce, 1993), the latter being deliberately aimed at social history curators, who seem particularly resistant to this approach. Both offer exemplary analyses of particular pieces of material culture, though they do not address each section of the model, and even the latter is perhaps insufficiently explicit in terms of museum practice for its audience. However, given the dominance of the analyst perspective, influencing social history curators in this way is a difficult task, as it requires many of them to make what amounts to almost a paradigm shift in their approach.

Pearce's model provides a structure whereby all facets of a piece of material culture can be explored in detail, to provide the fullest range of 'associated information', so that an object is not simply a curio. It would be invaluable if this was carried out for each museum object at the point of accession, even if this meant that far fewer objects could be added to collections. What percentage of current collections are little more than curios, because of the lack of such a detailed object analysis? I have modified the terminology of Pearce's model slightly to make it perhaps a little more user-friendly (see Figure 4.2), using single-word terms which seem to fit with each section. The model, by offering a thorough and logical approach to artefact analysis, gives a structure within which the value of the variety of material culture studies can be appreciated. But its value is much greater than this. What follows is an attempt to demonstrate that

1. Description	5. Location
2. Identification	6. Distribution
3. Construction	7. Significance
4. History	8. Interpretation

Figure 4.2 *Model of artefact analysis (after Pearce, 1986)*

by focusing minutely in this way on one object, a host of highly imaginative ideas for curatorial projects and exhibitions, of a very practical
nature, can be generated. This could be any piece of material culture,
whether high or popular culture. Applied to an artefact of high culture,
the model reveals the ordinary in the extraordinary; applied to popular
culture, it reveals the extraordinary in the ordinary.

By developing projects based on this method of object analysis, museums
can demystify curatorship, and reveal the processes and choices which lie
behind museum exhibitions – what Pearce has termed 'rhetorical curatorship' (Pearce, 1992, p. 264). This can be taken further, by enabling the
public to undertake aspects of the artefact analysis themselves in displays.
The fashion in museums currently is 'community involvement' or participation. Yet when the public are involved in the exhibition process, it tends
to be limited to the analyst approach, which involves community groups
producing their own 'book on the wall' exhibition. Curators do not tend
to engage the public in a detailed analysis of material culture, either as participants in the exhibition process or as visitors. Leon has argued that 'If
visitors are to analyze exhibits and set them into a broader context, they
must be taught the skills of analysis relevant to artifacts and other aspects
of material culture' (Leon, 1987, p. 138). Similarly, Schlereth has argued
that we need to develop the audience's '"object knowledge" – a special
type of literacy that would enable them to read both the museum's collections and the museum's context with greater interest and insight' (quoted
in Leon, 1987, p.139; see also Davis and Gibb, 1988). A good deal of
work along these lines has been developed by museum educationalists, but
the ideas are rarely integrated into exhibitions, symptomatic of how
museum education is still too often treated as an afterthought, once a
gallery is completed, rather than as a crucial intrinsic element. The model
for artefact analysis can generate many exhibition ideas and approaches
that do not just teach people how to look at and analyse material culture,
but enable them to learn how to develop such skills; museums can share
the skills of curatorship with their visitors.

Description

'The obvious starting point is the object's physical body, the components
from which it has been constructed, and any ornament which may have
been added ... a physical description of the piece' (Pearce, 1994, p. 128).
This in itself suggests a number of creative approaches to exhibitions by
engaging the public in this curatorial work. How often does the way that
objects are currently displayed lead visitors to focus sufficiently on a particular object to be able to describe it with any accuracy? Museum
education staff have produced a range of valuable approaches to this (see,
for example, Durbin *et al.*, 1990, pp. 20–5). Visitors, perhaps more usefully termed participants, could approach any particular piece of material

culture – say, a teapot, as this seems a popular example to take in material culture analysis! (see Pearce, 1993; Prown, 1993). They could be encouraged to draw it, photograph it or describe it in words. This would reveal how each of us perceives the object in slightly different ways. This first gallery might contain only a single teapot in the centre, with the walls filled with the equipment provided and the results of the public's activities. One might also suggest an introductory gallery prior to this which only reveals the subject of the exhibition, by displaying the written descriptions produced by visitors. The whole exhibition then becomes an experience of mystery and discovery.

Ideally this exploration of the object would not be limited to the purely visual, particularly as it is essential to meet the needs of people with sight impairments. We have up to five senses – if possible, the object should also be touched, smelt, listened to (if touch creates sound) and even tasted! We can be encouraged to explore an object in the way we first began to when we entered the world as a child. Such a hands-on (but not as yet tongues-on) approach, used increasingly in education work, is a key to attracting non-visitors in particular, who view the lack of such activities as a major weakness of museums (Fisher, 1990; Hooper-Greenhill, 1991, pp. 103–9).

Prown has argued that such a sensory approach to artefacts is perhaps the most powerful way to explore history as it was experienced by our ancestors, for 'Artifacts constitute the only class of historical events that occurred in the past but survive into the present. They can be reexperienced' (Prown, 1993, pp. 2–3). In an important passage, worth quoting at length, he argues:

> We are trying to understand another culture whose patterns of belief, whose mind, is different from our own. Our own beliefs, our mindset, biases our view. It would be ideal, and this is not as silly as it sounds, if we could approach that other culture mindlessly, at least while we gather our data. This is the great promise of material culture: by undertaking cultural interpretation through artifacts, we engage the other culture in the first instance not with our minds, the seat of our cultural biases, but with our senses. Figuratively speaking, we put ourselves inside the bodies of the individuals who made or used these objects; we see with their eyes and touch with their hands. To identify with people from the past or from other places empathetically through the senses is clearly a different way of engaging them than abstractly through the reading of written words. Instead of our minds making intellectual contact with their minds, our senses make affective contact with their sensory experience
>
> (Prown, 1993, p. 17)

When the object has been explored through the senses it can then be explored intellectually, by considering its design and ornamentation in relation to its function. What is this object for? Why does it look like this? If it didn't look like this, how alternatively could it look? Why is it decorated in this way? Why do you think it has its particular colour, texture, size, weight? The condition of the object could also be considered. Is it in good condition, or damaged in some way? What exactly do we mean by these terms? These questions of our teapot would be posed to the public, initially with only clues, to let them respond imaginatively.

Some would argue that we do not have five senses but six; certainly we should encourage an intuitive or emotional engagement with the object. What does it make you feel like? Do you like it or not? Do you consider it ugly or beautiful, and why? Perceptions of beauty and taste could be explored, as Suggitt has suggested (Suggitt, 1994b). The possibilities for exploring a single object in this way are limited only by our imaginations.

Identification

'Objects do relate to each other in an objective sense, they do fall into groups with shared characteristics' (Pearce, 1994, p. 128). Visitors can be encouraged to carry out this identification process for themselves, through visible storage of, for example, a collection of teapots, and associated documentary information. This process of identification could also explore the basis of typology. When is an object similar, but not quite the same? How do we know when it is exactly the same? What role do colour, material, texture, weight, shape, size etc. play within this? This could explore how we define things, how we know what they are by knowing what they are not. What exactly is the difference between a teapot and a coffee pot? Why are there so many differences in designs of teapot? How far can the definition 'teapot' be stretched until it becomes meaningless? What exactly do the differences in design indicate? A wide range of interpretative approaches could be used to explore this. Leon makes some useful practical suggestions, including possible interactive learning games with objects (Leon, 1987, pp. 141–2).

Construction

Sources could be made available for participants to discover when, where, how, why and by whom the object was made. This would reveal the technology, commerce, labour and social history of the time. Where possible, demonstrations of the making of the object by traditional methods could be used. Visitors could also be asked to consider the materials used in the object. The processes by which the provenance of the materials was established could be revealed, enabling an exploration of where each material came from geographically, how it was produced or extracted and transported, when and by whom, using which technology and under what social conditions. As participants have been asked to consider the function of the object, the analysis of the materials of the teapot inevitably broadens to a consideration of tea as a raw material. Our teapot thus leads us to consider the workings of the global capitalist economy and the history of imperial exploitation!

Considering the materials in any object is crucial, but 'it is ironic that studies of material culture should so neglect the actual materials that go into creating culture', being overwhelmingly concerned with 'form and design, rather than substance ... the material itself conveys messages, metaphorical and otherwise, about the objects and their place in a culture' (Friedel, 1993, p. 42). Friedel offers an invaluable discussion of this, considering how we might consider why particular materials are used (function, availability, economy, style); how this might change as circumstances change (geography, technology, science, fashion, competition); and how humankind has developed from using largely naturally occurring materials, to an almost limitless technical ability to create new materials. This is a key opening contribution to an area which deserves fuller exploration, in both material culture studies and museum projects.

Friedel also explores the issue that different values attach to different materials, and that rarity is only part of this (Friedel, 1993, p. 45). As Pearce comments, 'some kinds of objects seem to strike our human nature as desirable in the simplest sense. Most communities ascribe considerable value to artefacts made from bright and flashing or somehow intrinsically attractive materials like gold, pearl, shell, colourful feathers or ivory, and this value rests as much in the lust of the eye as it does in the comparative rarity of the materials concerned' (Pearce, 1992, p. 33). This could be explored through our teapot collection. Which are the most appealing to visitors, and is this a function of design or material? There are clearly endless possibilities for exhibitions in their own right which look at individual materials and their comparable uses in different cultures, or displays which focus on this issue of value in the apparently universal 'lust of the human eye'.

History

After the point of manufacture, what has been the history of the artefact? Who owned it and why? What do we mean by ownership? By what process did it pass from one person to another? Was it bought, given, loaned, donated, swapped, a bequest, stolen? What do we mean when we describe an object as a gift, a loan, a swap, a commodity, a stolen item? If we give a 'gift', do we still expect something in return? What are the power relations in these processes of transfer of ownership? How did the item accrue value? What do we mean by value? Is value a function of scarcity of the item, its material, its age or the craft required to produce it? What are the politics of value? (For a useful discussion of this, see Appadurai, 1994.) How did it end up in a museum? How far does this reflect its value, to whom and in what sense? Would you like to own it? If so, why? If not, why not? Do we not all pick out items in museums that we would like to take home? Alan Bennett, the English playwright, in a television documentary about the meaning that Leeds City Art Gallery held for him, admitted that 'My appreciation of painting is quite shallow. I find it hard to divorce appreciation from possession. So I know I like a picture only when I am tempted to walk out with it under my raincoat.' Visitors could be asked: 'Which objects would you like to steal?' Again the possibilities for exploration by visitors are enormous, and a variety of imaginative interpretative techniques could be used to explore these questions.

Location

'Objects exist in a locational relationship to other artefacts and to the landscape, and the study of these relationships can be very fruitful for our understanding of the role of the artefact' (Pearce, 1994, p. 130). Such information may not have been recorded with objects collected in the past, and it may be impossible now to piece this together, but it is possible in contemporary collecting. This involves a consideration of the other objects with which the object is associated, for objects tend to be understood in sets (Pearce, 1993). Ames has termed this association a 'constellation', for 'as with celestial constellations, artefact constellations yield a larger picture when read as a whole ... as indices of attitudes, values, and patterns of behaviour' (Ames, 1989, p. 209).

Again, this is not just an academic exercise, but something which could be imaginatively explored in displays. In one location, a teapot may be associated with a tea caddy, teacups, saucers, a milk-jug and a sugar bowl. In another, a packet of tea, a mug and a milk bottle. What would you read into this? To a British person, this suggests a distinction between middle- or upper-class habits of tea drinking in the former, and working-class habits in the latter. The relative degrees of poverty are acutely revealed by the various vessels used for drinking tea by the building workers in Robert Tressell's classic novel of Edwardian working-class life: 'old jam jars, mugs, dilapidated teacups and one or two empty condensed milk tins' (Tressell, 1965). Tea-making in different countries and cultures as well as classes could be considered in this way. Tea things could also be deliberately decontextualized, placed in the wrong sets, and participants asked to rearrange them. This might be linked to information about the different owners of each set. This can be taken a step further. How far can one object be extrapolated to reveal the particular taste and lifestyle of its owner? Participants could be asked to link individual teapots to photographs of domestic interiors. To which kitchen does this teapot belong?

The spatial location of an object is also revealing of social attitudes, values and patterns of behaviour. For example, taking tea with someone in different rooms in a house is revealing of the closeness of your relationship with them. Do you know someone well enough to have tea with them not in the lounge, but the kitchen? Or in the bedroom? Participants could be asked 'Do you have one of these? If so, where do you keep yours? And what does this say about you?' about a whole range of objects. For example, 'Do you have any condoms? If so, where do you keep them? In your bedside table or your partner's? In the bathroom? In your wallet or handbag? If you do not have any condoms, what does this reveal about you?'

It would also be interesting to consider how the placement of artefacts is viewed in different cultures. Feng shui, which originated in China 3000 years ago, is concerned with the layout of homes and workplaces and the arrangement of artefacts within them, and how they can enhance or sabotage your life. It is now fashionable as a kind of alternative therapy in the

USA and Britain. Whether you or I believe in it or not is irrelevant; it is significant because many people do. Through feng shui one woman realized her house was 'cursed':

> I'd been blissfully married for five years when we decided to buy a country cottage. Once we'd moved in, everything seemed to go wrong. Within 18 months my husband was having an affair and we split up. Just as I was moving out, I came across a book on feng shui and realised the house was a disaster area: there were loads of beams above the bed running lengthways between my husband and me, and the health, relationships and offspring areas were out in the garden!
>
> (*Cosmopolitan*, November 1995, p. 60)

Distribution

While the plotting of typological sets of objects in the landscape has long been a standard archaeological technique, Pearce notes that it has rarely been used in other material culture disciplines (Pearce, 1994, p. 130), though there is at least one notable exception, Deetz and Dethlefsen's study of distribution patterns in the designs of gravestones, and what this reveals of seventeenth- and eighteenth-century New England society (Deetz and Dethlefsen, 1994). Such an approach is arguably even more valuable and possible in twentieth-century consumer society, an age of mass-produced goods. The distribution of ownership of a single mass-produced object could be enormously revealing, not just geographically, although regional, national and even international differences would clearly demonstrate a great deal. Distribution is also revealing in terms of factors such as gender, age, ethnicity, class – indeed, any factor you would wish to choose.

Where is this object found? In every home? Only in certain homes? Which? Where? Why? What does this reveal about ourselves and our society? For example, Cohen has studied the material culture of American working-class homes, between 1885 and 1915, to reveal how middle-class notions of taste had little impact, but that the availability of cheap mass-produced consumer items meant that there was much less variety in the material preferences of the working class than the diversity of ethnic backgrounds would suggest (Cohen, 1989). Again, imaginative interpretative approaches could explore such notions in an exhibition. In doing so for the twentieth century, we have an enormously valuable potential source in the advertising industry, which seeks to forecast and plot distribution in terms of such factors. The burgeoning multidisciplinary academic study of consumption also has much to offer to curators (see Miller, 1995, for an excellent review of the literature).

Significance

What has been the significance of the object, in its time of construction, in its subsequent history and for us today? An almost endless variety of approaches can be used, but can be codified schematically, as we have seen, to nine by Schlereth and four by Pearce. However, the historical approaches will have been used in the 'history' section of the analysis, the environmentalist in 'distribution'. So here we are concerned with functionalist, symbolist and national character, structuralist and behaviourist approaches.

There is no doubt that the functionalist approach has value, since all objects do have a function, broadly defined. Pearce offers a thorough analysis of the strengths and weaknesses of functionalism (Pearce, 1992, Chapter 7). Functionalism is now intellectually unfashionable, and it does have clear weaknesses, most notably in terms of explaining change, the role of the agency of the individual and the assumption that artefacts chiefly or only have meaning through their ability to enable a society or an individual to survive as long as possible. Yet the approach has perhaps been too readily dismissed completely. Clearly, the function of artefacts can be revealing, particularly technological ones:

> Karl Marx suggested that 'it would be possible to write quite a history of inventions, made ... for the sole purpose of supplying capital with weapons against the revolts of the working-class'. Indeed, there are many examples of inventions made for the sake of taking power from workers by incorporating their skills into the mechanisms of the machine. Machine politics is the use of machines to mediate between groups with differing interests.   (Lubar, 1993, p. 200)

Yet technological artefacts also reveal the weaknesses of functionalism:

> English locomotives of the turn of the century look like a substantial building – very solid, very establishment; French locomotives are of a rational, extremely efficient design that shows off all their scientific improvements; and American locomotives are practical, easy to repair, only superficially decorated. The styles are sufficiently distinctive that it is easy to identify a locomotive's country of origin after looking at only a few exemplars. ... That there are social and cultural influences in design is easily seen in cross-cultural comparisons such as these.   (Lubar, 1993, p. 202)

Similarly, why do teapots differ so much?

The symbolist approach, sometimes combined with national character and elements of a structuralist analysis, can be revealing. For example, Maquet offers a decoding of the example of the three locomotives given by Lubar: 'The design of the British locomotive symbolizes the value of solidity; it corresponds to it by creating it. The visual forms stand for solidity and make the locomotive strong; the symbol (the English locomotive) is equivalent to the quality of solidity. The design of the French locomotive symbolizes the value of rationality. Here again the difference between the sign and the signified is blurred: The design stands for rationality and is rational. The design of the American locomotive symbolizes the value of practicality' (Maquet, 1993, p. 37). Similarly, differences in the design of teapots and the way that tea is made and drunk could reveal different cultures. Certainly the design and use of everyday objects are tremendously revealing of national differences: 'When you come back to England from any foreign country, you have immediately the sensation of breathing a different air. Even in the first few minutes dozens of small things conspire to give you this feeling. The beer is bitterer, the coins are heavier ... the advertisements are more blatant' (Orwell, 1982, p. 36).

Hawes has sought to explore the symbolic power of artefacts, particularly in their ability to be read in this way in terms of 'national character' (Hawes, 1986). However, he seeks to show that objects create myths about national character identity. Participants were asked to look at a series of objects deliberately chosen because they seemed to symbolize the mythic history of Americans in 'pioneer' or 'colonial' days. Participants responded to the artefacts in a fairly uniform way, which reinforced this mythic, heroic 'pioneer settlers' past. Yet even if these are myths (and Maquet's examples also), they are none the less important for being commonly held. It would be particularly interesting to explore the mythic quality of 'roast beef', long a symbol of Englishness, at a time of concern over 'mad cow disease'. Such mythic qualities of objects can be explored or demystified in a gallery:

> when planning an exhibit on the 1920s, we might consider our audience's image of that era. If we assume that the popular view of the decade features prosperity, speakeasies, flappers, jazz, Model T Fords, and F. Scott Fitzgerald, we might begin our exhibit with such unexpected topics as Alabama sharecroppers, the mah jongg craze, the expansion of the chemical industry, immigration restriction, and workers who struggled rather than prospered. 'New England Begins: The Seventeenth Century', an exhibition held in 1982 at Boston's Museum of Fine Arts ... forcefully challenged the popular view of the dour, stern, and frugal Puritans by showing the lush beauty of many seventeenth-century objects and the visual richness of seventeenth-century New England culture.   (Leon, 1987, p. 134)

Such approaches highlight the symbolic power that artefacts do therefore seem to have, but can be criticized for lacking a coherent theoretical basis. Why do we seem to share perceptions of the symbolism of certain objects, as Hawes's experiment demonstrated? Structuralism appears to offer an answer to this. Pearce has popularized structuralist approaches to material culture, and offered an invaluable critique (see Pearce, 1992, Chapter 8, 1993). In as simple terms as possible, Pearce comments that 'Structuralism depends upon the proposition that apparently "irrational" beliefs and actions (which is to say, beliefs and actions which apparently do not have a clear function of social survival) are obeying a logic of their own, that this logic can show that social beliefs and actions are reducible to sets or binary pairs which embody the "deep structure" of the society concerned, operating below the level of the infinitely various day-to-day events but giving rise to these, and that we can come to an understanding of the deep structure by applying appropriate analysis' (Pearce, 1993, p. 68).

The basics of the structuralist approach, in terms of *langue* and *parole*, metonymic and metaphoric sets, binary pairs and structuralist plots, are not essentially hard to grasp. But many, particularly British curators, when introduced to this approach, can be quite hostile, making comments such as 'Where do these binary pairs come from?', 'This doesn't logically follow', 'This is reading too much into things'. Structuralism necessitates the ruthless abandonment of 'simple commonsense' (Pearce, 1992, p. 182), but this is a particularly un-British thing to do, thinking, for example, of an ordinary terraced house as a 'transformation' of the body (Pearce, 1992, pp. 174, 176). This reaction to structuralism of itself perhaps reflects something of the way British people think, which brings the following binary pairs to mind:

> structuralism : empiricism
> impractical : practical
> unreal : real
> French : British
> intellectual : anti-intellectual
> illogical : logical
> nonsense : common sense

It is interesting that in Britain there is a similar reaction to the creative thinking ideas promulgated by de Bono in particular, which equally involve a rejection of 'common sense' (see in particular de Bono, 1992).

Another reaction is to find the structuralist approach intellectually stimulating, but to be unclear how the ideas can be practically implemented in museum work. Museum curators tend to be very practical, 'common-sense' people, and it is perhaps not surprising therefore that, as Schlereth notes, 'Although the monographic literature applying structuralism in material-culture research is growing, the theory has yet to inform a major history exhibition' (Schlereth, 1989b, p. 303). One must add *consciously*, for Pearce notes that binary pairs are used unconsciously all the time in current displays, which can be decoded to tell as much about how the curators think as about the subject matter of the exhibition (Pearce, 1992, p. 180).

Pearce has tackled the chief criticisms of structuralism as applied to the study of material culture (Pearce, 1992, pp. 180–91). To those who say it is too subjective, not subject to check or proof, Pearce argues that experiments with the method can be made, and the fact that it challenges notions of 'high' and 'low' culture can be seen as a strength, rather than a weakness. The approach can be most significantly criticized for its inability to account for change: 'Structuralism is a way of describing what (apparently) is, but it cannot relate this snapshot in time to the different system which went before and the equally different system which will succeed' (Pearce, 1992, p. 187). Despite this, Pearce concludes that structural theory in practice remains a useful '*technique* of analysis' (Pearce, 1992, p. 189). Yet while there is some literature which highlights the value of this technique in understanding the role of material culture in past and present societies, Pearce admits that it is not as yet particularly substantial (Pearce, 1992, p. 167; see Schlereth, 1989a, pp. 55–7). This, and the lack of conscious impact in museum work, has led Ames to conclude that structuralism is given too much credence by Pearce (Ames, 1994, p. 284).

It might be arguable whether structuralism can be used to decode an entire culture through an analysis of its material culture; but the insights it provides certainly are illuminating and thought-provoking. We may not be entirely convinced that, as Pearce suggests, 'the whole of a community's life is implicit in one black bow tie'; but it is convincing that it can help to explain 'why women's wedding dresses, once they were thought proper, were white and not red' (Pearce, 1992, p.191). A structuralist approach to material culture study is not something to be applied religiously by rote, but should be treated as a technique to be used creatively and intelligently, to spark tangential and lateral thinking. It shares a playful yet illuminating quality with de Bono's notions of creativity. Those who reject it out of hand have closed minds.

If it is already used unconsciously in museum display, then clearly it can be used consciously. Nor should it be limited to the study or display of 'traditional' societies, as Pearce has done with the Inuit, but could be illuminatingly applied to the analysis of any object in any society. Exhibitions could be deliberately structured in binary pairs (for example, by gender), or laid out in terms of the structuralist 'plot' of an entire society, and within this could explore notions of metonymic and metaphoric sets, or how far, for example, a terraced house can be seen as a transformation of the body. Such notions could be grasped by visitors, who could become involved in playful experiments with binary pairs to test the validity of the approach.

Turning to our tea exhibition example again, participants could be asked: 'What do you see as the opposite of tea? What words do you associate with tea and its opposite? Can these be matched in pairs? What does this tell us about the importance of tea drinking to us? How far does tea define us, and in opposition to what?' I would now like you to try this, and then compare your binary pairs with mine below. Do we overlap at all?

> tea : coffee
> home : abroad
> British : foreign
> biscuits : pastries
> toast : croissants
> ordinary : sophisticated
> unchic : chic
> old : young
> unsexy : sexy
> working-class : middle-class
> everyday : special

Several things emerge from this. Tea seems to strike me personally (and perhaps you also) as something defining in terms of national culture. Tea drinking is a metaphorical symbol of Britishness (or Englishness?). It also has connotations as a drink for ordinary, working-class people with plain food, as opposed to coffee, which is a European import for the upwardly mobile. Coffee is sexy, tea is not. As Boy George, the British pop star, famously confessed, 'I'd rather have a nice cup of tea than sex.'

This is made apparent in British adverts for tea and coffee. In the Gold Blend coffee commercial, sophisticated, sexy, young professionals are always jetting off to European destinations. You don't have to be Roland Barthes to decode a Gold Blend commercial. In the PG Tips tea commercial, chimpanzees dressed as people parody a British working-class family (the teenage son, naturally, is named Kevin). But how far have my or your notions of tea and coffee been defined or refined by such advertising? (For an analysis of the same advertising campaign from a slightly different perspective, see Pearce, 1992, pp. 174–7.) Gold Blend coffee is, according to its advertising slogan, 'rich, golden smooth' (and so are those who drink it). For the PG Tips drinker, 'it's the taste' that counts. Most other British tea and coffee commercials parallel my binary pairs. These differences are also revealed by considering other artefacts associated with tea and coffee. We have tea towels not coffee towels, teaspoons not coffee spoons, but we have coffee tables and coffee table books, not tea tables and tea table books. Such an analysis might also enable us to understand the elaborate rituals of tea-drinking in different cultures; why, for example, metaphorically, in British culture, fortunes can be read in tea leaves.

Perhaps you produced a different set of binary pairs to me, but with some degree of overlap. What does this tell us? Exhibitions could explore these similarities and differences, drawing on the perspectives of many different people – a fascinating experiment in the structuralist method.

While the degree of overlap will validate the approach, inevitably there will be differences between people, and over time. The process of change and agency of the individual in this needs to be accounted for, but structuralism can only help us to describe this. What does the behaviourist approach offer, through a focus on the relationship between the individual and an object? American studies have focused on the individual creator of craft products (Schlereth, 1989, pp. 57–63). Such studies have in some senses validated the structuralist approach. For the makers of items from baskets to houses, there is a set of rules or 'grammar' to follow, 'even if they cannot be explicitly stated by their users'. They cannot necessarily be verbalized, for this is a question of 'look' or 'feel' that something is 'right'. But neither is it simply intuition: the grammar can be decoded (Deetz, 1977, pp. 108–9).

Yet changes in design do occur, and things are slowly made slightly differently. How can this be accounted for? 'We need to find a way of uniting the behavioural process ... with the functionalist/structuralist analysis' (Pearce, 1992, p. 221).To answer this, Pearce broadens the behaviourist approach to consider not just the interaction of maker and object, but all our interactions with material culture, and also draws on phenomenological perspectives to explore this:

> the meanings of an object lie both in the object itself, with all the historical and structuralist/functionalist ways in which this meaning is constituted, and equally in the

process which the viewer carries out in relation to the object ... it is the *convergence* of object and viewer which brings the meaningful object into existence ... The object is inexhaustible, but it is this inexhaustibility which forces the viewer to his decisions. The viewing process is selective, and the potential object is richer than any of its realizations.   (Pearce, 1992, pp. 217, 219)

Objects are capable of 'realization' in an exhaustible number of ways; they are 'polysemantic'. Each of us experiences any object differently, and we also individually experience the same object slightly differently through time. But though objects are polysemantic, each of us reduces this to our own more manageable interpretation, structured in turn by 'the object itself, with its tangible and factual content', and the 'consensus within each individual's community', as to how the object should be interpreted (Pearce, 1992, p. 220). There is a dynamic here between the object, the individual and the society. The interpretation of objects in museums can be understood in this way. If an object is not interpreted, or interpreted only minimally – that is, in the formalist perspective – it is polysemantic, and each individual tends to interpret the object in his or her own way, or is even unable to interpret it, being too overwhelmed by its polysemantic quality. Alternatively, the museum, through the analyst perspective, can attempt to determine the interpretation strictly, to the point where the polysemantic quality would tend to vanish.

This consideration of the relationship between the object, the individual and society still does not account for change. Pearce turns to Gidden's notion of structuration (Pearce, 1992, pp. 221–2), which is helpful but not entirely convincing. In many senses this has long been an intractable problem. 'Structuration' appears to be little more than a reworking of Engel's 'parallelogram of forces' which addressed this same problem. Sartre grappled with this problem in examining the relationship between existentialism and Marxism, and it has continued to be a central debate in Marxist thought between those who emphasize human agency, such as E. P. Thompson, and those who favour structure, such as Althusser (Anderson, 1980, Chapter 2).

If this is still an intractable academic problem, consideration of the interaction of object and individual is essential, and can still be explored in museum displays. We have encouraged participants to consider that (passive) objects have a history. We can also encourage them to consider that, as this analysis suggests, objects are active, they have an impact on us too; as Pearce terms it, 'objects make history' (Pearce, 1992, pp. 224–7). The object has had an impact on those who have come into contact with it, and is doing so now. Of those who came into contact with this object, what impact did they have on it, and vice versa? What impact are you having on this object and it on you? The latter part of Pearce's study of the infantry officer's jacket is an invaluable discussion of this (Pearce, 1990). Why have people fought and even died for the possession of a particular artefact?

Interpretation

The final section of the model seeks to bring the various strands of the analysis together, to draw some conclusions about the role of the object in society. This would be particularly necessary in a museum display which approached one object in this way, given the huge potential variety of approaches that could be employed, and the fact that each individual will 'realize' the object in a slightly different way. In a sense this section is a form of self-evaluation. What is each participant taking away with him or her from this experience?

Conclusion

Use of Pearce's model of artefact analysis (with some minor revisions) has structured the innumerable possible approaches to a single piece of material culture, and, I hope, also demonstrated how these can be readily made accessible for museum visitors to participate in. If the object is 'inexhaustible', the role of the museum is to enable audiences to learn the innumerable ways by which this can be revealed. Complete exhibitions could be based around a single artefact.

This is not the only possible approach. Exhibitions could equally be based on one stage of the analysis for a number of objects, or even on just one approach or one question within each stage, such as the question of value. There could be, for example, exhibitions exploring all the areas outlined in Figure 4.3. These are the exhibition ideas that I have generated from an analysis of the model. How many yet more imaginative ideas could an exhibition team develop, particularly if employing techniques to aid creative thinking, such as brainstorming?

Exhibitions of this nature would represent a two-way process. They would bring material culture theory to the public. In return, the public would be making a major contribution to our theoretical understanding of material culture by being directly involved in research.

Objects can never be entirely understood in isolation, and elements of this model enable any artefact to be considered in relation to other material culture. Beyond this, however, it is important to recognize that much material culture is formed into what are considered collections. All material in museums is part of a collection or 'collections', and much of the material in museums was collected as a pre-existing collection (Pearce, 1992, p. 36). A single object in a collection can be analysed using the model. What is lacking is a model of collection analysis. The meaning of collecting is beginning to be explored. The seminal work of Pearce in this field in particular is highly relevant to museums (Pearce, 1995), but again the implications of this for curatorial practice need to be spelled out more directly if such research is to have a major impact on day-to-day museum work, particularly through the development of a model for collection analysis.

Exhibitions ...

of only one object

of no objects: deprivation from material culture

only written descriptions: participants have to work out what the object is

allowing only touch

allowing only taste: exhibitions of food and drink

of fragments to reconstruct

of objects participants are encouraged to destroy to explore their physical properties

objects of only one colour – why are they all this colour?

similarly, by texture or shape, weight or density

or by size: exploring our fascination with the miniature

exploring the symbolic meanings of contrasting or conflicting colours: black and white, orange and green

exploring the meaning of beauty and taste

similarly, what is considered normal or abnormal

exploring typology – when is a teapot a teapot, or not?

of objects of the same material and its meaning

of our fascination with bright shiny things

about what we mean by ownership: gifts, loans, swaps, stolen items etc.?

exploring value: which object in this display would you like to steal?

placing objects in sets

deliberately placing objects in the wrong sets

placing objects in locations: where do you keep your condoms? .

about feng shui

of the most common objects, rather than the rare

exploring the mythical power of everyday artefacts

consciously using binary pairs, as in a completely gendered display

examining techniques to 'read' objects

Figure 4.3 *Creative thinking around exhibition subjects and approaches, inspired by Pearce's model of artefact analysis*

There are an increasing number of displays which do approach material culture from at least some of the approaches indicated in this chapter (for example, Orna *et al.*, 1993; Callaghan *et al.*, 1994; Hartfield, 1994). No doubt there are many other imaginative displays that unfortunately I have not been able to see, or am unaware of. Museums have begun to offer what Pearce terms 'rhetorical curatorship', and to demystify the curatorial process, as, for example, in the Mankind Discovering Gallery at the Royal Ontario Museum in Toronto, and have begun to explore the meaning of collecting, by both the museum and private collectors (Pearce, 1995, pp. 142–5). It is noteworthy, however, that the most praised and praiseworthy exhibitions in the past few years which take material culture as their focus have often been by artists, such as Fred Wilson, and not by curators (Corrin, 1993, 1994; Garfield, 1993; Malbert *et al.*, 1995). The most interesting initiatives are very often in museum education, but educationalists are still all too often largely excluded from the exhibition process. The formalist and analyst perspectives remain overwhelmingly predominant. The inexhaustible possibilities of the object have only begun to be explored in the museum. But which objects should these be?

5

Sex and drugs and rock'n'roll ... and museums?

Introduction

'Sex and Drugs and Rock'n'Roll', the title of the classic punk anthem by Ian Dury and the Blockheads, is a parody of what popular culture is, but it emphasizes the aspects of everyday life that museums have ignored most, and in doing so have excluded a sense of youthful energy, excitement and danger. In fairness, museums have begun to reflect and explore these less 'safe' aspects of popular culture. There have been two, fairly distinct, approaches to popular culture in museums, which have followed the analysis derived from the plot developed by Pearce, utilized in Chapter 1: popular culture has been reflected in museums when it could be authenticated as either 'art' or 'history' (Figure 1.1). Which objects, which popular material culture, should museums be exploring, and why? At this point I give a reminder that the focus will be the museums and the popular culture of the UK, although examples from North America will be included as appropriate.

Pearce demonstrates the value of this plot in relation to an 'icon' of popular culture, a pair of 1950s Levi jeans, which begin as a mass-produced artefact, in the bottom right quadrant. In the 1980s Levis produced distressed jeans as a marketable heritage, a spurious masterpiece in the bottom left box. By the 1990s, 1950s jeans are considered worthy to appear either in the art gallery as significant in the history of design and taste, an authentic masterpiece, or in the history museum as an authentic artefact (Pearce, 1995, pp. 398-401).

One element missing from this analysis is that it would be possible for a particular pair of jeans to move in this way. Within this plot I would argue that it is possible for mass-produced items to move from the top right, as authentic artefacts, to the bottom left, as spurious masterpieces, through being 'customized' by their owner, individually altered and styled, to meet, for example, the fashion of a particular youth subculture. A major study of youth fashion and style contends that 'young people don't just buy passively or uncritically. They always transform the meaning of bought goods, appropriating and recontextualizing mass-market styles. That appropriation entails a form of symbolic work and creativity as young consumers break the ordered category of clothes ... personalising their purchases. Most young people combine elements of clothing to create new meanings' (Willis, 1990, p. 85). This customized pair of jeans could later find itself in a museum display on subcultures in either art or history. Pearce's analysis only allows for the deliberate marketing of 'heritage jeans' as spurious masterpieces, rather than their creation as such in the first instance.

One can take the analysis a little further and suggest that all kinds of further movements through changes in value are at least theoretically possible

(Figure 5.1). Take, for example, an everyday mass-produced artefact, a black plastic rubbish bag. This could be immediately disposed of, with its contents, falling into the rubbish at the bottom of the plot. Alternatively, in 1977 it could have been 'customized' as a piece of clothing by a punk, becoming a spurious masterpiece. This could then be thrown away, again falling into the rubbish. If it was kept as a souvenir, in the 1990s it could then have been displayed at the 'Streetstyle' exhibition of youth subcultures at the Victoria and Albert Museum (V & A) as an authentic masterpiece, or in a temporary social history display on youth culture, as an authentic artefact. If not added to the permanent collection, but returned to its owner, further movement occurs. The bag could also be displayed in an art context in a museum directly as an authentic masterpiece, as a 'classic' of design, or in a social history display on refuse disposal directly as an authentic artefact. The material culture identified as popular culture can be transformed and thus moved around the plot in almost any number of ways. How far has popular material culture been interpreted in these ways?

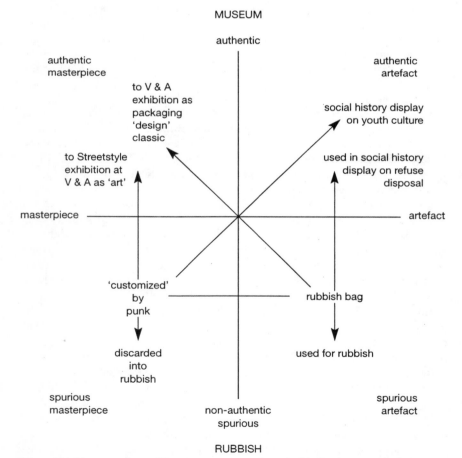

Figure 5.1 *Plotting of possible movements in value of a black plastic rubbish bag*

Practice: social history

The development of social history in British museums over the past three decades has brought a much-needed focus on the lives of working-class people, and therefore has included representations of popular material culture. However, the dominance of the analyst approach has meant that the material culture has been secondary, rather than the focus. Objects have rarely been interpreted as material expressions of culture. When social historians have focused on popular culture as a subject, it has usually been equated with a handful of stereotypical leisure activities, a very narrow definition, rather than the broader meaning as the culture of everyday life. Popular culture interpreted narrowly as leisure has been seen as slightly spurious, and also as something which is consumed rather than created. Perhaps not consciously, therefore, social historians have largely, until very recently, tended to interpret popular culture as an imposed mass culture, rather than a creative and vibrant cultural expression. This is paradoxical, given that the greatest influence on social historians has been E. P. Thompson, whose work pioneered the recognition of the richness of a culture he saw as largely created by working people themselves.

There is undoubtedly a sense in which the early folk museums could be said to have reflected certain aspects of the popular culture of the traditional rural societies which they interpreted. From the early 1970s urban social and industrial history museums such as Beamish and Ironbridge began to include aspects of popular culture in their displays, though it tended to be equated with leisure, and all too often confined to a reconstructed turn-of-the-century pub. Such displays also tended to be formalist. These representations were criticized, as part of a broader critique of the approach to history at such museums, as being depoliticized, and therefore fundamentally flawed (Bennett, 1988; West, 1988), a criticism which could equally be made of the folk museum tradition. As a reaction to this, labour history became an important museum movement in the early 1980s (Bott, 1988; Moore, 1994b). Yet in this concentration on the political and trade union aspects of working-class history, other aspects of popular culture tended to be ignored, as being by comparison rather lightweight, as King, curator at the People's Palace in Glasgow argued:

> Labour history studies usually concentrate on the action of organised labour in the form of trades unions, co-operatives and political parties, but one should bear in mind that in a lot of places the majority of working class people have spent their lives outside those organisations, in rank disorganisation, or have embraced other organisations – the church, the music hall, the cinema, the dance hall, the football field and the dog track. These organisations have likewise received short shrift in our museums but are, I feel, worthy of our attention.   (King, 1988b, p. 11)

The approach to working-class history at the People's Palace overcame this division between other aspects of popular culture and politics, by integrating them, reflecting both the politics of popular cultural activities, such as football, and the cultural aspects of political movements. A vigorous programme of contemporary collecting of popular culture heightened the popularity of this approach with the public. Billy Connolly's banana boots from his 1974 stage act became perhaps the most popular items on display. This is indicated by the fact that they feature on a badge currently sold at the museum, which reads 'I've been to the People's Palace'. The People's Palace gave museum form to the approach to working-class culture in E. P. Thompson's work (Moore, 1994b, pp. 157–8).

The People's Palace was influential in steering the development of labour history museums away from ghettoized histories of the labour movement and towards integrated histories of working-class life, such as the Merseyside Museum of Labour History, opened in Liverpool in 1986, and the People's Story, opened in Edinburgh in 1989. Furthermore, it was the major influence on the broader movement to establish social history displays of working-class life in many towns and cities which has followed these into the 1990s (Moore, 1994b, pp. 151–2). These integrated displays of working-class life, however, have failed to follow the People's Palace in viewing popular culture as cultural expression in all aspects of life. Popular culture has again almost uniformly been reduced to 'leisure', 'entertainment' or 'recreation', failing to consider, for example, the popular culture of the workplace. Popular culture as leisure has tended to be treated almost as an afterthought, as the least important topic, which has had the least research time devoted to it, is therefore the least effective and, tellingly, tends to be the last gallery visitors come to. The result of this approach has been displays which present a cold, almost 'cultureless' perspective, with a focus on the workplace and home life, but where neither come 'alive' as they are not treated as arenas of cultural expression. The displays at the People's Palace in the 1980s may have been a little shabby and anarchic, but this very quality enabled the perception of a living, vibrant culture which impinged on all aspects of life, and which was expressed as much in the home and the workplace as elsewhere.

Recent major social history displays have continued to 'ghettoize' popular culture in its definition as leisure, but have at least attempted to give it much greater prominence. The Museum of Liverpool Life has 'Mersey culture' as one of the three key themes of phase one of the project, opened in 1993, alongside 'Making a living' and 'Demanding a voice', with 'Homes and communities' to follow in the second phase. Though 'Making a living' and 'Demanding a voice' are highly impressive in their own terms, these representations of working and political life again lack their cultural aspects. Both the workplace and political life are potentially rich in popular culture, as the People's Palace demonstrated.

The 'Mersey Culture' gallery is based on the 'leisure' gallery of the Merseyside Museum of Labour History, which the Museum of Liverpool Life has replaced. It aims therefore to move beyond leisure to culture, 'Posing the question as to whether Liverpool has a distinct culture of its own' (Knowles, 1993, p. 9). Whether it succeeds in this has been questioned: 'Somehow the Liverpool culture to be found just outside the door was not captured ... the way people talk ... the way the women wear their clothes and hair ... the texture of people's interaction when they move about this remarkable landscape' (Trustram, 1993). Again, the displays, though much more effective than most, drift back to a focus on leisure, with popular culture as something to be consumed rather than created. Recent major displays have avoided ghettoizing leisure activities, as in the 'Great City!' exhibition in Newcastle, and the 'Lifetimes' gallery in Croydon. The former, however, is limited by its predominantly analyst approach. The latter in particular offers an encouraging approach, in making the material culture of everyday life much more the focus of the display, and in some senses therefore transcending the formalist–analyst binary.

While popular culture, at least until recently, has tended to be relatively neglected, marginalized or conflated to leisure in most general 'permanent' social history displays, temporary exhibitions have provided the scope for a wider range of topics and approaches. The importance of football to the culture of Merseyside was, for example, reflected in the 'Football Crazy' exhibition at Liverpool Museum in 1984. Sport has continued to be a popular choice for social history curators, with a significant number of exhibitions reported in the pages of the *Social History Curators Group News*, whether of individual sports or even particular teams. The 1989 Social History Curators Group Annual Study Weekend focused on museums and popular culture, and reflected on a number of temporary exhibitions, most notably 'That's Entertainment!' in Hull. Again, as the title implies, this tended to reduce popular culture to leisure, but drew record numbers to the museum (Wilkinson, 1989a). Pop music has been an equally popular theme as sport, perhaps most notably the 'Twist and Shout' display in Sheffield in 1993, the touring exhibition 'It's Only Rock'n'Roll' organized by West Midlands Area Museums Service, and displays at Stoke-on-Trent (Nisbet, 1993). A further common approach has been to focus on the popular culture of a particular decade, as in 'Back to the 1960s' in Dundee in 1993, and 'The 70s. A Celebration of the Decade' at Carlisle in 1995. Others have sought to go beyond the obvious yet popular choices of sport (particularly football) and pop music to look at less fashionable but no less significant leisure activities, such as pet keeping in Stevenage, pigeon fancying in Walsall or gardening in Stoke. Such displays have invaluably tackled new subjects, and switched the emphasis from popular culture as purely an act of consumption towards creation. Equally significant have been the number of displays which have sought to reflect the multiculturalism of the museums' community (for a useful review of these crucial developments, see Sykes, 1993).

This in one sense is a very healthy state of affairs, very much to be welcomed. Yet despite all this activity there remains the feeling that many social history curators in museums still do not take popular culture as a subject entirely seriously, as though it can be treated as a bit of light relief, or chosen as a topic for an exhibition a little unwillingly (even though it would clearly be popular with the public), primarily as it is still narrowly defined as leisure. The background to the 'That's Entertainment!' exhibition at Hull indicates this: 'When choosing the theme for the next exhibition it was considered important to select something lighthearted as a contrast to the relatively serious subject of education; popular culture was felt to be a suitable choice' (Wilkinson, 1989a, p. 39).

Perhaps most social history curators in Britain are driven by a political desire to reveal and popularize the harshness of working-class life in the past, and to a lesser degree in the present. At times the portrayal of social history has seemed almost to become a competition to reveal the worst social conditions in the past – 'No, infant mortality was highest in our city!' – or to stress that the curator works in the most socially deprived inner city borough in the country. This veers close to a Monty Pythonesque parody of the working-class past: 'Times were 'ard. We lived in a shoebox and licked the road clean for a farthing!' Times were – are – hard for many people, but too often the vibrancy of life and culture, the good times, or at least the escapism from the bad times, are missing from social history displays. Nor is poverty adequately explored as fundamentally a lack of material culture. The obverse of this is also problematic. Treating popular culture, defined as leisure, almost as light relief ignores the politics of the subject. Academic studies of leisure and popular culture emphasize that such activities are often the battleground between competing ideologies and class interests.

This is not to say that social history curators have not made a useful contribution to the representation of popular culture in museums over the past decade or so. Yet many subjects remain largely untouched, owing to being seen as too spurious, or unexciting. The dominant analyst approach also means that the material culture has not been adequately explored. The social history approach is fundamentally people-centred, focusing on the consumers, and still less frequently the creators, of popular culture, through oral history and other techniques. The actual material culture expressions of popular culture are often treated as secondary; they are illustrations, rather than the focus. Social history curators are concerned with 'history from below'; but they have paid too little attention as yet to the 'material culture from below'; that is, that from below the horizontal axis of the plot in Figure 5.1. In an overview of the SHCG Annual Study Weekend on the subject, Suggitt usefully sketched out the key problems and the possibilities, which remain as crucial today:

> We must consider the dominant mainstream forms as well as those that react against them. We will have to look at new 'sub-cultures' such as 'youth culture' and their obsession with objects and symbols, but we should not over emphasise these, simply because they are the most interesting. ... In order to produce a sensible coherent interpretation of our source material, be it pub culture, pop culture, car culture or home culture, we have to look for the way that so much of popular expression is transmitted through signs and symbols which give our objects a number of meanings.
>
> (Suggitt, 1989, pp. 3–4)

Practice: art and design

Simultaneously but separately, some art curators have begun to engage with popular culture, but in a very different way. In direct contrast, art curators focus directly on the material manifestations of popular culture, considering either their intrinsic artistic merit (spurious masterpiece becomes authentic masterpiece) or their significance in terms of their design and their impact on design more generally (spurious artefact or spurious masterpiece becomes authentic masterpiece) (see the examples in Figure 5.1). There is, conversely, in either of these art curator approaches, little or no emphasis on the creators or consumers of the material culture, which is clearly a profound weakness, as the objects become divorced from the living culture which produced them. Some merely present the material in a formalist manner, the classic example being exhibitions of folk art.

The first approach seeks to demonstrate that popular culture is art, and therefore worthy of a place in a gallery: spurious masterpieces are in fact authentic masterpieces. Comic art has been authenticated as 'art' in touring exhibitions of the work of Leo Baxendale, the creator of the best-loved characters in *The Beano*, and of Frank Hampson, the creator of Dan Dare of *The Eagle*, originated by Southport Art Gallery in 1990. Perhaps the best example to date of this approach in the UK has been the exhibition 'Bike Art: the Art, Craft and Lifestyle of the Custom Bike Movement', held at The Gas Hall, Birmingham Museum and Art Gallery, in 1994. According to the publicity leaflet, 'Bike Art presents the most outstanding examples of custom motorcycles. Bikes that feature exquisite paintwork, engraving and leatherwork. Works of art on two wheels. ... We find examples of delicate crafts, so beautifully and lovingly created they wouldn't look out of place in an art gallery. Or would they?' In the introduction to the publication which accompanied the exhibition, the originator of the display offers a very clear justification of this approach as a whole:

> Until now, museums have consistently ignored what has actually become a significant feature of contemporary life: the use of art to give personal meaning to activities well outside the conventional arenas of 'the arts'. Most of us need to express ourselves visually, especially in a world in which we are surrounded by the bland, mass-produced products of a materialistic age. We react by putting great energy into personalising our surroundings whenever we can, and whole industries have developed in some areas to support and exploit this effort. Few of us, however, have been aware of what has been going on in the world of the custom motor cycle. ... It is our view that the aesthetic quality of what is shown in this exhibition is of a very high order.
>
> (Birmingham Museum and Art Gallery, 1993, p. 3)

To try to argue whether 'bike art' is 'art' or not is, as I have suggested, to miss the point. Does it really matter whether it is or is not equal to 'high' culture? The importance of the exhibition lay not in whether it was art or not but in the fact that it explored the 'art' and 'craft' of a highly significant subculture. Whether visitors found it to their taste or intellect as 'art' or not was irrelevant. The great strength of the exhibition was that it explored the material culture first and foremost, seeking to explain the imagery used on bikes, clothes and even the skin, to reveal the inner workings of the subculture, something which is completely lacking in the social history approach: 'Read someone's tattoos and you have a route into their psyche, their personal philosophies, their beliefs.' This was devalued by an unnecessary attempt to make the visitor see tattooing as a respectable art form: 'Of all modern art forms, tattooing is probably the most misunderstood and misrepresented. Tattooing is still seen as synonymous with the criminal element or those of low intelligence, yet a modern tattooist is a highly skilled artist, working under the strictest conditions of hygiene and safety, producing stunning visual artwork of exquisite quality. No longer the province of sailors or drunks, tattooing nowadays appeals to people from all walks of life – housewife, managing director, building worker or biker' (Birmingham Museum and Art Gallery, 1993, p. 49). This may well all be true, but even if it was not, tattooing would still be a highly valid subject matter for museums, given its popularity in society.

This was a groundbreaking exhibition, a brave and bold attempt to explore an aspect of popular culture in a museum, particularly in choosing to focus on a subculture which is unpopular with the media and faces strong prejudice from society as a whole. The major weakness of the exhibition was that it did not, as its subtitle suggested, reveal much about the lifestyle of the custom bike movement. The bikes, clothes, jewellery, even the tattoos were reverentially treated as works of art. The consumers of this material culture were curiously absent, or present only in photographic images. The creators were present as artists or craftspeople in residence. The exhibition cried out for a behaviourist approach to reveal the experience and motivations of the members of this subculture. If you read someone's tattoos you may have a route into his or her psyche: but this by itself will not reveal why he or she wished to have a tattoo in the first place. 'Bike Art' was therefore the art, craft but not the lifestyle of the custom bike movement. Perhaps it was inevitable that, in claiming that its subject matter was art, the exhibition would fail to reveal these other aspects, and therefore tend to sanitize the subject matter.

The other approach taken by art curators is to consider popular material culture in terms of its design and its impact on design more generally: spurious artefact or masterpiece as authentic masterpiece. Notable examples have included elements of the 'Collecting for the Future' temporary display at the V&A in 1990, the V&A's twentieth century gallery, opened in 1992, and the Design Museum in London. But by far the most interesting example of this approach to date in the UK has been the much publicized exhibition 'Streetstyle: from Sidewalk to Catwalk, 1940 to Tomorrow', at the V&A in 1994–5. This again was a groundbreaking exhibition, as the first major display on largely working-class youth subcultures. Just as significant was that such a theme was addressed in a national museum, and one with an image as one of the bastions of the culture of the social elite: 'With Streetstyle the Victoria and Albert is dropping its aitches' (Feaver, 1994, p. 12). Yet it was also entirely logical and consistent with the overall purposes of the V&A. It was a *national* exhibition (one of the weaknesses being that it did not explore regional specificities in subcultures). Its natural home was also the V&A, in that it focused on the *design* aspects of the clothing of youth subcultures, and, as the title suggests, the impact of this on haute couture and the fashion industry. The exhibition very methodically traced the 'family tree' of youth subcultures in Britain and to a degree the United States. A strength, therefore, was that it broke away from the clichés of previous representations of youth subcultures on the occasions when they had featured in 'pop music' displays – teddy boys, mods and rockers, punks – to explore other subcultures which were the roots or antecedents of these, and which were also significant in their own right. It also brought the story up to today, whereas 'punk' had previously seemed as contemporary a youth subculture as some displays were willing to reflect, and very boldly, as the subtitle indicates, attempted to second-guess the future of style. The extraordinary popularity of the exhibition revealed the strength of public interest in this subject matter.

'Streetstyle' shared the weaknesses of the art and design approach of 'Bike Art'. The creators and consumers of each street style were largely silent, except on occasion to explain the particular choices behind their choice of design. This is not necessarily invalid. But we learnt nothing of the lifestyle of each subculture, the motivation for participating or even how the clothes related to other aspects, such as the music and the drugs. Again the full story of each subculture was sanitized through the narrow focus on design. What does it tell us about a subculture to see its fashions in isolation? We see mods, for example, as stylish dressers, influenced by Italian styles, but not taking drugs or fighting with rockers on Brighton beach. In a sense this is perhaps an unfair criticism, as the exhibition was not aiming to move beyond the design of the clothes, to even the design of other material culture of the subculture, never mind a broader consideration of lifestyle (unlike 'Bike Art', which aimed to do this). Within these relatively narrow objectives, it clearly succeeded, and perhaps this was enough to attempt in one temporary display. Yet this inevitably limited the depth of the display. 'Each mode gets a dummy or two, a caption, a backing photo or other accessory and maybe a sound bite. Fashion students are finding this brilliant' (Feaver, 1994, p. 12), but the general audience needed much more. 'Streetstyle', given either more display space, or less of a desire for encyclopaedic completeness, could have explored each or a smaller number of the subcultures in greater depth. As it was, like 'Bike Art', it remained a slightly soulless display. One can only wish, however, that this bold and fascinating display will act as the catalyst for many others on these themes.

Both 'Bike Art' and 'Streetstyle' assumed that popular culture is something which is created rather than imposed, without at least indicating how far this is a fundamental debate among academics writing in the field. 'Streetstyle', for instance, looked at the impact of street fashion on high fashion, but not at the fashion industry's commercialization of street styles, to sell to a mass market. Similarly, 'Bike Art' saw tattoos as a personal act of creativity: 'In a world of increasing conformity those who choose to be tattooed are making their own personal statements of individuality and freedom of expression' (Birmingham Museum and Art Gallery, 1993, p. 49). This fails to consider how the choice of designs might be structured in some way, or how far those who 'choose' to have tattoos can be said to be making an entirely free choice to do so.

The social history and art approaches therefore both have their strengths but also significant weaknesses. The social history approach has tended to see certain aspects of popular culture as spurious, although this is changing. The key problem has been the inevitable restrictions of the predominant analyst perspective. Some of the art displays have tended to be formalist, although both 'Bike Art' and 'Streetstyle' did move beyond this to a degree. Both, however, lacked the behaviourist element which is a strength of the social history approach. The main problem with both social history and art displays is that they do not take the material culture on its own terms: it has to be authenticated in some way to justify bringing it into the gallery, to bring it above the horizontal axis of the plot.

Neither art nor social history? The People's Shows

How can the strengths of art and social history be combined, and their joint weaknesses avoided? Suggitt has argued that the 'People's Show' exhibition at Walsall Museum and Art Gallery in the West Midlands in 1990 was 'Neither art nor social history, it had lessons for both' (Suggitt, 1990, p. 32). This was an exhibition of some of the private collections of ordinary local people. The success of this first exhibition led to a second in 1992, which was part of a People's Show Festival across the English Midlands, with 13 museums and galleries all holding their own shows. By 1994 this had developed into a national festival with over 47 museums taking part (Digger, 1994). The People's Shows phenomenon, I would argue, has been the most significant attempt by public museums in Britain to reflect popular culture to date, for a number of reasons: its scale; its focus on a key aspect of popular culture, popular collecting; because the displays do seem to a degree to combine the strengths of the art and social history and behaviourist approaches; and perhaps above all because they take the material on its own terms.

As we have seen, around 30 per cent of the population describe themselves as collectors (Pearce, 1995, p. vii). In reflecting popular collecting, therefore, the People's Shows have begun to reveal perhaps the most significant, in that it is perhaps the most popular, aspect of British popular culture. Simply by displaying popular collections without interpretation, the People's Shows would have made an important statement. Some, par-

ticularly the earlier displays, did little more than this. In one sense, therefore, they were formalist, but by displaying material of this nature and
not claiming that it was art, the exhibitions completely subverted the formalist perspective. Some of the exhibitions, particularly those at Walsall,
have aimed to move beyond this to say much more about the collectors,
their motivations and lifestyle, and their relationship with their collections. In doing this they have, as Suggitt has suggested, combined social
history techniques with those of art curators, which has reflected the com-
position of the exhibition teams. However, Digger recognizes that 'there is
a need for a much more analytical approach to collecting and collections
in The People's Shows' (Digger, 1995, p. 10). This may be so, but in fairness, when the People's Shows began in 1990 there was little academic
literature on the subject. The first major academic study of collecting as a
social phenomenon has only recently been published (Pearce, 1995). It is
to be hoped that future displays looking at popular collecting will be
more informed by such research.

Many of the collections in the People's Shows have been of material
that even museums with a willingness to reflect themes of popular culture
would deem far too spurious to collect or even display in another context,
such as '*Smartie* tops', the plastic tops of the tubes of a popular brand of
sweets, and airline travel sick bags in the first Walsall show in 1990. The
display of such collections in the museum was therefore inherently a challenge, a subversion to traditional museum practice. It has been a
deliberate aim of the displays, at least at Walsall, to subvert the distinction between 'high' and 'low' culture, and the relationship of this to the
perceived status of museums in society. Such material was not displayed
as art or for its significance in design terms; it was displayed on its own
terms. This was, at least at Walsall, a celebration of spurious artefacts and
masterpieces *as* spurious artefacts and masterpieces, as part of the democratizing vision of the museum service. According to one of the exhibition
team, 'In accepting collections of all types as valid objects for display in a
museum, The People's Show is working towards changing the traditional
value creating role of a museum, moving from upholding and reinforcing
the culture of the power elite towards valuing and celebrating cultural
activities which cross boundaries of social class, age and gender' (Digger,
1995, p. 35). The exhibitions also emphasized creation as much as consumption in popular culture: 'Collecting is a playful activity ... it is
consumption as fun, allowing the collector to joyously manipulate a
symbol system. ... *The People's Show* becomes a celebratory statement
about people's control over their own lives and the world around them'
(Digger, 1994, p. 43). In allowing and encouraging collectors to be
involved in the display arrangements of their collections, the People's
Shows also sought to democratize the museum process.

The achievements of the People's Shows have been questioned. While
at Walsall collectors have been encouraged to take part in the exhibition
process, this has not always been the case elsewhere. The choice of collec-

tions has also been criticized. Many of the shows seem to have deliberately chosen the 'wackiest' collections, and publicity materials and the resultant press coverage have sometimes played up the popular image of the collectors as eccentrics. While this might be good for visitor figures, 'are we being encouraged to laugh with the collectors or at them? ... Is the People's Show egalitarian in practice as in spirit or does it, perhaps, entail an element of exploitation?' (Francis, 1994, p. 45). Not all the participating museums seem to have entertained the same democratizing spirit as Walsall, the impression given being that the People's Shows have been used in some cases as a vehicle for a quick improvement in visitor figures, with no further involvement planned with the participating collectors. However, I would argue that these are drawbacks of approach and practice rather than fundamental challenges to the validity of the concept, which has perhaps done more than any other initiative to promote popular culture in public museums.

The People's Shows have highlighted the enormous potential for public museums to work with private collectors in reflecting popular culture. The responses to the appeals for collections for the shows and the research being undertaken on popular collecting at the Department of Museum Studies, University of Leicester, have suggested that the most significant collections of material culture relating to popular culture are not in museums but in private hands. The weakness of the displays has been the tendency merely to celebrate popular collecting rather than to explore its significance; but perhaps the celebration had to come first, to establish the validity of the subject.

This is not to say that museums had not sought to draw on such collections before the People's Shows. Many of the successful exhibitions initiated by social history curators on sport in particular in the 1980s were based on the loan of such collections. The idea for the first People's Show at Walsall grew out of a previous exhibition of a collection of Native American material owned by a private collector. The People's Shows, however, have highlighted such possibilities to curators. The result has been what can best be described as 'themed' People's Shows in a number of museums, displays of a number of collections on a single popular culture theme. Perhaps the best example of this has been 'Thunderbirds Are Go! The Worlds of Gerry Anderson', a temporary display at Wolverhampton Art Gallery and Museum in 1992. The exhibition 'celebrates the career of television producer Gerry Anderson, and looks at some of the puppets, models and vehicles that starred in his television and film work', most notably the classic 1960s series *Thunderbirds, Stingray and Captain Scarlet* (Wolverhampton Museum and Art Gallery, 1992). The material used mainly came from the private collection of one individual. In terms of the plot this represents spurious masterpieces (original artwork, puppets, models etc. from the shows) as authentic artefacts. They were seen as historically significant items, because Gerry Anderson's work is regarded as important in the history of television.

Unrealized potential

Despite all this activity, one is still left with the feeling that public museums have as yet only scratched the surface of the possibilities in reflecting popular culture. There is enormous potential. Does this really matter? Simply because the potential is there, is this the right course for museums to pursue more fully? In the current climate, to do this will surely mean directing resources away from a fundamental museum activity. How exactly can this be justified?

Public museums should reflect the needs and interests of those who pay for them through their taxes. Yet too few museums have ever effectively asked the public through marketing research what those needs and interests are. In the past, curators held the view that this was unnecessary: their job was to share with the public what they, the curators, felt the public needed to know, which largely equated with high culture, the 'highest and the best'. While over the past two decades social history curators in particular have sought to democratize the museum, this has still rarely been backed up by adequate marketing research. The new breed of community-oriented curators still assume that they know what people want, or base their view on small and often unrepresentative community groups. Some of the marketing research that has been carried out by individual museums in recent years has led them to put on displays of popular culture, as in the pop music displays at Stoke-on-Trent.

Clearly, further research is required to answer how far the public wish to see popular culture represented in museums. In the meantime the public are voting with their feet. Again, research is needed to quantify this, but the impression is that museum exhibitions on popular culture themes appear by and large to have been extremely popular. 'Star Trek: the Exhibition' at the City Art Centre, Edinburgh, in 1995, a touring exhibition organized by Paramount Pictures, makers of the television series and films, was targeted to attract 11,000 visitors; the attendance was 192,000, with nearly 60 per cent of visitors on a day trip to see the exhibition, their only reason for visiting Edinburgh that day. The Edinburgh hosts should perhaps have been a little more positive in their forecast: the exhibition attracted almost a million visitors at the Smithsonian (Pavlidou, 1995, pp. 23–4, 34).

Such displays are popular because they reflect things which people feel astonishingly passionate about, such as *Star Trek*. Ettema recalls that an analyst exhibition at the National Museum of American History, 'A Nation of Nations', which sought to demonstrate what the various ethnic constituencies had contributed to American culture, had to have an *ad hoc* sign put at the entrance to direct visitors to what they most wanted to see: 'This way to A Nation of Nations, for: Judy Garland's ruby slippers (as worn in the film, *The Wizard of Oz*) ... Fonz's leather jacket ... Muhammad Ali's boxing gloves' (Ettema, 1987, p. 77). The People's Shows in contrast have aimed to reveal this passion, this desire for certain kinds or pieces of material culture. This fascination for material culture on a particular theme is not limited simply to those who might collect it; it is shared by others who feel passionately about that aspect of popular culture. For example, collectors of football memorabilia, though significant in number themselves, represent only a small proportion of those who are passionate about the game, and who as a result are fascinated by the material culture associated with it. Similarly, I drove for over two hours to stand in a queue outside the 'Thunderbirds Are Go!' exhibition among ten-year-olds who were dressed as one of the Tracy brothers, but it is not the driving passion in my life, only one aspect of my interest in popular culture among many.

The power of this material culture is revealed by the fact that many exhibitions of popular culture are curatorially rather weak. 'Thunderbirds Are Go!', for example, was formalist, and in Agren and Carlsson's terms only a 'label' display. Such was the appeal of the material culture, however, that the exhibition was still extremely popular and enjoyable. Many of the People's Shows can similarly be criticized for the lack of context or analysis, without this being reflected in the visitor figures. Conversely, 'analyst' social history displays often have disappointing visitor figures, despite the quality of the research and interpretation, because, I would argue, they do not contain material culture of great public appeal.

One indication of the value that the public place on popular material culture is to consider the high monetary value of such items, even of relatively recent origin. Some material is valued very highly because it is unique. When in 1995 Sylvia Anderson, co-creator with Gerry Anderson of *Thunderbirds*, sold the original puppet of Lady Penelope used in the film *Thunderbirds are Go* at auction, it fetched £34,000 (*Daily Mirror,* 20 September 1995, p. 3). In the past few years one of jazz legend Charlie Parker's alto saxophones has been valued at £30,000 to £40,000 (Gelly, 1994, p. 5); screenplay writer Herman Mankiewitz's 1941 Oscar for the film *Citizen Kane* was valued at £130,000 (Mullin, 1995, p. 7); three gold medals, including one from the Olympics, won by British ice skater John Curry, fetched £22,000 at auction (*The Guardian*, 6 July 1994, p. 3); baseball legend Babe Ruth's bat, with which he hit a record-breaking 56th home run in 1921, sold for £35,930 (Ellison, 1994, p. 3); the original manuscript of lyrics for the song 'Getting Better', written by Paul McCartney for the *Sergeant Pepper* album in 1967, was expected to fetch £47,000; and the Stratocaster guitar Jimmy Hendrix used at Woodstock sold for £198,000 in 1990. Even 'relics' of apparently little direct significance to the achievements of their owner can be valued highly, such as: a small leather container which John Lennon used to stash his marijuana, £350; a door from Paul McCartney's childhood home, £2500; a piece of the stage from the Cavern Club in Liverpool where The Beatles played their early gigs, £500 (Jones, 1995, p. 31).

It is not just the unique items of popular culture which have gained what might seem to curators, if not to collectors, an unexpectedly high market value. Mass-produced items of fairly recent origin have reached seemingly high prices in the past few years if sufficiently rare or in good condition. A 1966 model of Thunderbird 2 is worth £150; an early version of Lady Penelope's pink Rolls Royce, £100; a 1966 sweet wrapper featuring the Thunderbirds characters, £44; a 1972 playground set of the children's television series, the *Magic Roundabout*, £600; a copy of the first issue of the comic featuring Superman in 1938 sold for £14,300; Biffo the Bear's second appearance in the classic British comic *The Beano* has fetched £1,980 at auction; a British poster for the 1952 film *Singin' in the Rain*, £800 (Kelly, 1994, p. 7; *The Guardian*, 4 March 1996, p. 7; *The Observer Review*, 12 March 1995, p. 3). Such items are therefore prized by a significant number of collectors, which drives up their value. As a result collecting in this field has become commercialized, attracting the attention of dealers and the auction houses. In the USA collecting popular culture can be considered as an industry. An advertisement in a guide to Las Vegas asks you to

> Let America's Premier Collectibles Wholesaler Help You with your next Acquisition or Liquidation. The National Collector Corporation is a Worldwide Distributor of Popular Collectibles New and Old ... Pre Paid Phone Cards ... Movie Memorabilia. Animation Art. Barbie and Character Dolls. Star Trek. Star Wars. Sports Cards. Gold and Silver Age Comics ... We specialise in servicing: Private Collectors. Retail Dealers. Corporations. Museums. Restaurants and Nightclubs.
>
> (*The Insider Viewpoint Las Vegas*, April 1995, p. 33)

These developments have profound implications for museums. They are at the root of a paradox: many of the things that people care most passionately about are unavailable to museums because the degree of that particular passion and its popularity drives up the monetary value beyond a price many museums can afford. This assumes that museums are actively looking for such material in the world of the dealers. Perhaps the more usual reaction of curators is not to realize that such material exists, simply because it is not being offered to them. And here we have a second paradox: the material that people offer to museums is often that which they care least passionately about! In terms of the plot, it is on its way down into the rubbish category, the last stop being to offer it to the local museum!

Competition

While *public* museums have only slowly come to recognize the importance and popularity of such popular material culture, a *private* museum sector has begun to develop in this field. Often these are relatively small-scale, based on one private collection, which is opened to the public as much out of enthusiasm as for financial gain. It would be interesting to note how many of these exist, since they do not seek to be part of the 'official' MGC-registered museum sector; and, furthermore, how many were opened after the collector offered the collection to a museum, only to be rebuffed. One intriguing example is the House of Hemp, a cannabis museum in London (Mills, 1995, p. 9). The classic example is the Robert Opie Collection Museum of Packaging and Advertising in Gloucester. Opened in 1984, it is based on Opie's collection of over 250,000 items of advertising and packaging, begun in 1963 when he kept a Munchies sweet wrapper, because he thought, 'If I throw this away I will, never, ever see it again, and yet here is a whole wealth of history' (Elsner and Cardinal, 1994, p. 33). A fetishistic collection, displayed in a formalist, label or even mass style, it attracts over 60,000 visitors a year. In terms of the plot it is spurious artefacts as authentic artefacts: the mass-produced items are seen as historically rather than aesthetically significant because of their design. Conversely, when some items from Opie's collection were displayed at the V&A in 1976, their authentication was as masterpieces.

Other private museums are based on the collection of an organization, such as the Museum of the Moving Image (MOMI), established by the British Film Institute, or the sports museums set up by The Royal and Ancient Golf Club of St Andrews, the Marylebone Cricket Club (MCC), the Wimbledon Lawn Tennis Association or football clubs such as Manchester United and Arsenal. Some of these seek to be considered part of the museum mainstream, as non-profit making and registered with the MGC, such as MOMI and the British Golf Museum at St Andrews. Others, particularly the football club museums, are quite deliberately commercial ventures, to cash in on the popular appeal of the material. They may employ 'professional' standards of collection care and interpretation, but do not see the need to seek MGC approval. Even the conservative National Trust has leapt ahead of public museums in this field, in purchasing the home Paul McCartney lived in between 1957 and 1964, where The Beatles practised and composed.

There are also displays based on the private collections of individuals or organizations which do not aim to be seen as museums as such at all, the exhibitions being just a part and not necessarily the focus of a larger commercial leisure venture. At one end of the scale is The World and Sooty in Shipley, which features displays of the sets and props of the popular children's television puppet series, which has run since 1952, in a complex with the world's only Sooty factory and factory shop. At the other end of the scale are high-profile leisure attractions such as Rock Circus in London, run by Madame Tussauds Group, where memorabilia take their place alongside audio-animatronic moving and static wax figures, lasers, videos and archive film.

The danger is that, since they did not take popular culture seriously enough, it is now perhaps almost too late for public museums to do anything to redress this. Historical material is often too expensive at auction for most museums, even if they were interested, given its value to private collectors, denying public access to material of great appeal. Further private museums which are planned, such as a national museum of football, involve their originators in high financial bidding against each other for the private collections of individuals, syndicates of collectors or football organizations. Other organizations have already seized the initiative to produce highly popular museums or displays as part of commercial attractions. Aside from the cost of admission, the key issue is what kind of interpretation is being presented to the public. At museums such as MOMI, the intention is to be as objective and as educative as is possible in any public museum; at the commercial attractions, the aim is entertainment, which tends towards a misleading and romanticized portrayal. The material culture of popular culture is thus privately or commercially controlled. Sheffield City Council is planning a museum of popular music, the subject of a lottery bid, but 'may find that the really worthwhile artefacts have already been snapped up by the Hard Rock Cafe, which hangs Buddy Holly's guitar over the hamburgers and fries like a relic of the true cross' (Sudjic, 1996, p. 5).

Museums have also lagged behind the media in reflecting popular material culture. Television programmes such as *Small Objects of Desire* have explored the history of everyday items such as the tampon. *Sign of the Times* and *From A to B – Tales of Modern Motoring* examined the way we decorate our homes and the fetishization of the motor car. *The Antiques Roadshow* attracts an audience of over ten million people, and often features popular culture items alongside traditional high culture. *Through the Keyhole* attracts a similar audience, to second-guess, from the clues of the material culture, which celebrity owns the house we are invited to snoop around. *Hello!* magazine plays on the same fascination. Guessing what a person is like from his or her clothes, car, decor or possessions is a popular feature of magazines. One of the new breed of men's magazines (that is, not of the top-shelf variety), has featured the 'Secrets of a woman's bedroom'. Waking up in her flat after a one-night stand, only to find that she has popped out to buy a newspaper,

> how do you go about deciding what sort of person she is, whether you've struck lucky or made some terrible mistake? ... her flat may well provide many of the answers you need, especially her bedroom and bathroom, two very personal environments that can reveal a lot about a woman and her character ... to decode from her natural habitat the secrets of her personality.   (Smith and Sherwood, 1995, p. 72)

In a quiz form, offering a range of options, a range of material culture is explored. How much more powerful would this be as an exhibition, as long as the gender roles were also reversed, and the assumption of heterosexuality was removed?

As some of the examples used in the analysis thus far have indicated, the representation of popular culture in the USA is in some senses much more advanced than in the UK. In part this would appear to be because of a much less rigid distinction between high and low culture, perhaps in turn a product of its being a less overtly class-bound society in cultural terms. This is not to say that curators did not face opposition when beginning to collect in this field in the 1970s. When staff in the Community Life Division of the National Museum of American History collected Fonz's leather jacket from the television show *Happy Days*, they had to spend a great deal of time justifying this within the museum (Mayo, 1982, p. 10). Yet this, as we have seen, was to become one of the most popular exhibits with the public. Encouraged by the popularity of such exhibits, the museum has continued to do a great deal of collecting and exhibiting in this field.

The more commercial environment in which cultural services operate in the USA has also encouraged the development of a private museum sector, sometimes in partnership with the public sector, to seize the opportunity which the high public appeal of popular culture represents. Many of these museums aim to work to accepted professional standards and are non-profit making trusts. The approach has most often been from the history perspective, particularly in the field of sport. A Muhammad Ali Museum and Education Center is the latest planned in a long line of such developments. The co-founder of Microsoft is funding a museum in Seattle based on a private collection of material associated with rock legend Jimi Hendrix (*Lord Cultural Resources, Planning and Management* Newsletter, Spring/Summer, 1995). A major new museum has been something of an exception in taking more of an art-oriented approach. The first Rock and Roll Hall of Fame opened in 1995 in Cleveland, Ohio, USA, at a cost of $100 million. The brainchild of the founder of Atlantic Records and the founder of *Rolling Stone* magazine, the museum is based on a 'mammoth' collection of rock memorabilia, held in trust by a foundation. The museum came to be sited in the unfashionable Midwest because the city put up $65 million, anticipating the tourist potential of the project. It marks a deliberate attempt to raise rock and roll to high culture, beginning with the building itself: 'There's little doubt that the building marks an impressive statement about the artistic credentials of rock'n'roll. It suggests, by using the architect who designed the Louvre expansion, that the artifacts of rock'n'roll are every bit as important as the art of Picasso' (Lee, 1995, p. 10).

While this is a very welcome development in many senses, given that, as one of the curators, an ex-*Rolling Stone* journalist, argued, 'Rock music has been around a long time and has had a huge impact on our culture and it's time to recognize that' (Lee, 1995, p. 10), at the same time, why should rock music have to be considered as 'art' in order to be taken seriously in a museum? Maybe Lennon and McCartney can be ranked as composers alongside Beethoven, but is it necessary to make such a judgement in order to reflect their work in a museum, given its enormous cultural impact? The danger with this approach is also that, as with 'Bike Art' and 'Streetstyle', popular culture is therefore sanitized by being placed in a gallery: 'Whatever happened to the first two elements of sex and drugs and rock 'n' roll?' (Lee, 1995, p. 10). In the turning of spurious masterpieces into authentic masterpieces, something of their essence is lost.

Beyond these private institutions which aim to be museums, as in Britain, there are commercial leisure attractions which exhibit popular material culture as part of a broader themed experience, if on a much larger scale, as in some of the film studios' theme parks. Disney, as we shall see in Chapter 7, is more concerned to reflect high culture. The World of Coca-Cola in Atlanta features, according to its publicity leaflet, 'the largest collection of Coca-Cola memorabilia ever assembled'.

If material in all of the above displays, with the exception of the People's Shows, is moved from spurious to authentic, there are some displays which quite deliberately do not attempt to do so, as indicated in Figure 5.2, which also demonstrates the position of the People's Shows on the plot. Sometimes this is done with a sense of irony and playfulness, as at the Museum of Bad Art in Boston, USA. This private museum, which began as 'a kind of private joke', is based on selecting pieces which the artists aimed to be authentic masterpieces, but which are rapidly falling towards rubbish. The works are found in skips or bought at church sales. The criteria for inclusion are severe: 'No kitsch, no velvet clowns, no syrupy kittens and poker-playing puppies. Prints are banned. All works must be original and must be purchased for less than $6.50. Above all, to be truly bad, the work has to be sincere. "The artist did it with the enthusiasm, courage, and passion that can sometimes make great art", explains ... [the curator], "but something went horribly wrong" (Freedland, 1995, p. 8). Deliberate spurious masterpieces are therefore excluded, even where they are originals, and particularly where the artist solicits inclusion for the ironic cachet; they must be intentionally

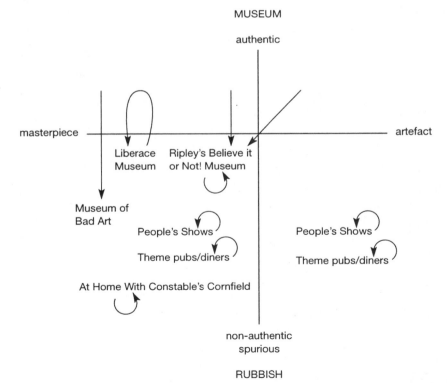

Figure 5.2 *Museum displays and attractions which consciously or inadvertently explore the spurious*

authentic but accidentally spurious. In terms of the plot, therefore, artwork which was intended to be an authentic masterpiece, but which was falling into the rubbish category, is rescued and revalued as a spurious masterpiece.

Other displays set out to occupy the bottom left quadrant, but from a desire to make money out of the public's fascination with kitsch. One example is the 'Ripley's Believe It or Not! Museum' chain, which has branches in key tourist locations in the USA, such as San Francisco and Niagara Falls, and Blackpool in the UK. This involves collecting spurious masterpieces, if of a different kind, and emphasizing them as such: 'I savoured every tasteless oddity. It was outstanding. I mean honestly, where else are you going to see a replica of Columbus's flagship, the *Santa Maria*, made entirely of chicken bones?' (Bryson, 1994, p. 96). Based on the collections of 'curios' gathered by Robert Ripley in the 1930s, 'the modern Marco Polo', who 'travelled to 198 countries', these 'museums' also feature items which in another context might be considered authentic museum pieces, such as 'A fabulous hand blown glass replica of Prince Charles' and 'Lady Diana's wedding coach crafted by England's finest glass makers', or, more controversially, 'a genuine Jivaro shrunken head from Ecuador' (Ripley's Believe It or Not! Museum, publicity leaflet, 1991). Authentic artefacts or masterpieces are therefore included if they can be revalued as spurious. There is common territory with mainstream museums in this. Such 'curios' have long been popular display items in museums. A feature at Ripley's is a two-headed calf, billed as ' "Pranks of Nature" turn the ordinary into the extraordinary'; this is also a key attraction at the public-funded Melton Mowbray Museum in the UK. Both museums are playing on our fascination with the abnormal as a way of defining what is considered normal (Pearce, 1992, pp. 57–9).

Displays of 'antiques' and 'curios' found in theme pubs, restaurants and wine bars in Britain and North America are also below the horizontal axis of the plot, as they involve displaying both spurious masterpieces and spurious artefacts as such. This was a significant economic activity in its heyday in the 1980s, one firm alone supplying over fifty pubs a year in Britain, with a typical spend of £30,000 to £60,000. It is part of what Pearce has termed marketable heritage (Pearce, 1995, p. 400), for the aim is to 'resemble a pub that's been here since early in the century, where people have kept on bringing items' (Windsor, 1992, p. 37). Clients such as American diners, opening branches in Britain, specify a very exact list of the hundreds of items of nostalgic urban Americana that must appear in each outlet (Windsor, 1992, p. 37). Why such material is appealing to customers requires further research. One of the designers explains his aims as 'I like to show them something they would have seen in their early lives – something not quite remembered but capable of jogging their unconscious' (Windsor, 1994, pp. 55–6). The irony is that this has pushed up the price of such items considerably, to the point that in some cases replicas are being used. Such commercial collecting therefore has an impact on both private collectors and museums, and reflects the commer- cialization of popular culture collecting discussed above.

Some displays find themselves in the spurious masterpiece quadrant not by intention but by how they are perceived by at least some of their visitors. For example, in Las Vegas The Liberace Museum, according to its publicity leaflet, displays '"Mr Showmanships's" dazzling jewellery, priceless antiques, million-dollar wardrobe and rare classic cars ... from one of a kind Rolls Royces with thousands of mirror tiles to a rhinestone covered customized car' (The Liberace Museum, 1995). This is a serious non-profit-making venture, donations going towards The Liberace Foundation for the Performing and Creative Arts, which provides grants to students. This is therefore spurious masterpieces displayed as authentic art, but to many visitors it remains 'a palace of kitsch', 'the tackiest place in the tackiest town in the world. ... Not all the visitors, said to total 150,000 a year, are blue-rinsed faithful. The museum has attracted a different kind of customer, present all over Las Vegas: the irony tourist. These Generation X-ers particularly enjoy ribbing the curators about the fact that no explanation is given for how Liberace died. "He was old, he just died", say the staff. Aids is never mentioned' (Freedland, 1996, p. 2).

The popularity of these approaches indicates that this is fruitful territory for museums; but it is clear that public museums would need to adopt a more objective approach to the exploration of kitsch. Some of the People's Shows can be said to have done this, as discussed above. A further groundbreaking exhibition of particular relevance was 'At Home with Constable's Cornfield', at the National Gallery in London in 1996. This displayed reproductions of this famous painting on a range of items, such as firescreens, jigsaws, cushion covers and wallpaper, alongside the original, and explored the meaning of these for their owners. Over 500 people responded to the appeal for material. Many did not know that the original was in the National Gallery, some even that it was a painting (Kennedy, 1996, p. 7). This exhibition is interesting in terms of the plot, for it is spurious artefacts and spurious masterpieces featuring reproductions of an authentic masterpiece, displayed in terms of their own value, alongside the authentic masterpiece, in a temple of high culture.

Realizing the potential

The plot has enabled us to map the approaches that have been taken, and to analyse their respective strengths and weaknesses. What conclusions can be drawn? I would argue that it is unnecessary and unhelpful to attempt to identify those elements of popular culture that can be deemed worthy of their place in the museum as art or history. The subject matter of the museum is material culture in all its variety. The horizontal axis on the plot can simply be removed. This chapter has emphasized how, in doing so, public museums would begin to reflect the interests of all of society. True democratization in museums surely lies in opening up all kinds of decision making – including even collecting policies – to public involvement. While I do not wish to deny curatorial expertise, there surely needs to be more of a balance between what curators perceive as significant and what the public do. The deliberately commercial displays of popular culture are at least responding to public interest, reflecting marketing research. If the public wish to see temporary displays or entirely new museums related to popular culture, the public museum sector needs to respond as far as is possible. Marketing research is required to indicate what the public desire, or could desire, in this respect. Should public museums fail to do so, they will be bypassed by a private museum sector, with no public accountability or necessarily any attempt at objectivity.

In meeting public needs museum workers will inevitably be forced to cover topics of no interest to them, material not to their taste or that they may even find offensive. This will reflect regional and local particularities. A curator in Walsall has to become interested in pigeon fancying and a curator in Market Harborough in boxing, because these are key aspects of local popular culture (Copp, 1994). The other alternative is to train and recruit museum staff in future who already share the public's passions.

Public museums, unlike the private sector, however, also have a responsibility to reflect aspects of popular culture which may be unpopular or even considered offensive by many people. The Rock and Roll Hall of Fame in Cleveland plays safe so as not to offend any of its audience. It largely excludes punk, rap and grunge, and 'No gangsta lyrics are on display (this is the very white Midwest, after all)' (Lee, 1995, p. 10). 'Streetstyle', in contrast, included all subcultures, including those predominantly lesbian and gay.

Alongside a sometimes potentially provocative subject matter, public museums must also reflect popular culture in a way which the audience will sometimes also find unexpected or even challenging. Unlike the private sector, it necessitates a critical analysis of the broader social meanings of the material, as outlined in Chapter 4. This has been undertaken for one piece of popular material culture in the next chapter as a concrete example of the appropriateness and value of such an approach. This will reveal a range of meanings beyond those held by the owner or creator, which may even be unpalatable to these, for they may challenge their understanding of the material and their motivation for ownership or creation. Conversely, as a part of this process, curators must also make an attempt to understand the meaning of such material from the perspective of its owner or creator, without making a curatorial judgement of value. This would mean, for example, exploring the meanings to their owners of items generally considered to be kitsch, without patronizing, with respect for those who acquire such material without a sense of irony, as exemplified by both the People's Shows and 'At Home with Constable's Cornfield'. It would also mean a respect for the fetishistic impulse of collectors, revealing their passion, as the People's Shows have done.

The natural corollary to the removal of the horizontal axis from the plot is the removal of the vertical. The distinction between masterpiece and artefact is arguably an artificial construct of the museum, which in turn reflects the deeply entrenched boundaries in curatorial subjects, between fine and applied art and the rest. Who is to make such judgements? Even if they are still valid, a masterpiece can be considered as an artefact, as a painting is when made the subject of Pearce's model of artefact analysis. On the other hand, all artefacts can be considered in terms of their aesthetic or design qualities, as they already are in Pearce's model. Objects currently held by different departments for often arbitrary reasons could be brought together. An invaluable move towards a much more interdisciplinary approach to museum work would be encouraged. This would be particularly useful, indeed essential, in terms of popular culture, given that this is inherently multidisciplinary, neither art nor history, but both. It could also include other disciplines, particularly science and technology (Woroncow, 1989). As part of their course work, exploring the use of creative management techniques in gallery development, a group of students in the Department of Museum Studies considered the re-display of the Rutland Dinosaur Gallery in New Walk Museum in Leicester, under the expert guidance of Mike Ross, a Canadian consultant in the field. The key elements to emerge were that we should 'listen to the dinosaur', for what it revealed in terms of 'life's delicate balance – rebirth and/or extinction'; and 'seeing it differently – dinosaurs in traditional and popular cultures'. Popular culture could be integrated into all science displays.

One exhibition which has taken an interdisciplinary approach is 'Fluffs and Feathers: an Exhibit on the Symbols of Indianness', originated and toured by the Woodland Cultural Centre, Brantford, Ontario, Canada. The aim was to consider how the dominant white European culture of North America had depicted Native Americans in material culture over four centuries, and what this therefore revealed of the relationship between the cultures. The exhibit drew on a wide range of contemporary and historical popular material culture, a huge range of mass-produced goods which had depictions in toys, ornaments and souvenirs, comics and books, film and television representations, and also some 'high culture' material in the form of paintings and sculpture. It also featured a section on how Native Americans were 'displayed' as live performers in Wild West shows. The display revealed nothing of Native American culture but much of that of the white culture through its need to mythologize the Native American as the 'other', either as '"savages" below Euro-Canadian "civilization" or as "noble savages" who are more moral, faster, stronger, kinder than any Euro-Canadian'. Aside from its specific subject matter, the exhibit has a wider significance: 'At its heart this exhibit ... is about the creation and manipulation of symbols. It is also about the power of symbols to justify what is and to control what will be' (Doxtator, 1992, p. 14). The display took material from all four quadrants of the plot to explore the theme, from existing museums and private collections. There was no attempt to consider the relative value of the material, for its significance lay in its symbolic qualities.

This exhibition also highlighted the relationship between museum representations and collectors. Collecting Native American and 'Wild West' artefacts is increasingly popular and commercial in both Britain and North America (Lewis, 1981, p. 75). It would be interesting to know what motivates such collectors and whether they have considered the implications of the depiction of Native Americans in some of this material. Some at least may have been disarmed to see material similar to their own collections interpreted in this way. Indeed, 'Fluffs and Feathers' could have usefully extended its remit to move beyond the symbolic meanings to consider why such material is so eagerly sought by collectors.

Collaborating with collectors

The relationship between museums and collectors will be a crucial one in attempting to develop displays of popular culture. Much of the material which is sought by museums is already in private hands, whether individuals or commercial organizations, and increasingly when it comes on to the market it is at a price few museums can afford. Private collections are forming the basis of the growing private sector of museums and display centres in this field. Is it already too late for the public museums, or are there still opportunities to work with private collectors?

Museums have a long history of working with collectors of high culture, with many of today's most significant public museums having been established by a private collector or collectors. Museums continue to court such collections as bequests. The People's Shows marked the first notable relationship between collectors of popular culture and public museums, followed by the 'themed' versions such as 'Thunderbirds Are Go!' Collectors are undoubtedly initially flattered to have their collections 'authenticated' by museums to a degree in this way (Fardell, 1995; Lovatt, 1995). However, from the collector's perspective the interest the museum shows is often transitory. There may be a feeling among collectors that they have been patronized, used as a novelty feature to boost visitor figures, and though they would welcome a continued relationship with the museum, this is not always reciprocated: 'Certainly some of the People's Shows have implied that the contributing collectors have been the subject of a controlled experiment, or have been best kept at arm's length' (Martin, 1995, p. 83). Despite the People's Shows, museums have not begun to take such private collections seriously, in the sense that they do not deem them worthy of permanent display or addition to the museum's collections. The curators remain the gatekeepers to the museum. As a consequence, collectors who feel that their collections are of strong public interest have established their own museums, or worked in partnership with a commercial organization to display their material.

From the perspective of the curator, the argument is that private collections of popular material culture can only be displayed occasionally, as part of a temporary exhibition programme, as the museum through its mission has a much broader remit. Collecting popular culture rarely features prominently in collecting policies. Even if such material fell within the collecting policy, and was offered for sale by the collectors, the museum may well not have the resources to purchase. If collections were offered as a gift, perhaps as a bequest, curators would only probably be interested in a small selection of material. The collection as a whole would be regarded as a fetishistic product of the collector's psychology, of significance in its totality only to the individual.

It is perhaps not surprising therefore that the relationship between collectors and public museums, despite the People's Shows, remains an uneasy one, if there can be said to be a significant relationship at all (Martin, 1995). This is graphically highlighted by the attack by Neil Cossons, director of The National Museum of Science and Industry, on steam buffs (railway enthusiasts), whom he described as being a 'self-centred self-serving movement that does little or nothing to further the knowledge of serious railway history' (Mason, 1994, p. 14). Yet museums are going to have to radically alter their attitudes towards collectors, if representing popular culture becomes an important part of their mission. Many of the assumptions about collectors are based on prejudice rather than fact. A major research project is beginning to reveal that the differences between public and private collecting practices have been exaggerated (Martin, 1994, 1995). Despite collecting policies, public museum collections all too often merely reflect the fetishistic whims of curators, something which was even more marked in the past, or of the private collectors whose collections of high-culture material form the basis of many museums. Many private collections can be considered just as 'systematic' as those in museums. The current director of the V&A has commented that 'Objects in private hands can be, and often are, better looked after than in museums.' While he undoubtedly had collections of 'authentic' material in mind, the same can be said for popular culture. Collectors often document their material, in their own way, but to standards that would still shame many museums. Collectors in a particular field also have specialist knowledge that perhaps no curator in the country is likely to be able to match. Collectors very often are concerned with the original social context of the object. At a time when 'access' is such a fashionable word in museums, 'many private collections are already more accessible to interested enthusiasts than the basements of museums' (Borg, 1991, p. 31). The popular material culture already in museums is often neglected and inaccessible, owing to a lack of curatorial expertise, interest and resources, whereas collectors, through their organizations, exchange access to collections and information. Collectors would also have the expertise to interpret the 'orphaned' material in museum stores.

Public museums would appear to need private collectors more than collectors need public museums. Collectors hold the material, the expertise and knowledge of the source of such material, the market, the dealers and the prices. Perhaps the most notable example of how valuable collectors are to museums is that of the collector who in 1994 found the two earliest surviving films in the UK, dating from 1895, which he has kindly donated to the British Film Institute collection (Hattenstone, 1995, p. 10). That there is currently an imbalance in what each brings to the relationship is demonstrated by the way in which particularly fine private collections of popular culture are being sold or leased to the highest bidder for display in many of the new commercial museum ventures. What, then, can the public museum offer?

Public museums will need to enter into a partnership of equals with collectors, 'to celebrate their mutual interests and establish a knowledge sharing nexus', something not unlike outreach work (Martin, 1995, p. 82). In return for the collector's expertise, museums can provide their expertise, in the fields of collection management and interpretation, an exchange which would have limited resource implications. Access, in its broadest sense, to private collections for both curators and the public could be negotiated in return for greater access for collectors and the public to museum collections. This need not be gallery display directly, given the inevitable limitations. A detailed national register of public and private collections could be established. If information technology has the potential to open up museum collections to the public, with suitable security precautions private collections could similarly be made accessible, as Martin has suggested. Museums and the collectors could benefit equally from any funds raised from the sale of CD-ROMs or other licensing agreements. Such an approach might militate against the need for museums to collect directly much material at all, given the high cost. In the short term a low-tech solution, after due consideration of security requirements, is to have guided tours for the public of museum reserve collections on open days, as already sometimes occurs, in tandem with guided public access to private collections in their stores, most often in the collector's home. This would be a collections equivalent of the national gardens scheme, whereby private gardens are open to the public on certain days of the year. For particularly significant collections, public museums can also emphasize that, unlike many private sector developments, collections offered as a bequest would be given a secure future, with no threat of their being broken up by a future sale.

The interpretation of collecting as a practice should not be overlooked in this process. Collectors should be open to learning about their own motivations through the growing study of the psychology of collecting, but only if curators are too. Some displays have already begun to explore this territory (Pearce, 1995, pp. 142–6). An example which reinforces the prejudices about collectors, but which makes this point particularly well, is that of a man who lived alone for most of his life in the same house in London:

> He was a loner, so much so that it was some weeks after his death before neighbours noticed a lifelessness about the house and called the police. They broke in to find the place stuffed from floor to ceiling with paper. For nearly half a century the man had

subscribed to magazines and journals on a variety of subjects, throwing none of them away and so accidentally providing complete runs of by now very rare material. Most interesting of all were the glossy fashion magazines because from one of these each week he had ordered an expensive pair of high-heeled ladies' shoes, as advertised. The shoes had been taken out of their boxes, worn perhaps once or twice round the house, and then replaced in mint condition. Here was a hoard which was instantly transmogrified, by the mere light of day, into a costume collection of extreme importance. It has gone to a larger home where it is more widely appreciated – the Victoria and Albert Museum.   (Gascoigne, 1986, p. 11)

If the collector was a fetishist in more senses than one, is this not in itself of interest? And what are we to make of the curators at the V&A, who felt that it was necessary to acquire the entire 'set'?

Public museums must also seek partnerships with consortia of collectors or major commercial organizations which hold private collections, such as film studios. The *Star Trek* exhibition is an excellent example of this, but these relationships need to go beyond temporary exhibitions, for these organizations will eventually move to establish permanent displays. Public museums cannot compete with such developments but could become major partners, by emphasizing their unparalleled expertise, and the kudos which they carry in the eyes of the public. For example, the next time a football club decides to set up a museum, the local museum must seek to be directly involved as far as possible. This involvement will benefit the public, by seeking to ensure that professional standards are maintained, that access to all as far as possible is ensured and that the interpretation is not simply a public relations exercise but a balanced portrayal.

If any of this rethinking of the relationship with private collectors seems too radical, the message is clear: there is no alternative. Alongside this strategy a much greater emphasis could be placed on contemporary collecting, along the lines of the SAMDOK programme in Sweden. Imagine if curators in Liverpool had collected material relating to The Beatles in the early 1960s. But as this is so hit and miss – what if they had chosen the wrong group? – valuable though it clearly would be, it would not negate the need to work with collectors. Museums must stop patronizing collectors of all kinds, especially trainspotters, and begin to try to learn what it is that makes people so passionate about certain kinds of material culture. Isn't this after all what museums are all about?

And academics from cultural studies?

Collectors are not the only potential source of expertise for the museum in relation to popular culture. It has become an important field of academic study. Museums should similarly seek to develop partnerships to mutual advantage with academics. Some have already been made, as in the 'Streetstyle' exhibition, which was co-curated by an academic. The relationship is a delicate one, because academics inevitably perceive the subject and its representation in a very different way, producing literature, not exhibitions, for a limited specialist audience, rather than the public in gen-

eral. The effectiveness of the 'Streetstyle' exhibition, for example, was
hampered by an overly academic approach. 'Household Choices', an exhibition at the V&A in 1990, usefully sought to explore the same territory as
the BBC television programme *Sign of the Times: the way we decorate our
homes.* But in being curated by the academics leading the project, it ended
up as a book on the wall. The accompanying publication said everything
the exhibition could (Putnam and Newton, 1990). 'Harmonious Relations:
Popular Music in Family Life on Merseyside', at the Merseyside Museum
of Labour History in 1991, again co-curated by academics, contained
some material culture, but only as illustrations to the analyst book on the
wall. Though some writers, as we have seen, have defined popular culture
as its material culture, the general neglect of objects as a source is shared in
this field, with some notable exceptions. There are significant limitations,
therefore, on what such partnerships can achieve. Curators and collectors
are much closer in what they are seeking to do, and that is therefore a far
more significant potential partnership. Academics of popular culture do,
however, have something to offer, in terms of both subject matter and
methodology; what is appreciated even less is that museums probably have
as much, if not more, to offer in return.

Academics have made the study of popular culture acceptable, even
respectable, in the university in a way that it is still not in the museum.
Yet the study of artefacts has been relatively neglected, a reflection in part
of a lack of awareness of the methodologies which can be employed to
interpret them. Studies of British youth subcultures, which preceded
museum interest in the subject by over a decade, have included an exploration of the meanings of their clothes (see, for example, Hebdige 1979;
Cosgrove, 1989; Willis, 1990). There has been a little more attention to
objects in the USA, a reflection of the higher profile of material culture
studies in North America (see, for example, Fishwick and Browne, 1970;
Gilborn, 1989).

Much more interest has focused on more comparatively academically
mainstream sources, such as popular literature, popular music, especially
the lyrics, and films and television. This has been invaluable in establishing the validity of studying: teenage girls' magazines such as *Just
Seventeen* and *Jackie* (McRobbie, 1991) or football fanzines (magazines
produced by the fans themselves; Haynes, 1994); the lyrics of punk songs
(Laing, 1989) or a Madonna video (Fiske, 1989a); films, not simply those
considered 'art', but the popular, such as James Bond; and television,
again not just 'quality' drama with artistic aspirations, but popular programmes such as *Coronation Street*, *Dallas* or *Doctor Who* (see Turner,
1990). All emphasize that the study of such material is far from spurious,
for popular culture, it is argued, reveals much about the power relations
in our society.

The implication for museums in terms of subject matter is that there is
some, if limited, common ground in the study of artefacts. More significant is that museums can draw on such work to explore aspects of

popular culture that they have particularly neglected, most notably film and television. In Britain as many people visit the cinema each year as go to museums, and they all pay for admittance; 98 per cent of homes have a television set, and almost two-thirds a video recorder, and on average every member of the population watched over 26 hours of television a week in 1992 (Strinati, 1995, p. 263). The National Museum of Photography, Film and Television and MOMI are exceptional in the UK in looking at these areas. There is clearly much more that museums could do to reflect the media (Wallace, 1995). When they have done so, their approach has been largely analyst, so that the programmes and films themselves are secondary to the narrative history to be told, rather than being analysed individually in detail as the prime material evidence. Museums need to make the films and television shows, and their associated material culture, the focus, as in the *MASH* and *Star Trek* exhibitions at the Smithsonian. Other examples of note include the touring exhibition of costumes from the BBC television costume dramas *Pride and Prejudice* and *The House of Elliot,* and the costumes, set designs and artwork from the international hit Australian film *Strictly Ballroom* at the Powerhouse Museum, Sydney, in 1992. Yet all of these highly popular displays tend to be formalist, and many possibilities for the exploration of their subjects through the material culture remain unexplored.

The academic study, on the other hand, could benefit from moving away from textual sources to also consider artefactual evidence. Even the study of popular fashions and styles has been extremely limited, in looking at subcultures, which only directly involve a fraction even of youths, though they can have a wider cultural impact. More mainstream, high-street fashion is relatively neglected. A useful starting point is Fiske's analysis of 'jeans' (Fiske, 1989b, Chapter 1). Popular culture academics have failed to acknowledge collecting, despite its immense significance. When, for example, 'Trekkies' (*Star Trek* fans) have been studied, their collections, arguably the most significant aspect of their fandom, have been ignored in favour of an analysis of literature they have produced (see Fiske, 1989b, p. 150).

What can museums learn from the theoretical approaches employed by the academics in the field? A wide range of often contradictory theoretical positions from other fields have been applied to and developed within the study of popular culture, as indicated in Chapter 1. Museums must be aware of and use the variety of approaches as appropriate. Strinati offers a perceptive critique of each approach, Turner a highly readable introduction to the field which is wider in scope (Strinati, 1995; Turner, 1990). The multiplicity of approaches to the study of popular culture can, however, as we saw, be characterized as adopting one of two fundamental positions. It tends to be viewed either as a mass culture imposed by a culture industry to maintain the power of a ruling elite, or as a genuine, creative cultural expression from below, a form of consumer subversion in opposition to the dominant ideology. The first of these positions has a long tradition, from the mass culture approach, which in its British form feared the Americanization of youth culture, to the Frankfurt School, which saw popular culture as a form of industrial production, securing the stability and continuity of capitalism, something shared to a degree with other strands of Marxist theory, such as Althusserian, and to a degree, Gramscian. Some structuralist approaches have seen popular culture as an expression of universal and unchanging mental and social structures, while Barthes's highly influential semiological approach argued that this was historically and culturally specific. Some feminist approaches similarly see it as an imposed culture, this time in the service of patriarchy (Strinati, 1995, *passim*). All these approaches share the perspective that aspects of popular culture can be read as 'texts' to reveal that they are products which ultimately support the holders of power in society, even if the techniques used to 'read' the 'text' vary, and the definition of the power relations in society, and how these are created, also varies significantly.

The alternative and, at least until the past two decades or so, weaker tradition has been termed 'cultural populism', that which sees popular culture as a creative force from below, often resistant to the dominant ideology. In cultural history this is best exemplified by the highly influential approach of E. P. Thompson; in the sociological approach to contemporary culture, in the ethnographic work of Paul Willis; in some elements of the focus on subcultures, such as the work of Hebdige; and in the media studies analysis of television audiences (Turner, 1990, Chapters 3, 4 and 5). Postmodernist thinking broadly also relates to this approach, but little of any significance has been contributed directly by this to the debates around popular culture (Strinati, 1995, Chapter 6). 'Cultural populism' has invaluably counteracted the excesses of the mass culture perspective. This has not been entirely difficult, given the crassness of much of this. It may, for example, have come as a surprise to academics that each individual does not simply swallow wholesale the ideological messages of television programmes, depending on whether he or she is middle-class or working-class, but that individual reactions vary considerably, but not to anyone who has ever watched television in company (Turner, 1990, Chapter 4). Yet the cultural populist approaches are not a mirror image of imposed mass culture (Strinati, 1995, p. 257); almost all share, to varying degrees, the acceptance that while popular culture is in part self-created, this is not on terms independent of broader relations of power. To paraphrase classic Marx, we make history and therefore culture, but not in circumstances of our own making. Where such approaches can be criticized is in overemphasizing the politically oppositional nature of popular culture. Whereas the mass theories have often seen audiences as 'full of passive unthinking dupes, open to manipulation and ideological control by the mass media and the culture it spreads, cultural populism has turned this around, seeing audiences as self-conscious, active subversives, exploiting media culture for their own ends, and resisting and reinterpreting messages circulated by cultural producers. Whereas elitism patronised the audience by calling it stupid, populism has patronised the audience by calling it subversive' (Strinati, 1995, p. 258). Some have come to recognize this. Hebdige, for example, has back-tracked on his earlier reading of the politically oppositional nature of the punk subculture (Hebdige, 1979, 1988; Turner, 1990, pp. 113–17). Others have sought to establish a middle-ground, a neo-Gramscian approach which insists that there is a dialectic between the processes of production and the activities of consumption (Strinati, 1995, pp. 160–75).

I hope this has at least indicated that there are a wide range of conflicting theoretical perspectives. There is clearly a delicate balance between popular culture as mass culture or a creative culture in its own right, if not on its own terms. Yet this is not a problem for museum interpretations, but an opportunity. Museums can potentially play a major role in the debate, by exploring whether an interpretation of the material culture supports or refutes either of the perspectives. In the past museum displays have unwittingly either tended to follow a mass culture perspective, as in design-oriented displays, or taken a cultural populist approach, as in the People's Shows. Museum workers need to be more aware of the academic debates, in order to avoid unconsciously adopting a position, and also to explore the debates in their interpretation.

This interpretation could be informed by the methodologies used by academics. Many, such as structuralism, and the many variants of this, have already been considered in museological literature, if not significantly in practice. Ethnographic and anthropological methodologies, including participant observation, have been used by museums in relation to 'other' cultures in developing countries, but rarely in relation to popular culture in our own society, and could be invaluable in programmes in the badly neglected field of contemporary collecting (Turner, 1990, Chapter 5). These could, for example, have informed the analysis of the teapot in Chapter 4. Media studies approaches to both text and audience could prove very useful as museums seek to move beyond the analysis of artefacts to other aspects of material culture in its broadest definition, such as films and television programmes.

What specifically might museums learn from the methodologies of the comparatively few academics that have specifically analysed artefacts? The structuralism of Levi-Strauss and more particularly the semiological approach of Barthes (1973) has been particularly influential, but it is not simply its impenetrability that limits its value to museums. Barthes's renowned analyses tell us more about himself than they do about the artefact in question: 'What validity does Barthes's interpretation of a particular cultural item possess? He does not attempt to indicate why his interpretation is to be preferred to others' (Strinati, 1995, p. 123). Hebdige has offered a critique of Barthes's analysis of the Citroen DS 19 motor car, arguing that 'To reconstruct the full "cultural significance" of the DS Citroen we would have to do more than merely "demystify" its reception in the marketplace. ... The "cultural significance" of the Citroen DS 19 might be defined as the sum total of all the choices and fixings made at each stage in the passage of the object from conception, production and mediation to mass-circulation, sale and use' (Hebdige, 1988, pp. 81–2). What is needed is a 'comprehensive and unified account of all the multiple values and meanings which accumulate around a single object over time, the different symbolic and instrumental functions it can serve for different groups of users separated by geographical, temporal and cultural location' (Hebdige, 1988, p. 80). These remarks presage such an analysis of the motor scooter in Britain over three decades, but rather than adopting an ethnographic methodology, as this might suggest, semiological analysis still remains a significant part of his approach, as in his previous study of subcultures (Hebdige, 1979). Hebdige is struggling here with the notion of polysemy, which, as we have seen, Pearce has brought more fully to material culture analysis. To a large degree, therefore, what is offered by Hebdige and others has already been taken on board within the museological literature.

Ethnographic methodologies have been employed by those closer to a 'cultural populist' perspective. As part of a major research project into 'the symbolic creativity' in the everyday life of young people, Willis considered the meaning of style and fashion, largely through interviews, concluding, as we have seen, that young people do not just passively consume but 'recontextualize' to create new meanings (Willis, 1990). Critics argue that this does not reveal the underlying relations of power that provide the boundaries to such 'symbolic creativity', yet if polysemy is a key part of the analysis, this methodology is very helpful. How do a range of people relate to a particular object or objects in their everyday lives? It does not equate to oral history, unless the focus of the interview is the relationship with material culture. Reminiscence work is perhaps the closest museums get to this at present. Major research surveys using questionnaires rather than interviews have been undertaken by Pearce on a cross-section of the population's relationship with collections and objects.

It would appear that museological methodologies to artefact analysis have more to offer to the academics of popular culture than vice versa. Hebdige's search for 'cultural significance' equates to 'significance' in the Pearce model of artefact analysis. He fails to consider the other stages in the analysis. Pearce's model offers the most comprehensive guide in seeking the full cultural significance of an artefact. One might suggest that it could also be usefully applied to the analysis of other, non-artefactual forms of material culture, such as film and television.

Museums offer an environment to explore the meanings of popular culture in ways that academic texts cannot, primarily because the material culture can be directly experienced. How can we fully understand Hebdige's analysis of a Lambretta scooter without being able to see it, smell it, hear it and touch it? The second advantage of the museum is as a public space, open potentially to the widest possible audience, presenting a dissection of the meaning of popular culture in an accessible manner. The academics have failed to touch the public's consciousness; if their goal is ultimately to enable us all to understand the significance of popular culture, then they have failed miserably. Museums offer a unique forum to succeed where the academics have failed. Those who work in museums have no need to fear any of this, for they have nothing to lose but their aitches.

6

It's coming home, it's coming
home, this football's coming home

That ball's part of Geoff.
(Alan Ball, Daily Mirror, 26 April 1996, p. 2)

Introduction

This chapter aims to elaborate on the analysis in Chapter 5 by focusing
on one particular but significant aspect of British popular culture: football. Within this I will further focus the analysis on one individual object,
for two reasons: to demonstrate that the material culture of popular culture can be subjected to exactly the same kind of curatorial analysis and
interpretation as more traditional museum objects; and to demonstrate
the value of Pearce's model of object study, as discussed and refined in
Chapter 4, and, I hope, as a consequence to popularize its use within the
profession, by applying it to a particular object. The variety of ways in
which the ball could form the centrepiece of a display will be apparent,
but this time the details of this will be left to the reader's imagination.

The item in question is the football used in the final of the Fédération
Internationale de Football Association (FIFA) World Cup at Wembley
Stadium, London, on 30 July 1966, when England beat West Germany by
four goals to two, to become the holders of the Jules Rimet Trophy, the
World Cup. This, I will argue, is an extremely important artefact in
English post-war history, the value of which has been shamefully ignored
by museums. The ball, as we shall see, became a major talking point in
England in April 1996, when for the first time plans were made for it to
appear on public display, though not in a museum. The ball in the inter-
vening 30 years had been held in private hands. It is therefore in part a
symbol of the wider neglect of popular culture by museums. Some of the
details provided will inadvertently be a source of amusement to football
fans reading this, but it is deliberately written assuming no previous
knowledge on behalf of the reader, that you are not an initiate of this particular 'subculture', if it can be described as such, given the enormous
popularity of the game. I would argue that football is too central to
English cultural life to be marginalized by the use of the term 'subculture'.
It is the national sport, but perhaps also the most popular aspect of
English culture.

Description

It would be extremely difficult if not impossible for me to see the ball before it shortly goes on public display. At the time of writing I have only seen the ball in photographs and television clips. It is orange in colour, and apparently made of leather (*Daily Mirror*, hereafter *Mirror*, 26 April 1996, p. 3). It is ornamented with the autographs of several of the players from the 1966 final, including Bobby Moore of England and Uwe Seeler of West Germany, and also other top footballers from the tournament, such as Pele of Brazil (*Mirror*, 27 April 1996, p. 2).

Identification

The object is a football, from its size, weight, materials and design. The size and weight are determined by the governing bodies of the game. The history of the football as an artefact has only been sketched, rather than fully written (Hale, 1996, pp. 92–3), and there are certainly too few balls in museums to establish the position of the ball in a typographic sense, given that museums have so far taken comparatively little interest in the game. There are two possible sources for pursuing this kind of research: private collectors, of whom there are many; and the original manufacturers, who may still hold examples.

Construction

This step involves first a consideration of details of how the object was constructed, by whom, when and where. Second, it involves analysing the materials of which the object is made, in order to establish their provenance, and the way in which these have been treated in the process of manufacture. Fortunately, the answers to the first set of questions are known, which means that the second can also be tackled more easily. The ball was made by Malcolm Wainwright at the firm Slazenger in 1966 (*Mirror*, 27 April 1996, p. 3). Research could reveal much about the techniques of manufacture, the origins of the materials, and hence how this industry related to others, and the social relations of production. It would also reveal why such a ball from this company was chosen for the final, as opposed to those of other competing manufacturers.

History

The ball was purchased by FIFA, which supplied all the balls for the tournament. Three balls were used for the final, apart from the balls used in the kick about (practice on the pitch) before the game. The two reserve balls were kept by the fourth official (the reserve to the referee and the two linesmen) (*Mirror*, 26 April 1996, p. 2). Balls are kept in reserve at football games in case a ball bursts or is lost in the crowd, or even goes over the roof of a stand and out of the stadium. It is part of the folklore of the English game that at Shrewsbury Town Football Club, a coracle (a small roundish boat) is used to retrieve lost balls from the River Severn, which passes behind one of the stands. In the 1966 final, only one ball was used throughout the game. At the end of the game, the referee has a duty to collect the ball, but on this occasion the official, Gottfried Dienst, failed in his duty. Instead, one of the West German team, Helmut Haller, jostled with him to get the ball: 'I ran off with the ball because it is an old German tradition – if the winners get the cup, the losers keep the ball' (*Mirror*, 26 April 1996, p. 2). Haller was photographed with the ball when receiving his loser's medal from the Queen in the Royal Box immediately after the game. At the official reception after the game, Haller sought and got some of the top players in the tournament to autograph it. Haller then took the ball home as 'a present for my son ... a gift on his fifth birthday' (*Mirror*, 27 April 1996, p. 2). For the next thirty years the ball was kept by the Haller family, through three house moves in Italy and two in Germany. Haller's son Jurgen recalls that 'even when we lived in Italy it was never far away from me. When we came back to Germany, we lent it out to local businessmen, pubs and close friends. But I always made sure I got it back' (*Mirror*, 26 April 1996, p. 3).

Haller took the ball because of a 'tradition' of the German game. Yet there is an equally strong tradition in English football that if a player gets a 'hat-trick' in a game (scores three goals) he or she gets to keep the match ball. Such is the strength of this unwritten but deeply entrenched tradition that there was outrage when, after the Reading player Trevor Senior scored a hat-trick against Cardiff City in 1985, the club told him he would have to pay £40 for the ball, presumably its market price (Hale, 1996, p. 94). In the game in 1966, the English player Geoff Hurst became the first (and to date still the only) player to score a hat-trick in a World Cup Final, making it probably the most famous hat-trick of all time. Hurst did not claim the ball at the time, apparently because amid the euphoria of this exceptional game, this being England's first (and to date only) appearance in the final, this was not uppermost in his mind (The *Sun*, hereafter *Sun*, 25 April 1996, p. 4). However, when Haller and Hurst met at a reunion dinner in London in 1988, Hurst made a claim for the ball. Haller responded with another German tradition of the game: 'The first man to score in the final always gets to keep it' (*Mirror*, 27 April 1996, p. 2).

In April 1996 Hurst made a further appeal for the ball in the British press. England's victory in 1966 was topical for two reasons: the thirtieth anniversary of the final was approaching, and for the first time the European Football Championships were to be held in England in June, an event termed Euro 96. This is generally considered to be the most major international sporting event in England since 1966. Spotting the public appeal of this story, on 25 April the *Sun*, Britain's most popular newspaper, in its lead headline on the front page, announced that 'Geoff Hurst gets his ball back'. The ball had been tracked down 'after a massive search led by The Sun', though it admitted that the search had been triggered by soccer magazine *Total Football*. Finding the ball, despite this headline, had clearly not been a difficult task, as Hurst had known for years that Helmut Haller had the ball. Hurst admitted to a *Sun* reporter that 'amid the euphoria of the World Cup win, he did not try hard enough to retrieve it. ... "It's only now, after 30 years, that I am realising how much it means to me"' (*Sun*, 25 April 1996, p. 4). Despite the headline, at this stage Hurst had not got his ball back, though he had 'high hopes' it would be handed over to him (*Sun*, 25 April 1996, p. 1). In later editions the *Sun* was slightly more circumspect, changing the headline to 'Sun finds Geoff Hurst's lost ball'. This reflected that the *Sun* now faced competition from its biggest rival tabloid newspaper, the *Daily Mirror*, for the return of the ball.

On Friday 26 April, the *Daily Mirror* on its front page announced a 'world exclusive' story, 'I get my Hans on Hurst's ball, by Daily Mirror Man Peter Allen', the 'Hans' being a pun on what English people generally regard as the most popular name for German men. According to Allen, 'the supreme symbol of English football glory was on its way home last night' (*Mirror*, 26 April 1996, p. 2). The following day the *Mirror*'s front page pictured Geoff Hurst kissing the ball, with the headline 'World exclusive. They think it's all over ... it's his now. The Daily Mirror gets Geoff his ball back.' This was a pun on what since 1966 have become for English football fans the most famous words associated with the victory that day. As Hurst strode forward in the dying seconds of extra time to score England's fourth goal and secure the victory, BBC television commentator Kenneth Wolstenholme said, 'Some people are on the pitch. They think it's all over. It is now!', as Hurst lashed the ball into the net. These are words which every English football fan can recite.

The *Mirror*'s story continued: 'It's the moment all England has been waiting for – soccer legend Geoff Hurst reunited with his World Cup hat-trick ball. ... Overjoyed Geoff Hurst lovingly cradled his 1966 World Cup football for the first time in 30 years and said: "It's like I've won the Cup all over again"'(*Mirror*, 27 April 1996, pp. 1–2). Haller, with the agreement of his son Jurgen, had decided to 'give the ball back' to Hurst because 'The Daily Mirror is right – 30 years is a long time. It's about time I handed it back. It deserves to go home' (*Mirror*, 26 April 1996, p. 2). Haller had apparently been offered 'a fortune' for the ball, but agreed to hand it over to the *Mirror* in return for a donation to a children's cancer charity. The *Mirror* had done this deal in partnership with Richard Branson's Virgin business empire and Eurostar, the operators of the Channel tunnel rail service. The ball 'will now be put on display at London's Waterloo international rail station ready for Euro 96' (*Mirror*, 27 April 1996, p. 2). The *Sun*, meanwhile, stung by the *Mirror*'s stealing of the story and the ball from under its nose, retorted that Haller and his son Jurgen had been attempting to exploit the ball for money, demanding £80,000 just for a *photo* of the ball. The *Sun* reported that the *Mirror* and its partners had, in fact, paid the Hallers £80,000 for the ball, *including* a donation to children's cancer charities of £20,000 (*Sun*, 27 April 1996, p. 11).

Location

This could involve a consideration of the ball in relation to the other artefacts required for the game itself, such as the shirts, shorts, socks and boots etc. of the players and officials, even the pitch and goal posts, or a wider examination of the material culture surrounding the final, including all scarves, flags, rattles etc. of the 93,000 fans in the stadium, or even of the estimated 400 million who watched the final on television. In Germany the ball was kept in the Haller home but occasionally loaned to local businessmen, pubs or close friends. When the media interest in the ball became apparent, Helmut Haller initially did not know where the ball was, but his son Jurgen said, 'There is no mystery. I had the ball all the time. ... It was in a box in the cellar, along with another ball my father gave me. I treasure this one too because the famous Brazilian star, Pele, played with it' (*Sun*, 25 April 1996, p. 4). Geoff Hurst, however, has not 'got his ball back', for the ball is to be 'given pride of place' in a glass case at Waterloo international railway station, 'the most modern terminal in the world', belonging to Eurostar, one of the sponsors of the deal. Exactly why Eurostar got involved in the deal will be discussed below, but this was an obvious location to place the ball, particularly given that, according to the Eurostar spokesperson, five million people had passed through it in the past year, and it was hoped that this would be ten million next year. During Euro 96 thousands of fans from Europe would also pass through the station, and 'On their way, they will now see the greatest football on earth' (*Mirror*, 27 April 1996, p. 3).

It is important to consider the immediate location, a glass case, suggesting that the ball has been 'museumified'; in our culture we place important objects in glass cases. The fact that this process had taken place is indicated by the way in which Peter Allen, the *Mirror*'s reporter, interacted with the ball in the cellar of the Haller's home. Here it was not seen as a 'museum piece': 'There was a lump in my throat as I threw it in the air and gently volleyed it towards the ceiling' (*Mirror*, 26 April 1996, p. 3). Note, however, the word *gently*, suggesting that he already felt that the ball needed to be treated with at least some degree of care. This certainly does not mean that the Hallers did not treat the ball with respect. According to Helmut, 'Jurgen played with it a few times but was always scared of damaging it so we ended up putting it in our cellar.' During the flight over to Britain the ball was still to be 'museumified', but was treated with care, being strapped into its own seat next to Jurgen (*Mirror*, 27 April 1996, p. 5). Whether the ball will be kept in something like an ideal museum environment is not clear, but access had been negotiated. A Eurostar spokesman commented that 'when Geoff Hurst wants to borrow it, he'll be very welcome' (*Mirror*, 27 April 1996, p. 3). Hurst, however, would have preferred to have the ball at his home. As the story first broke he had commented to the *Sun*: 'if I get it back I'll give it pride of place in my home in a special case' (*Sun*, 25 April 1996, p. 1). It is very common for footballers to keep souvenirs of the game, such as medals, caps and hat-trick balls, in display cases in their homes; they mimic museums. Hurst has 'seven or eight balls from my hat-tricks for West Ham', the London football club he played with for many years (*Sun*, 26 April 1996, p. 4). We can learn much about the ball and its wider significance, therefore, from its location.

Distribution

If we could plot from the manufacturer Slazenger's order book from 1966 where balls of this type had been purchased, it would tell us much about the geographical spread of the game, particularly if allied to studies of other manufacturers. This could also be expanded through time. If orders were made from overseas, this might reveal much about the professionalization of the game, particularly in developing countries.

Significance

The examination of the significance of this ball depends first on whether it can be proved to be the actual ball used in the final, since clearly much of the analysis hinges on this. This is not an idle question, as Geoff Hurst's agent has expressed his concern (Editorial, 1996, p. 4). We know that there are photographs and also television footage of Haller on the steps of the Royal Box with *a* ball under his arm after getting his loser's medal, but can we be sure this was the match ball? Ken Aston, the World Cup referee whose job it was to look after all the referees in the 1966 tournament, has commented that 'If Haller had a ball under his arm at the end when he got his medal, he must have got the match ball', but adds a slight doubt, in relation to the two reserve balls that were not used: 'He couldn't have got his hands on the other balls and even if he did it wouldn't make sense to get one of those' (*Mirror*, 26 April 1996, p. 2). Television evidence could probably prove beyond all doubt that Haller got hold of the match ball. Since that day the ball has not always been in the possession of Haller or his son, for it was loaned out on occasion. So how can we be sure that the ball that Jurgen Haller got out of the box in the cellar was still the 'real thing'? *Mirror* reporter Peter Allen, on seeing the ball for the first time in the cellar of the Haller home, commented that 'It was scuffed and stained but unmistakably the bright orange leather which helped put English football at the top of the world. Fading signatures of wonderful players who took part in the tournament, including Brazil's Pele, could just be made out' (*Mirror*, 26 April 1996, p. 3). It is still possible, however unlikely, that this is a clever fake. After all, the 'real' ball is worth £80,000. Perhaps one final act of provenance is required. Malcolm Wainwright, the maker of the ball, claimed that 'I'll know right away that it's one of mine. I made about 100 by hand and I know my own work' (*Mirror*, 27 April 1996, p. 3). A close relative of Mr Wainwright, speaking on BBC Radio Five Live on 27 April, said that Mr Wainwright would be able to identify the ball from a production number inside that only he knew.

What, then, is the significance of the ball? One approach is to consider its function. The function of the ball has changed greatly during its 30-year history. Serving its purpose as a football for just 120 minutes during the final, the ball then became a souvenir for Haller, and indeed a vehicle for other souvenirs (the autographs of famous players). It was only used as a football on a few occasions by Jurgen. In 1996 it has become a vehicle for a further round in the circulation war between England's top-selling tabloid newspapers, and finally an object for display to the public at one of Britain's busiest railway stations. It remains a football, but is no longer used as such. Yet this approach by function reveals only a fraction of its full significance.

Rather than utilizing in turn the range of theoretical approaches, such as functionalism, that could be used to help establish the significance of the ball, I will draw upon these as appropriate, in considering what the ball has meant or means to the various parties with an interest in it. This will reveal its polysemantic qualities.

To the man who made it, Malcolm Wainwright, its significance is that 'It's part of our heritage. An English craftsman made it, an English player scored three goals with it' (*Mirror*, 27 April 1996, p. 3). Its significance rests for him not just in its use in the game, but in the fact that he made it by hand, with a skill that is now redundant – balls are no longer made of leather and are mass-produced. The ball is thus tied into the decline of the craft worker.

To Helmut Haller, immediately after the game its significance was that it 'belonged' to him as a result of one of the 'traditions' of German football, that the losing team keeps the ball. Haller, however, as we have seen, later drew on a different tradition, that the first man to score in a final gets to keep it, to justify his possession. In either case, it was a souvenir of the game: Haller has described it as 'my little memento' (*Mirror*, 27 April 1996, p. 2). The ball gained extra significance for him as a souvenir when, at the official reception after the final, he got it autographed by up to thirty top players, not just from the two teams in the final. It was now also a souvenir of the tournament as a whole. Yet it was not simply a souvenir for himself: 'To be honest it was a present for my son' (*Mirror*, 26 April 1996, p. 6). While over the next 30 years the ball remained in the family as a souvenir for Helmut Haller, possession had, at least in part, passed to his son. By April 1996, Helmut Haller was willing to give way to a stronger claim to the ball, but interestingly this was not that of Geoff Hurst. Haller was reported as feeling that he had to bow to the wishes of the English people in general: 'The football means a great deal to me but I never really appreciated how much it meant to the people of England'; 'I can't believe how passionate you can be about a little old football. There are wars around the world, even mad cow disease, yet the interest in my little memento is just incredible. But I've come to realise over the past few days that this isn't just a football. It's a symbol of your biggest sporting success. It's only right you should have it back'; 'this ball should be in England. It deserves to go home' (*Mirror*, 26 April 1996, p. 2; 27 April, p. 2). However, he was apparently only willing to part with the ball for £80,000, which he claimed was for charity. Does every souvenir have a price? But by now the ball was not his to return: it belonged, at least in part, to his son Jurgen. To Jurgen, the ball still had ' huge sentimental value'. Aged five in 1966, he recalled that 'It is a very personal thing – I can only remember the game very vaguely ... but the ball has been my most treasured possession ever since' (*Mirror*, 26 April 1996, pp. 2–3). His father, however, was soon able to convince him to part with the ball, in exchange for the donation to 'charity'.

Geoff Hurst had not claimed the ball on the day despite the hat-trick tradition, apparently because of the euphoria of England's victory. He had, however, as we have seen, asked for the ball from Haller in 1988. By 1996, he commented that 'It's only now, after 30 years, that I am realising how much it means to me' (*Sun*, 25 April 1996, p. 4). Again, for Hurst it was a souvenir of the final, with the added piquancy of his hat-trick: 'It will be the greatest memento of my football career' (*Sun*, 25 April 1996, p. 1). On learning from a *Sun* reporter that Haller had refused to return the ball, he commented: 'I would hope he had regard for the tradition of this country – if you score a hat-trick you keep the ball. ... This ball would have been a fantastic memento and must mean more to me and the England team than to Helmut. I am very disappointed he is hanging on to it' (*Sun*, 26 April 1996, p. 4). But in thanking the *Mirror* for securing the return of the ball, Hurst slightly played down its significance: 'I think it's probably the most important memento you could get from that game apart from the medal', referring to the medals received by each player at the end of the game (*Mirror*, 27 April 1996, p. 2). This may be either because, while Hurst has got his medal, he does not get to keep the ball, or because he views the victory by the team as more significant than his individual achievement.

Hurst suggested that the ball in 1996 has more significance to players in the England team than to Haller. Is this the case? According to Bobby Charlton, immediately after the game, 'I didn't even think about it ... I won't lose a great deal of sleep over it. ... Having said that, I'm delighted if the ball is coming back to England. I'll be glad if Geoff gets it eventually.' Nobby Stiles did not know until recently that Hurst did not have the ball, and recalled that, 'To be honest winning the World Cup was more important at the time.' Alan Ball was much more positive: 'I'm delighted. People who score hat-tricks normally get the ball, so it's only fair it's on its way back', and, in an interesting comment on our relation to material culture, 'That ball's part of Geoff' (*Mirror*, 26 April 1996, p. 2). The ball therefore has polysemantic qualities for even members of the England team, and those meanings have changed through time.

For the two newspapers the ball represented an opportunity to score a victory over the rival in a circulation war. On 27 April, the headline on page five of the *Mirror* was 'Daily Mirror 1 The Sun 0. The greatest win since 1966'. In flying over with the ball, Jurgen was guarded by *Mirror* staff. At Stansted Airport he was aggressively questioned by two *Sun* journalists: 'Police called to the disturbance by airport staff led the two over-tired hacks away and warned them about their behaviour' (*Mirror*, 27 April 1996, p. 5).

The *Mirror* continued to milk the ball for all it was worth as the Euro 96 tournament began, bringing in another key player. On the day of England's opening game of the tournament, Uri Geller, top international 'mind-bender', joined the paper for the 'Great Euro 96 Psychic Experiment'. Readers of the paper were urged to 'use their powers to take England to victory', for

> The master of the paranormal has 'energised' the famous orange ball used in the nation's 1966 World Cup win. ... At 3.00 pm today – when England kicks off against Switzerland ... look at our picture of the ball, rub it ... and think of England. The result could be sensational. Soccer-mad Uri tells readers: 'I have filled the ball with my positive energy. Touch and rub the picture and concentrate for two minutes on England winning. ... You can even bend the ball towards the goal if you try hard enough!' ... Uri ... believes the World Cup ball is especially lucky. It symbolises our greatest sporting moment and has special 'psychic' powers because of its colour.

Geller was pictured holding the ball with the headline, '3.00 pm. Rub that ball and think of England'. He was seeking a meeting with the ball with the England squad, to 'help psych them up for the big game ... even if they gaze on the ball they will gain inspiration'; but if they touched it, after he had, this would be even better (*Mirror*, 8 June 1996, pp. 2–3). After England's disappointing 1–1 draw with the Swiss in the opening game of the tournament, the *Mirror* led on its front page with the story 'England call-up for Uri Geller'; England officials were apparently trying to arrange for Geller to meet the squad with the ball to give them a 'psychic boost' (*Mirror*, 11 June 1996, pp. 1, 5). With England leading Scotland 1–0 in the next match, Scotland were awarded a penalty. Just before Gary McAllister struck the ball, it moved slightly in a windless Wembley Stadium, possibly just enough to put him off, and was saved by the England goalkeeper David Seaman. Gazza (Paul Gascoigne) almost immediately scored a goal of pure genius to give England a priceless 2–0 victory. Geller, speaking on BBC television's *Fantasy Football League* on 21 June, described the slight movement of the ball as 'solid proof that the power of the mind can move balls'.

Virgin boss Richard Branson and Eurostar bosses may well have felt very strongly that the ball should come back to Britain. Additionally, their share of the £80,000 gave their organizations some excellent press cover-age. A sub-headline in the *Mirror* incorporated the Virgin and Eurostar logos, and proclaimed that the ball had been 'Saved for the Nation' by the three partner organizations. Branson was photographed with Helmut Haller and Hurst holding the ball. Eurostar was quoted as saying that 'the ball would be given pride of place in the most modern terminal in the world'. *Mirror* Deputy Editor Brendon Parsons said, 'We are also extremely grateful to Richard Branson, our most dynamic entrepreneur, and Eurostar' (*Mirror*, 27 April 1996, pp. 2–3). One can suggest that with many thousands of football fans due to travel to Britain in June for the European Football Championships, many using Eurostar, the further publicity benefits for the company are clear.

The ball will have particular significance to collectors of football mem-orabilia. That there are a great number of collectors is indicated by the fact that much historical football memorabilia now has a high financial value. A prominent collector of football cards has recalled that

> I well remember the cards being given away with the 'Adventure' and the 'Rover' and the black and white Famous Footballers in packets of Barratt's Sweet Cigarettes. The cards were thrown out or given away at a later stage and are now in many cases worth £30 or £40 a set. The financial value of such material is something of a two-edged sword to the collector, for while it is pleasant to feel one has a collection of some worth, inflationary costs mean that the amount of new items which can be acquired is that much more limited ... many older collectors deplore these rising prices.
>
> (Ambrosen, 1989, p. 6)

It would be interesting to see, however, if values are lower than for, say, cricket or golf memorabilia, the theory being that collectors connected with these sports are likely to be of a higher social class, and therefore to have greater financial resources. Some football material culture at auction does, however, reach very high prices, particularly medals. For example, George Cohen, one of England's World Cup winning team, believes that his winner's medal is now worth £50,000 (*Sun*, 26 April 1996, p. 5). There is no doubt that the ball would be a prize possession for many seri-ous collectors, who would be prepared to pay a significant sum for it. Helmut Haller had already apparently been offered 'a fortune' for the ball, though presumably less than £80,000.

What of the significance to English football fans in general, and not just the collectors among them? Some grandiose claims were made by many of those involved about this. To Hurst, 'The 1966 final was the biggest day in our sporting history. People remember it like the day of the Kennedy assassination. ... It's a piece of our history' (*Mirror*, 27 April 1996, pp. 1–2). Helmut Haller called it a 'symbol of your greatest sport-ing success'; *Mirror* reporter Peter Allen described it as 'the ultimate symbol of English sporting triumph'; a Eurostar spokesman as 'the great-est football on earth'; the *Mirror* Deputy Editor Brendon Parsons as the 'ultimate symbol of British sporting achievement'; Malcolm Wainwright, its maker, as a 'part of our heritage'; the *Mirror* considered it 'English football's most famous memento' (*Mirror*, 27 April 1996, pp. 1, 2, 3, 5). The paper's editorial focused on the ball:

> The 1966 World Cup Final was England's proudest sporting moment. Soccer is the country's national sport and all fans could rejoice in the magnificent victory at Wembley. So it is not surprising that 30 years later there is so much excitement about the ball used in that historic match. Perhaps the most amazing thing is that so long has passed without anyone realising that it was hidden away in a cellar in Germany ... even if no hat-trick had been scored, that ball should have stayed in this country. It is part of our history.   (*Mirror*, 27 April 1996, p. 6)

Is this simply hyperbole by those with an interest in talking up the significance of the ball? Football has long been unquestionably England's number one sport, with hundreds of thousands attending live games every week, and millions more watching on television. When the England team all too rarely does well, interest is intense. In 1966, 25 million people are estimated to have watched the final on television, over half of the population, with a further 400 million viewing around the world in 30 countries, 'about 50 million more than for the funeral of Sir Winston Churchill' (*Daily Mail*, 29 July 1966, p. 12). When England lost to Germany in the World Cup semi-final in 1990 on penalties, the viewing figure in England was of the same order as in 1966. Since then the game has become even more popular, with attendances and television audiences rising significantly. Football is probably the most popular aspect of English culture, and arguably world culture. Games during Euro 96 were estimated to be watched on television by a total worldwide audience of seven billion people; the 1990 World Cup in Italy attracted a total audience of 15 billion.

Those who are not football fans cannot readily understand the passion for the game, the quasi-religious fervour of its fans. This, as we shall see, has begun to be explored by academics. Two stories in the *Sun* in the same week as the 1966 ball story indicate this. A dummy of Eric Cantona of Manchester United, currently the most popular player in the English Premier League, was to be the new star attraction at Madame Tussaud's (*Sun*, 25 April 1996, pp. 2–3). The previous day the paper ran the story of a Manchester United fan who had had a nine-inch tattoo of Cantona put on his back, and had named his son after Cantona. The paper had previously reported that a female Newcastle United fan had had an eight-inch portrait of the team's manager, Kevin Keegan, tattooed on her thigh (*Sun*, 24 April 1996, p. 3).

The ball clearly does have a special significance to millions of English football fans; otherwise neither of the two top-selling tabloid papers would have run the story. The fact that it got caught up in a circulation war between them only highlights this. This is demonstrated by the fact that on the Friday the *Sun* again led with the story, even though it had lost out in getting the ball. The ball surely is, as the *Mirror* claimed, 'part of our history', for the 1966 final *was* the biggest day in English sporting history. Hurst, I would argue, speaks for millions in singling out the day as being as memorable to English people as Kennedy's assassination.

Indeed, it has been argued that these are two of only three single days since VE day for which a majority of English people can remember 'where they were', with the Coronation in 1953 being the only other comparable day (Clarke and Critcher, 1986, p. 112). The ball, as the most important symbol of that day, is 'the ultimate symbol of English sporting triumph', and as such is one of the most significant artefacts in English post-war history. As a football fan myself, the ball does have this meaning to me. Born in 1960, I have as my first clear memory Kennedy's assassination. In 1966 I watched the final on television at home with my mum, my dad and my sister. It is a profound memory for me, and as for many of my generation was the moment which ensured that football would become one, if not the, dominant passion in my life thereafter.

There is only one artefact that might be considered a greater symbol of the day, and that is the World Cup itself, the Jules Rimet trophy. However, the winning country only got to hold this for four years, until the next World Cup, or until a country won the trophy three times, in which case they would get to keep it permanently. Brazil achieved this feat in the next World Cup in 1970. The trophy, however, was linked to all the finals up to 1970; the ball is a unique symbol of 1966. The ball is also a symbol of the most common popular memory of the final, which has entered English folklore, as Hurst lashes the ball into the net for the fourth goal, and commentator Kenneth Wolstenholme proclaims, 'They think it's all over. It is now!' The moment when Bobby Moore, the captain of the team, received the trophy from the Queen is a lesser event in popular memory. Further research is required to establish the full significance of the ball to football fans and the wider public.

A further key area of analysis which can reveal even more of the significance of the ball is the question of *ownership*. At first glance this is straightforward. The *Daily Mirror*, Virgin and Eurostar have bought it from Helmut and Jurgen Haller. But was it the Hallers' to sell? Keith Cooper, FIFA director of communications, has argued that the balls in the tournament belonged to FIFA, for, as the organizers of the tournament, they had purchased them, and therefore 'Legally it belongs to us.' However, he backed Hurst's claim to the ball in terms of the unwritten traditions of the English game: 'spiritually it belongs to Geoff ... if it was returned to us we would make sure Geoff got it at a special presentation'. This view was backed by a spokesman from the English Football Association (FA), and Ken Aston, the referee in charge of all referees at the tournament in 1966, who said that although the ball should have been handed in by the referee to the organizing committee, 'I would have given it straight to Geoff Hurst.' Unsurprisingly, Hurst's right to the ball was backed by his team-mates and other figures in the English game, on the grounds of the hat-trick tradition (*Mirror*, 26 April 1996, p. 2).

Helmut Haller claimed the ball, as we have noted, on the strength of an apparently equal, unwritten German football tradition: 'It saddens me that stupid people have branded me a thief for taking it. It is a German tradition that the first scorer in a game gets the ball' (*Mirror*, 27 April 1996, p. 5). So why should the Englishman's claim come ahead of the German's? It is the ultimate irony of the saga that despite the *Mirror*'s headline, Geoff Hurst has not got his ball back, only apparently access to it. But the debate has ceased to be about the rights of one Englishman against one German, but of one *nation* against another.

At this point the ball becomes embroiled in a claim of 'cultural restitution'. This piece of English history, the symbol of our greatest sporting achievement, had been wrongly held in another country. Unlike the Elgin Marbles, the ball was on the other foot, as the old saying (nearly) goes. The ball had to be 'saved for the nation', 'it is back where it belongs. In England, in the hands of Geoff Hurst' (*Mirror*, 27 April 1996, pp. 2, 6). Haller was soon convinced, whether from an acceptance that the English football tradition should take precedence at a game in England, or thanks to the 'charitable' donation, that 'This ball should be in England. It deserves to go home' (*Mirror*, 26 April 1996, p. 2). A prominent collector of football memorabilia, interviewed on BBC Radio Five Live on 26 April, stated that 'the ball is as important to English football fans as the Elgin Marbles are to the Greeks'.

Having lost out on the ball, the *Sun* played up the fact that the ball should never have left England in the first place: it was not Haller's to take and ask for money for its return. On 26 April its front-page headline accused the Hallers of being the 'Greediest Krauts on Earth' (Kraut being a derogatory term for Germans used by the English): 'The grasping German who nicked England's 1966 World Cup Final ball yesterday demanded £80,000 – just for a *photo* of it.' Under the headline was a 'world exclusive' photo of Jurgen with the ball that the paper had 'snatched' (*Sun*, 26 April 1996, p. 1). The *Sun* is renowned for poking fun at foreigners, particularly the French and the Germans. A cartoon portrayed Haller at the 1966 final as saying 'Enjoy your triumph, Hurst ... soon you will be more upset than if I had taken ze last sun bed', something which German tourists are stereotyped as doing by their English or British counterparts, who believe that the German practice of booking sun beds by putting their towels on them the night before is unfair and certainly 'not British'. Two further phrases which immediately come to mind demonstrate how sport is ingrained in British culture: this practice by the Germans is 'unsporting', 'just not cricket'.

Popular comedians not renowned for their political correctness were encouraged by the *Sun* to join the fray. Stan Boardman, whose act is largely based around the Second World War, his catch-phrase being 'The Germans bombed our chippy' (fish and chip shop), was pictured in a German soldier's uniform, commenting that 'National pride is at stake here ... it's typical of the Jeermans [*sic*] to try and rip us off like this.' According to Bernard Manning, 'This is ridiculous. We should wheel Vera Lynn over there and sing the Huns into surrendering the ball for nothing', and added an inevitable pun: 'It's a lot of money to pay a German for a ball – I'd sell two of my own for half that price.' Prominent figures in football joined the xenophobic attack on the Germans, Tommy Docherty (a Scot) commenting that Haller should have given it back, 'But if you wait on the Germans for sportsmanship you'll wait forever' (*Sun*, 26 April 1996, pp. 4–5). The *Sun* also encouraged its readers to have their say in a similar vein: 'Tell Krauts where to stick their ball! Is grasping Helmut Haller kraut of order by demanding a huge ransom for the ball? Tell us what you think by ringing our hotline or sending us a fax' (*Sun*, 26 April 1996, p. 4). The responses included: 'Let's sue the Germans for the ball'; ' Police should arrest Helmut Haller for theft'; and 'I am willing to put my £1,000 savings towards a private prosecution of Haller. I have already been to the police'; though a Welshman commented that 'If I was Haller I would tell Geoff Hurst to go and get stuffed' (*Sun*, 27 April 1996, p. 11).

The ball had therefore become a symbol of something much greater, the uneasy relationship between the English and the Germans. Many people in England currently fear what they see as the growing dominance of Germany within the European Union. Alongside the 'Greediest Krauts on Earth' headline on its front page, the Sun reported on its previous phone poll: '31,000 readers say no to single EU currency. ... An astonishing 31,270 responded to fears of a German takeover of Europe by voting overwhelmingly against economic union' (*Sun*, 26 April 1996, p. 1). This popular mistrust and even antipathy towards the Germans, whipped up by the *Sun* and other papers, ultimately, as we have seen, has its roots in the Second World War. German reunification has reawakened latent feelings. Even some of those 'celebrities' asked to comment on the return of the ball in the *Mirror* reflected this. Footballer Vinnie Jones said that 'This bloke Helmut Haller obviously still had the hump about the war and was trying to level things up.' Radio DJ Johnnie Walker commented, 'I am delighted that Geoff has got all his balls intact. After all, Hitler only had one' (*Mirror*, 27 April 1996, p. 3), a reference to a still well known wartime anti-German ditty: 'Hitler has only got one ball, Goering has two but very small, Himmler has something similar, but poor old Goebbels has no balls at all.'

The *Sunday Mirror*, the *Daily Mirror*'s sister paper, dug out an anti-German wartime story with a football connection. Under the headline, 'The day we soccered it to the Huns', it told the tale of a First World War regiment who kicked a football ahead of them on the first day of the Battle of the Somme. There were 57,000 casualties that day, 'but in the end we won the battle, World War One, World War Two and the 1966 World Cup' (*Sunday Mirror*, 28 April 1996). The popular tales of English and German troops playing football between the trenches in the First World War during the cessation of hostilities on Christmas Day were not reprised. Both tabloids were criticized for their xenophobia in relation to the 'battle for the ball' by the leading national football fanzine, *When Saturday Comes*: 'a football tournament called Euro 96 will be taking place simultaneously in 1966, 1939–45 and 1914–18'. The tabloids were accused of providing licence for English hooligans through such stories (Editorial, 1996, pp. 4–5).

We can take the analysis even further, without, I believe, falling into the common trap of most sociological writers on popular culture, of reading far too much into too little. There is a strong popular feeling in England that, although we won the war, Germany has won the peace, by becoming, with allied assistance initially, far more economically successful than England in the post-war years. This jealousy has been heightened by our growing failure to beat the Germans at *our* national game, the game we invented and gave to the world, most recently in the World Cup semi-final in 1990 and the Euro 96 semi-final, made even more galling by the fact that the Germans went on to win both finals. There is only one exception, one moment in post-war history when the English scored a significant victory: 1966. Football and war have become entwined in the popular consciousness of the relationship with Germany, particularly among football fans. A popular chant among English fans in the 1990 World Cup was 'Two World Wars, one World Cup, do da, do da', the three great victories over Germany. The ball is the symbol of the last time England beat Germany at anything.

Football has been likened to war by other means, as part of the 'civilizing' process (Morris, 1981, pp. 17–20). As one Scottish supporter told John Motson, the BBC television football commentator, just before the crucial England versus Scotland game at Euro 96, presumably with a sense of irony: 'We Scots went one up at Bannockburn, and you English equalised at Culloden. And then from 1872 we decided to settle it on the football pitch instead.' The *Mirror* on the day of this game featured leading English and Scottish players Paul Gascoigne (nicknamed Gazza) and Gary McAllister wearing appropriately historic military uniforms, under the headline 'Cry God for Gazza, England and Tel' (Tel being the nickname of the England manager Terry Venables – I am struck by just how much needs to be explained to those of you who are unfamiliar with all this!), a play on the most famous speech in Shakespeare's Henry V, under the sub-headline, 'Battle of Wembley' (*Mirror*, 15 June 1996, p. 36). If Scotland is England's oldest enemy in both football and war, for the English this rivalry has been supplanted by that with Germany. But whoever England plays against, old conflicts will be recalled by the popular press. Before England played Spain in the quarter finals, the inevitable references to Sir Francis Drake and the Armada in 1588 were made (*Mirror*, 22 June 1996, p. 2). With England due to play Germany in the semi-final, the tabloids went into overdrive. The *Mirror* caused an outrage by its front-page headline: 'Achtung! Surrender. For you, Fritz, ze Euro 96 Championship is over ... *Mirror* declares football war on Germany' (*Mirror*, 24 June 1996, pp. 1–2). In 1969 riots at a World Cup qualifying game actually led to a war between Honduras and El Salvador.

The shine is slightly taken off the victory for England in 1966 by the fact that the third English goal is heavily disputed by the Germans, who claim that the ball never crossed the line, although the referee awarded it after consultation with the Russian linesman. The linesman's nationality is popularly seen as significant, in terms of who was fighting with and against whom in both world wars. Television, photographic and film footage, despite what many Germans claim, is ambivalent. Thus even this 'victory' over the Germans is a little tarnished. Hurst's third goal and England's fourth, in the dying seconds ('They think it's all over ...'), therefore assumes greater importance, as it provided an unequivocal margin of victory, and therefore also heightens the significance of the ball.

The significance of the ball goes even further than English rivalry with Germany. The English invented the game of football itself, but have only won the World Cup once, and hence the special poignancy of 1966. Since then fans have endured 30 years of relative failure. The official England Euro 96 squad song, with music by the group the Lightning Seeds and words by Frank Skinner and David Baddiel of the BBC television football comedy programme *Fantasy Football League*, captures these feelings perfectly. As a result it went to number one in the charts, and was easily the most popular chant at the England games in Euro 96:

Everyone seems to know the score
They've seen it all before
They just know,
They're so sure
That England's going to
throw it away,
Gonna blow it away
But I know they can play,
'Cos I remember ...
Three lions on a shirt,
Jules Rimet still gleaming
Thirty years of hurt
Never stopped me dreaming

It's coming home, it's coming home,
It's coming
Football's coming home

Apart from revealing our fascination as a species for bright shiny things – 'Jules Rimet still gleaming'; why else are trophies silver or gold? – the song claims that football is 'coming home'. The return of the 1966 ball – *this* football is coming home – is linked to this in some way. The ball symbolizes the game of football itself. At a deep level it links to the English self-perception as a 'nation of inventors', but nowadays we feel we fail to gain the fruits of such inventions, which are taken up by other nations. The ball, I would argue, has become a symbol for England's post-war decline; or rather, it is an object to stand against this. It has come to represent a time when England was more successful than it is today, when our footballs were made of leather by craftsmen rather than mass-produced in plastic, our footballers were the envy of the world, and our fans were fans and not hooligans. In recent years, so-called supporters of the England team have been involved in disgraceful scenes of hooliganism across Europe, most recently the riot during the 'friendly' international against Eire in Dublin in February 1995, which caused the abandonment of the game. Football as a game has become symbolic of the popular perception of the decline of England, the relative failure of the national football team inextricably linked with our decline as a country, and the end of empire. The ball represents a supposedly more positive and hopeful past. A structuralist analysis would suggest the following:

> past : present
> success : failure
> authentic : inauthentic
> leather : plastic
> hand-crafted : mass-produced
> skilful footballers : unskilful footballers
> fans : hooligans

A columnist in the *Guardian* newspaper has made a similar reading:

> At the time the 1960s seemed like a generational break with the war-dominated past. In retrospect I'm not nearly so sure. In a ridiculous but nevertheless real way, 1966 kept alive this country's great 20th century curse, the myth of English superiority over Germany.
>
> Thirty years later we still can't let go. In a debased and trivial way, the tabloid hunt for Geoff Hurst's ball is part of the desperate clinging to the national past. It says: if only it could always be like it was then. If only we could always live in 1940 or 1966, defying the world and time. Hurst's ball is a metaphor for a much wider English nostalgia. ... Can We Have Our Ball Back? is the latterday English equivalent of Faust's fatal wish for the beautiful moment not to pass away. They think it's all over, said the man that sunlit day in 1966. But it isn't. And that's exactly the problem.
>
> (Kettle, 1996, p. 23)

The significance of the 1966 final to English history has been similarly examined by sociologists: 'The connections between football, its cultural processes and symbolic moments, and the national sense of England as a political, economic and social entity, seem especially close in the 1950s and 1960s. ... 1966 was, or could be taken to represent, not merely a moment of football history, but a moment in the history of English culture as a whole' (Clarke and Critcher, 1986, p. 113). Clarke and Critcher suggest that there were parallels in the national consciousness between the failure of the national football team in the post-war era and England's decline as a world power and the loss of the empire. They also draw parallels between the England manager Alf Ramsey's 'modernization' of the tactics of the England team and Prime Minister Harold Wilson's attempt to modernize Britain as a whole through 'the white heat of technology'. Yet neither man's programme of modernization succeeded. Though

England's post-war 'crisis of national identity seemed to have found its symbolic resolution in the 1966 victory' (Clarke and Critcher, 1986, p. 121), the England team failed to build on this success, even failing to qualify for the World Cup Finals in 1974 and 1978, a bleak decade for the country economically. The 1966 victories of both Ramsey in the World Cup and Wilson in the general election were achieved not through a radical change, 'not slavish imitation of our competitors but the harnessing of the "best of British", by a "remaking of tradition" which served to obscure the deeper conditions of decline and fostered illusions of a return to greatness' (Clarke and Critcher, 1986, pp. 125–6). This was a view echoed in football terms at the time: 'It was a victory for preparation, organisation, dedication, spirit, heart and teamwork; admirable attributes which could not be quarrelled with but unfortunately without the show of all round skills one would have expected from the football champions of the world' (Rollin, 1966, p. 11). If Clarke and Critcher are guilty of pushing their analysis too far at times, there are clearly important and reciprocal links between football and English culture, with 1966 as a crucial moment, further enhancing the significance of the ball.

It's coming home ... but not to a museum

There is one final 'player' I wish to consider in relation to the ball, and that is museums. I trust that I have demonstrated, even to the most sceptical, that the ball is a highly significant artefact in English cultural life, even if you do not agree with my personal view that it is the most important post-1945 object. Museums, surely the natural place to hold and display such a venerated piece of material culture, appear, however, to have shown no interest at all in this object. Football, along with other aspects of 'low' culture, was outside of the remit of museums as temples of high culture. As so often in the area of popular culture, the exception was the People's Palace museum in Glasgow, which developed a collection of football memorabilia long before any others (King, 1988a, p. 90). As was briefly discussed in the previous chapter, only in the 1980s did this slowly begin to change. In 1984 a major temporary exhibition, 'Football Crazy', was held at Liverpool Museum, with the support of the three professional football clubs on Merseyside, Liverpool, Everton and Tranmere Rovers, who loaned trophies, including the FA Cup and European Cup, and other material. The exhibition was highly popular, reflecting the fact that Merseyside is one of the hotbeds of football in England, with particularly fervent supporters. This has been followed by a number of temporary exhibitions on either football or sport more generally, usually organized by social history curators, who are anxious to broaden the appeal of their museums to all sections of the local community.

Football has also come to be featured alongside other aspects of popular culture in the permanent displays of social history museums, most notably in the Museum of Liverpool Life, which has a section of the gallery called

'Mersey Culture' on 'Going out to the match'. Yet the feeling remains that even many social history curators regard football, like other aspects of popular culture, as slightly spurious and perhaps only of value in increasing attendances and drawing in those who would not normally visit the museum, in order that they will then be exposed to the mainstream, 'serious' displays. I hope that this chapter has demonstrated that to its fans football is a serious matter. Some curators are even more negative about the game. On the eve of the crucial game between England and Scotland in Euro 96, the director of Berwick Museum told the *Guardian* that 'I take no interest in football. It is a minority interest. Ten times as many people go to museums as soccer games' (15 June 1996, p. 22). This was despite the fact that the border town of Berwick, which changed hands 14 times in wars between the two nations, and now in England, was fascinatingly divided in loyalties between the two teams.

Football has had rather less impact in public art galleries than in museums. There are, however, some artists who have been focusing on the game, and have exhibited their work. Perhaps the most notable example is 'The Homes of Football' exhibition by photographer Stuart Clarke, which began a lengthy tour of over twenty galleries and museums in 1992. The exhibition looks at the fans' relationship with the stadium of their team, as the symbolic 'home' of their support.

The year 1996 marked a significant shift in museum attitudes to the game. Major exhibitions were to be held in museums in many of the cities in which games in the Euro 96 tournament were held, including 'The Homes of Football' in Liverpool. Museums were reacting to several factors, not simply the fact that this was the first major international football tournament to be held in the country since 1966. Football is enjoying an almost unprecedented increase in popularity in the 1990s, following England's relative success in the 1990 World Cup (and Euro 96), and the creation of the Premier League. The game is increasingly fashionable among a number of disparate groups in society, which are all fuelling this upsurge. Football since the late 1980s has become much more integrated with other aspects of youth culture – drugs, fashion, music – than perhaps ever before. The game is fashionable with 'celebrities' – pop stars, television stars and presenters, politicians and the like – for the first time since the mid-1960s, when footballers such as George Best first became celebrities in their own right. The hooligan problems and consequent tragedies that beset the game in the 1980s led to a 'politicization' of many fans, which led to the creation of independent supporters' associations at many clubs, the football fanzine phenomenon (an independent fans' magazine culture which in turn had its roots in the fanzines of the punk rock movement of the late 1970s) and the Football Supporters Association, a national pressure group for the rights of supporters. Supporters organized in these ways are now an important force in the game. The 'politics' of this can be overstated, for the fanzine culture is one based primarily on humour, as has been reflected in the popular BBC 2 show *Fantasy Football League*.

The blurring of 'high' and 'lows' culture means that the game is also fashionable as never before among the liberal intelligentsia, with novelists of repute lining up to proclaim their lifelong support for Chelsea or Manchester United; and partly as a consequence, for the first time the game has produced literature which is being taken seriously, particularly following the publication in 1992 of the best-selling *Fever Pitch*, Nick Hornby's account of his own fanatical obsession with the game and Arsenal Football Club in particular (Hornby, 1992). The recognition of football as key part of cultural life is being actively promoted by an organization called Philosophy Football, which sells shirts adorned with epithets on the significance of the game by footballers, philosophers and those, like real-life goalkeeper Albert Camus, who straddled both of these worlds: 'All that I know most surely about morality and obligations, I owe to football.' For Euro 96 Philosophy Football organized, in association with the *Guardian* newspaper, 'Europe United: a day for everyone who loves football', presumably deliberately at a centre of 'high' culture, the Royal Festival Hall on the South Bank in London, and 'featuring plays to fashion shows, debates to comedy, poetry to music. ... With a crèche too' (Cornwall, 1996, p. 18). Football has also become an acceptable, and indeed trendy, subject matter for artists, and this is to be reflected in a number of exhibitions at public and private galleries in 1996 (Cornwall, 1996, p. 18; *Four Four Two*, June 1996, pp. 20–1). These attempts to emphasize the cultural significance of the game, including *Fever Pitch*, would be derided by many if not most working-class fans, who still make up the majority of supporters, but have raised the profile of the game in certain circles. In such a climate museums ignore the game at their peril. It also represents a tremendous opportunity, for while the average fan would be unlikely to overcome the cultural barriers to view an installation in a private gallery, he or she could be tempted to see a display of more familiar material in a much less intimidating place.

To argue that football has a place in the museum – and museums need football far more than football needs museums – there is no need, as some writers have done, to argue that football is 'art'. The analysis in the previous chapter made it clear that the material culture of the game is of interest to museums regardless. It is not necessary, as some have done, to compare football in some way to poetry or ballet: 'Football is great not because of its similarities to other pursuits but because of its differences to them. In the end if people cannot recognise that greatness it's because they are idiots. Admittedly this is not much of an argument, but it has worked pretty well for modern art over the past half century' (Pearson, 1996, p. 7). The difference is that football has several billion more people interested in it. Curators may not agree with Pearson or myself that in Pele's famous phrase it is the 'beautiful game', but they cannot ignore its profound cultural significance.

Despite this flurry of activity in 1996, museums have only belatedly and perhaps a little half-heartedly become interested in football, even though these displays have demonstrated intense public interest in the history and material culture of the game. This is only partly because curators have seen popular culture as marginal. Even curators who are football fans have been reticent to develop exhibitions. A commonly held view among museum staff is that there is little material culture connected with the game, and what few objects there are cannot adequately reflect it. This view is shared outside museums, most notably by Nick Hornby, who has summarized it particularly well:

> Football Museums have a handicap that the British Museum or the Science Museum do not. An antique pot or painting is a direct and meaningful articulation of an ancient culture, and a working model of a steam engine is an adequate and instructive representation of the real thing. But football is necessarily about movement, athleticism, fleeting moments and huge crowds; a couple of old medals, a few international caps and a pile of old programmes – the staple of football collections – hardly capture the essence of the game.   (Hornby, 1994, p. 43)

This widely held view can, however, be criticized on a number of grounds. I hope that this chapter has made it clear that there is no difference between 'an antique pot' as 'a direct and meaningful articulation of an ancient culture' and the 1966 ball as an articulation of its culture. Both need to be adequately interpreted to reveal the culture from which they came, if they are to be more than simply a pot or a ball. If the 'movement, athleticism, fleeting moments and huge crowds', the 'essence' of football, cannot be revealed in some way through its material culture, then neither can an ancient civilization from a pot, or, for that matter, any culture from any object in a museum. The problem with current displays of football is not the inadequacy of the material culture but its interpretation. Much can be revealed from just one piece of material culture, such as the 1966 ball, if a wide range of interpretative techniques are employed. What could be more central to the game of football than a football? Furthermore, this chapter has suggested that the ball can tell us as much about English history and culture in general as it can about football.

Much more could therefore be achieved with just 'a couple of old medals, a few international caps and a pile of old programmes' with more effective interpretation. But the most effective displays will employ the widest range of material culture. Contrary to the commonly held view, there is a wealth of material culture associated with the game, both historically and today, held in innumerable private collections, by the clubs, players and, above all, the fans. This ranges from material directly associated with the playing of the game, such as shirts, boots, balls etc.; to directly associated items, such as programmes, match tickets, trophies, caps, medals, even parts of the stadia, film and photographs; to the wider culture of the fans, such as scarves, banners, football cards, board games and the like.

The material culture of the fans is the element which has been most overlooked in displays to date. Fans symbolize their 'love' of their team, 'objectify' their support, through a wide range of material culture. This has most usually been a scarf, though there are of course trends within this over time, and in the 1990s the scarf is being supplanted by the wearing of the team's shirt. Such items are powerful, for they are souvenirs not just of one moment but of the hundreds of games when the fan has given his or her support. Other items are kept by fans as souvenirs, such as programmes and match tickets, but these are less powerful, as they reflect only individual games, no matter how significant, not years of support:

> there's one item I own that is the repository of all my feelings about my team. In itself it holds a wealth of memories; it has been an almost constant companion since early adolescence; it symbolises my allegiance, privately and publicly. It's my scarf. My scarf. It's old, it's filthy, it's horrible. No one else in the world would dare go near it, let alone want to wear it. But then I wouldn't let them. It's mine and it's sacred.
>
> (Wicken, 1992, p. 22)

This is heightened for some fans not just by the accumulation of dirt but by attaching the pin badges of other clubs, particularly from away games. The material culture of fans has a long and as yet largely unresearched history. The Sheffield football newspaper reported in 1928 that 'People dress themselves up in strange garb, carry painted umbrellas, blow bugles, swing rattles and handbells, and perform in a manner they would never think of doing at any other time' (quoted in Fishwick, 1989, p. 59).

The Museum of Liverpool Life has a display of such items. This includes a sample of the many thousands of scarves and other 'signifiers' of support left on the pitch at Anfield, the ground of Liverpool Football Club, as a mark of respect and an act of mourning after the Hillsborough stadium tragedy in Sheffield in 1989, when 95 Liverpool supporters died. Over one million people visited the Anfield stadium, supporters of a huge range of clubs coming from all over the country. Fans of Everton, Liverpool's other leading team, and therefore Liverpool Football Club's greatest rivals, shared in this mourning by organizing a one-mile long chain of scarves knotted together from Everton's ground to Anfield, the last scarf being tied on the Kop end of the ground at 3.06 p.m. at the beginning of a two minute silence. An editorial in the *Museums Journal* recently asked 'When did you last weep in a museum?' (*Museums Journal*, September 1994, p. 7). I was moved to tears in front of this display, not just because of the tragic death of the fans, but because I knew how much it had meant for the other supporters to leave these items which were so precious to them, and therefore I knew just how much the tragedy had affected them.

Such items represent the fans' support. Many fans also acquire items which represent an individual player or even the football club as a whole. For a player this would usually be an autograph, but exceptionally and ideally this would be a shirt worn in a game or a boot. The exhibition in Leeds Museum for Euro 96 featured the prized possession of one ten-year-old supporter: a napkin that his favourite Leeds United player, Tony Yeboah, had used in a restaurant. These items are powerful relics to their owners and other fans. Items to reflect the club as a whole can be either a piece of the stadium or a part of the pitch. In recent years, when clubs have been redeveloping their stadia or relaying their pitches, they have often auctioned off such items to fans, the proceeds going to charity. Such auctions are hugely popular. At Tranmere Rovers in 1994 the pitch was sold off immediately after the last home game of the season. My partner and I queued with hundreds of other fans to buy a one foot square piece of turf each, which are now a carefully marked and tended part of the lawn in our garden. Each fan was given a 'certificate of authenticity', signed by the head groundsman. Two fans bought enough of the pitch to completely re-turf their gardens. Why? We now own a real, tangible part of Tranmere Rovers Football Club, we have bought in, we belong to the club, it belongs to us. If we ever moved house, we would dig it up and take it with us. This in turn reflects the fact that football grounds can be considered as quasi-religious sacred spaces, often referred to as 'cathedrals' by football journalists. When Chester City's ground closed in 1990, a fan commented: 'Sealand Road has been part of my life for 30 years; it's more than a football ground; it's a way of life not just to me but to thousands of people alive and dead whose lives have revolved around a match at the stadium. It is more than bricks and mortar, it's almost something spiritual' (quoted in Bale, 1991, p. 131).

Some football and sporting exhibitions have come to recognize the power of such relics, particularly those associated with an individual. 'Sporting Life', the largest and longest running exhibition on sport in general in Britain to date, at the Old Grammar School Museum, Hull, in 1995–6, reflected this in its promotional material: 'We have ... Linford Christie's spikes, Virginia Wade's tennis dress ... Bryan Robson's football boots.' A collection of shirts worn by famous players was displayed in the first People's Show at Walsall Museum in 1990. As a member of the exhibition project team, I interviewed the collector in his home. He offered that I could put on a shirt worn by Pele, the Brazilian footballer generally regarded as the greatest of all time. I refused, because I felt I was 'not worthy' enough. I could only bring myself to touch it and be photographed with it. I ascertained that it had not been washed and therefore still contained Pele's sweat, which somehow seemed to be significant to me. This reaction may seem like madness to you, but I do not think it would be untypical of football fans. Would a Christian put on the Turin Shroud?

The business world (and football clubs) has long played on this 'fanatical' devotion, which is, after all, the derivation of 'fan', designing an increasingly diverse range of memorabilia for all clubs, including kits, scarves, baby clothes, lampshades, mugs, key rings, duvet covers, computer mouse mats, juggling balls, slippers, miniature figures, toilet seat covers, sunglasses, sexy underwear, jewellery, perfume, aftershave, ashtrays, playing cards, watches, popcorn and crisps, to name but a small sample (*Four Four Two*, October 1994, pp. 74–5). This commercial activity has also involved designing collections for fans which involve either direct purchases of the items to be collected, such as cards or stickers of players, or the encouragement of the purchase of a particular product. These play on the fascination that young boys (rather than girls) seem to have for completing sets. I still possess my (sadly incomplete) *Wonderful World of Soccer Stars Picture Stamp Album: England First Division, 1968–1969*. This was 'hugely influential. … There had of course been football cards before, but never had they been so comprehensive or so comprehensively marketed. From Highbury to Molineux there can have been few school playgrounds that year that did not boast clusters of boys muttering eagerly, "Got, got, got, haven't got", as they shuffled through Jim Montgomery, Ian Ure and the rest' (Sturgis, 1992, p. 30). The clever direct marketing ploy was that we received a 'personal' letter from England stars Gordon Banks and Bobby Moore, to encourage us to build a similar album collection for the teams in the World Cup in Mexico in 1970. This tournament opened up a whole new phase of football material culture consumption. I have in front of me my complete set of Texaco Famous Footballers medals, given free with Texaco petrol in 1969. After this experience, my father refused to drive out of his way to only Texaco stations the following year, so I was unable to collect the medals of the 1970 England World Cup squad. Others were more fortunate, as novelist Roddy Doyle has recalled: 'My parents fed my habit. My father, I suspect now, filled his Volkswagen with Texaco petrol, siphoned it, dumped it and went back for more. By the end of the Mexico World Cup I had the full squad. I had seven Alan Mullerys and four Bobby Moores. … My sisters got me "Back Home" by the England World Cup Squad, my first record' (Doyle, 1993, p. 12). 'Back Home' (I still have my copy) went to number one in the charts. This shared experience, this 'common heritage', expressed in part in material culture, has led to the now thirty-something generation who have responded to the nostalgia in Nick Hornby's *Fever Pitch* and have helped make it a bestseller, and have played a key role in the football fanzine movement (Sturgis, 1992, p. 30).

Fans who would not describe themselves as serious collectors (including myself) accumulate over time significant collections of souvenirs of their support of their team, or 'relics' of the club, or 'fetishistic' collections of items designed by commerce. For example, a Newcastle United fan for thirty years had turned his attic into a 'personal shrine' to his club, a '"Tyneside Temple", filled with scarves, shirts, books, programmes and even newspaper hoardings nicked off lampposts!', which earned the accolade of 'Fan of the Week' in the *Daily Mirror*, in its regular feature, 'Superfan '94' (*Mirror, Score Supplement*, 3 December 1994, p. 8).

Such collectors are fetishistic, in Pearce's non-derogatory sense (Pearce, 1992, pp. 73–84) about items connected with their team. There are other collectors who are fetishistic in a different sense, collecting as much as possible of a particular kind of material culture, most usually programmes, or more purely fetishistic collectors, who acquire anything connected with the game. This involves collecting items of all teams, and indeed such collectors rarely support a particular team. Programme collectors collect from games they did not attend, again often beginning in male childhood (Smith, 1994). The game here has almost become secondary to the passion to collect. A particular form of football collecting, known as ground-hopping, is akin to trainspotting, as the aim is to attend matches at the grounds of all 92 professional league clubs. Collectors of certain kinds of material have established organizations, such as the Association of Football Badge Collectors (*Four Four Two*, March 1996, pp. 78–9). Further research in progress at the Department of Museum Studies in Leicester is examining the relationship between collectors and the game.

Contrary to the view expressed by Hornby, shared by many curators, there is therefore a wealth of material culture associated with football, and not simply film and photographs. Museums potentially have a wide range of possibilities in display. Displays could also reflect collecting as a popular activity associated with the game. The problem for museums is that, because they failed to collect the material culture of the game in the past, it is now unavailable to them. Private collectors have acquired the kinds of material that museums are becoming interested in. As a result, the market prices are already too high in many cases, even for a major museum service, such as Glasgow. They find it difficult to acquire material for their permanent collections, which in part explains the focus on temporary exhibitions, where material could be borrowed from private collectors, ex-players or the football clubs. Where museums have been unable to borrow from collectors, the displays have been little more than 'books on the wall', with reproduction photographs and a video showing archive film.

While public museums have ignored such passions, at least until 1996, a private museum sector has developed to fill this void. This has paralleled the rise of sports museums in the USA. This was initiated by the football clubs themselves, who have seen the potential for income generation that displays of their existing but privately held collections of memorabilia represented, after viewing the success of such ventures at the top clubs in Italy, Spain and Portugal. Manchester United led the way in England, opening a museum and visitor centre in 1986, with a second phase added in 1992. Arsenal followed in 1994, with a museum built into the development of a new stand, as 'an integrated part of the marketing machine and the product mix on offer' (Hall, 1994, p. 45). Jon Hall, the designer of both museums, and also well known in the public museum sector, forecasts that 'As more clubs, propelled by the Taylor report, seek to maximise their investment in new stands and facilities, museums will be seen as cost effective use of some of the space ... with benefits extending far beyond the gate receipts as they feed both catering and retail outlets and add novelty to the sponsorship and corporate packages' (Hall, 1994, p. 45). Developments are planned at several other clubs.

The clubs' exhibitions are 'museums' in the sense that they employ professional standards of collection care, professionally trained staff and high-quality museum design, and utilize the latest interpretative techniques, such as interactives and multimedia. They might be criticized, however, in terms of the 'histories' they portray, which are official, highly partial, uncritical celebrations of the club in question. Perhaps to criticize them in this way is to miss the point. Their popularity suggests that this is what fans want to see. Yet given the rise of the independent supporters' associations, football fanzines and the Football Supporters Association, all of which are often highly critical of the actions of the clubs, there is surely a need for such museums to present more objective histories. The museums too rarely reflect the fans and their material culture, which again would have to be 'warts and all', reflecting also the problem of football hooliganism. But wishing to have the fans represented in a club museum, is 'a bit like going to a church ... to find out about the churchgoers as opposed to the religion' (Pes, 1993, p. 11). In any case it is probably naive to think that the club museums will ever present such objective histories, given that their primary role is public relations and income generation, adding 'novelty to the sponsorship and corporate packages'.

The club museums, whatever the approach, would still not provide a suitable home for the 1966 ball, which is of national significance. Two clubs in the north-west of England, Preston North End and Carlisle United, have recognized the apparent need for a national museum of football as an opportunity, again as part of the redevelopment of their grounds. Cynics would suggest that this is because neither club has a sufficiently glorious history of its own, though this is unfair to Preston, a founder member of the Football League in 1888 and the first champions. The Preston proposal is for an MGC-registered national museum, comprising a gallery telling 'The Story of Football', a 'Gallery of Greats', focusing on the finest post-war players, equivalent to the 'Halls of Fame' at sports museums in the USA, an 'Interactive Area', a cinema and, intriguingly, a gallery devoted to permanent and temporary exhibitions of 'Football Art'. The aim, according to the promotional brochure, is to attract 100,000 visitors each year, a not over-ambitious target given Preston's excellent road and rail connections (National Football Museum, n.d.). While the initiative in England has come from two clubs, in Scotland, by comparison, the Scottish Football Association (SFA) is spearheading plans for a national museum in Glasgow, as part of the redevelopment of the Hampden Park stadium, based initially on the SFA's own collection. This project has received significant support from Glasgow Museums, which is currently providing gallery space for a pilot display. Both the Scottish and English projects are dependent on raising private funding, primarily from the National Lottery. The English initiatives are negotiating the loan of one or more of the very major private collections which exist, as providing a basis from which to open, and then develop, their own collections in the future. One wonders why the English Football Association (FA) is not seeing the potential in such a museum, unlike its Scottish counterpart; instead, it appears to being doing sweet FA. It is to be hoped that the proposed national museum will avoid the purely celebratory, partial histories of the club museums and portray a much fuller picture of the meaning of football in English society through the interpretation of the full range of the associated material culture, both that of the clubs and that of the fans. The Preston museum is entering into partnerships with private collectors to gain public access to historical material. A programme of contemporary collecting should be an equally important part of its strategy. Will the museum have the courage to present football 'warts and all' and display the weapons and 'calling cards' of the football hooligans?

While the proposed national museum would play the key role in the representation of the game, this still leaves room for local initiatives, as is taking place in 1996. The strength of football support is divided over 92 league clubs in England, which means that a significant number of museums have yet to seize the opportunity this presents. Successful exhibitions have also been held on non-league clubs, as at Trowbridge Museum in 1995 on Trowbridge Town Football Club. There is probably not a museum in the country that could not hold a popular temporary exhibition on the game. The rationale for such exhibitions would not simply be their expected popularity, but that football is a central part of English cultural life, and an interpretation of its material culture reveals a great deal about society as a whole. The object analysis of the 1966 ball has indicated what is possible from the interpretation of a single piece of material culture. Future exhibitions could benefit greatly by reflecting each aspect of the object analysis. Visitors could be enabled and encouraged to do this actively for selected objects, carrying out the 'curatorial' stages of analysis for themselves. The burgeoning field of material culture studies can not only inform approaches to interpretation, but also be made accessible to the public, who can develop the skills of material culture analysis in their own right, as was argued in Chapter 4.

Such interpretation could to a degree be informed by the growing historical and more especially sociological study of sport, and football in particular. Some work has valuably focused as much on the fans as other aspects of the game, including studies of fans in other countries (for example, Lever, 1983; Taylor, 1992). Yet for museums what these have to offer is limited. Partly this is because most of the major studies so far have focused on the hooliganism problem, and therefore the literature over-emphasizes its importance in the game. It is also because the sociological cultural studies approach is riddled with jargon and betrays a failure to appreciate the game as it is enjoyed by the fans (see the review of Haynes, 1994 by Ticher, 1996). More problematic still is the almost total disregard for the significance of material culture in such work, failing to address the questions of interest to museum staff. Some research has been carried out on the football fanzines, but these are treated as literary texts (Jary *et al.*, 1991; Haynes, 1994). The culture of the fans as expressed through material culture is not considered, though it is clearly a crucial part of football culture. The acts of mourning following the Hillsborough

disaster have been analysed in terms of their wider sociological significance, but the material culture is secondary to this analysis (Walter,
1991). Yet the material culture was the most astonishing part of this
public mourning. This features more prominently in a study of the close
interrelationship from the mid-1980s between football, pop music and
youth culture, which links a consideration of fashion to fandom and its
material expression (Redhead, 1993). A major new bibliography of football reveals only a very small and non-academic literature on the material
culture of the game and collections, though such works, produced in the
main by collectors, are of great value to curators (see Seddon, 1995). The
material culture of the game as collectable has also featured regularly in
the prominent magazine *Four Four Two*. The material culture of the fans
has appeared in a humorous way in fans' literature, including how to
wear your scarf; there is a similar history of the football boot, and an
anthology of terrace chants (Bulmer and Merrills, 1992; Baldwin, 1995).
The exception to all of this is a fascinating study by the popular anthropologist Desmond Morris, *The Soccer Tribe*, which analyses all aspects of
the game, including the full range of material culture, including that of
the fans (Morris, 1981). Although now a little dated, this is a hugely valuable work for curators.

Where does this leave the 1966 ball, in relation to museums? As yet the
ball has no museum home, not even in the private sector. Being on display
at Waterloo International means that it has the potential to be the most
viewed object in the country, by up to ten million people in 1996. Even
displayed on its own, with little or no context, it is capable of being
viewed in a multiplicity of ways, it is polysemic. Few objects have such
resonance in English post-war history; few are capable of still meaning so
much with such little interpretation. But is this the best place to display
it? There are potential environmental problems, but only if the owners
wish to keep it under museum conditions. Security is an issue for such a
valuable object, and may be an issue of concern to members of the public,
particularly as many will recall that in 1966 the Jules Rimet Trophy, the
World Cup, was stolen from a private exhibition, only to be found under
a hedge by a dog called Pickles. But would it necessarily be more secure in
a museum? Yet aside from any environmental or security considerations,
or the lack of contextual interpretation, this is still surely not the best
place to display it. It is too important not to be in a museum. The proposed national museum at Preston would be a natural home for the ball,
and had the museum already been established, it may well have been able
to join the *Daily Mirror*'s partnership.

Maybe football is too central to English history and culture to be ghettoized in a specialist museum. If there was a national museum of English
history, the 1966 ball would be a crucial acquisition. In the absence of
such an institution, where could the ball go? The British Museum is the
only candidate, for though its name is a misnomer, it does hold and collect important British material, including twentieth-century objects

(Carey, 1991), and 'Britain rightly tries to protect its own heritage. The British Museum plays a major role in this process. ... Some things must be protected at all costs' (Wilson, 1989, p. 117). The British Museum holds the three oldest known playing balls in the world, from ancient Egypt (Morris, 1981, pp. 187–8).

Why does it seem so absurd therefore to suggest that the British Museum would take the ball? In a dream similar to that experienced by William Morris in *News from Nowhere* I awake back in 1966 as director of the British Museum, and arrange for the Jules Rimet Trophy to be displayed in the museum before the tournament begins, though unfortunately this means that Pickles the dog loses his five minutes of fame. I also prearrange for the ball from the final to be donated to the museum, which means I get a ticket for the final. What could be more natural than for this 'Museum for all Nations' (Wilson, 1989, p. 106) to collect and display this symbol of the World Cup, the greatest international event of that year? But then the dream turns sour. Hurst does the unthinkable and scores a hat-trick in the final. Haller 'steals' the ball, and the museum is forced to buy it from him. The museum then becomes embroiled in a claim of 'cultural restitution' from Geoff Hurst. 'Give me my ball back,' says Hurst. 'If you score a hat-trick you keep the ball.' 'But Mr Hurst,' comes the reply, 'the British Museum certainly always asks the question of provenance before it buys and always rejects objects for which there could be the slightest question of illegality' (Wilson, 1989, p. 117). 'And in any case your living room lacks adequate security and environmental control.' However, I awake back in 1996 to find that my dream has come true, as the British Museum's real director personally collects the ball from the pitch after the Euro 96 final 'as a symbol of European unity' and announces that it is time for the museum to lose its marbles to make way for the balls.

7

Real things, real places, real people

That looks excellent. Your theme park idea, you could have a reconstruction of Old Croydon High Street and go down it.
(Family museum goer, in Fisher, 1990, p. 71)

It's like Yorvik. It's a Viking village and you get all the people talking and all the smells and everything.
(White teenager, in Fisher, 1990, p. 68)

They should have people in the museum who would dress in the period clothes but you should know they're museum staff, so you can ask them things.   *(Black teenager, in Fisher, 1990, p. 38)*

Introduction

The analysis thus far has aimed to demonstrate the power of material culture, the sense in which 'objects make history'. We have considered how museums benefit from the power of 'the real thing': 'They alone have the power, in some sense, to carry the past into the present by virtue of their real relationship to past events' (Pearce, 1992, p. 24). Here, however, I wish to challenge this notion, or at least significantly broaden it. Alongside the power of the 'real thing', we also have, I will argue, the power of the 'real place', and the power of the 'real person'. What is proffered is a 'triple notion of the power of the real'. It is my contention that the most successful, the most effective, representations of the past, whether in museums or elsewhere, are those which employ this 'triple power'. This has profound implications for museums and, indeed, all forms of heritage provision, whether in interpreting high or popular culture, which are explored in the second part of this chapter.

The power of the real place

By this I mean how a geographical site which has a historical connection seems to have the power, in some sense, to carry the past into the present by virtue of its 'real' relationship to past events. If, as Pearce argues, objects to some extent make history, then so also do sites and structures. Partly this involves broadening the definition of the 'real thing' from the 'discrete lumps', the movable pieces of material culture which museums are intended to hold, to include material culture in its widest sense, whether it be, for example, a historic house, a castle or an industrial archaeological site. These are also the 'real thing'. What this highlights is what Sola has termed 'The nonsense of division between movable and immovable heritage' (Sola, 1992b, p. 399). All historic material culture, from the smallest museum object to the largest building, can be considered as part of the same process and for the same purpose. This leads, as we shall see, to the argument that the distinction between museums and other forms of heritage preservation is arbitrary and entirely artificial, and should be removed. At what point on which scale does material culture cease to be movable? There are, after all, museums of historic buildings, plucked out of their original context.

If the power of the 'real thing' and the 'real place' are the same in this sense, there is a distinction. Places still seem to have a degree of 'real' power even when little or no material culture remains. Battlefield sites, for example, still have some real power even when the landscape itself can have changed considerably in the centuries after the event. Places retain power because although we may not be able to see very much (if anything), what are perceived to be important historical events happened there. Of all the senses activated by such sites, it is perhaps the sixth that is most important, as evinced by the 'intuitive experiences' many people claim to have at battlefield sites. Clearly, however, places where buildings, even if ruins, remain tend to have a stronger sense of the 'real place'. Yet just as some 'real things' are regarded as more historically significant than others (though, this is always a matter of interpretation), so some 'real places' are seen as more significant than others. There comes a point where a particularly notable battlefield site, such as Bosworth, becomes more powerfully a 'real place' than a historic house which, although well preserved, has no intrinsically strong connection to significant historical events.

I would argue therefore that the 'real thing' is one sort of power, the 'real place' another which is equally significant. Objects in a museum have lost part of their power by being decontextualized from their 'real' place – unless they are at a site museum, or in a historic house, where they remain in their historic setting. 'Objects can tell us much about past and present societies, but their power is seldom realised. Part of the problem is that objects that so often come under study are in museums, divorced from the social and cultural environment responsible for their existence' (Brown, 1993, p. 141). Similarly, entire buildings which are moved from their original site to an outdoor museum elsewhere also lose some of their 'real' power. What this leads to is the view that the most potent museums or heritage attractions are where the two 'real' powers – 'thing' and 'place' – are combined: real things in their real context.

This is demonstrated by the grid in Figure 7.1, where the horizontal axis is power of the 'real thing', running left to right from 'no real things' to 'excellent collections of real things', and the vertical is the 'power of

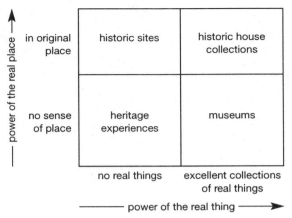

Figure 7.1 *Plot of 'real things' and 'real places' to give a fourfold division of heritage provision*

the real place', running from bottom to top from 'no sense of place' to 'in original place'. This gives rise to a fourfold division of heritage provision, between the four quadrants: heritage experiences, historic sites, historic house collections and museums. Museums typically have the real thing, but not in the original place. Heritage experiences, the theme park rides which have a historical theme, have no real things, and often little or no connection to the real place. Historic sites, such as ruined castles or battlefields, have a strong sense of place but no collections. Finally, there are historic houses which possess their original collections, which combine the real place and the real thing.

Of course there are variations within each quadrant, and a schematic fourfold division of the two scales has been provided in Figure 7.2 to demonstrate this. Left to right now reads 'no real things', 'some real things', 'good collections' and 'excellent collections', and bottom to top reads 'national/international context', 'local/regional context', 'real site but few physical remains', 'real site with physical remains'. A number of museums and other heritage attractions can then be placed on this grid to demonstrate this. The examples are drawn from the UK and North America.

In the bottom left corner would be a heritage experience which has no real things and also only a national or international sense of place. A good example is the complete reconstruction of Tutankhamun's tomb at the moment it was discovered by Howard Carter in 1922, which is in 'Luxor', a huge holiday entertainment centre on the theme of ancient Egypt in Las Vegas. It is an impeccably researched reproduction, with an audio tour. Above this would be a heritage experience such as The Oxford Story, a theme park style time-car ride through the history of the Oxford colleges, which has a local sense of place, but no collections. In the top left-hand corner would be, for example, a castle, perhaps a ruin, but still possessing a stronger sense of place, though it has no collections.

power of the real place	no real things	some real things	good collections	excellent collections
real site with physical remains	Stonehenge Coronation Street	Castle Rushen	The Tenement House Mr Straw's House	Buckingham Palace
real site but few physical remains	Bosworth Battlefield	Jorvik Plimoth Plantation		
local/ regional context	The Oxford Story		typical local museum	Beamish Sturbridge
national/ international context	Tutankhamun's Tomb at Luxor			CMC British Museum Horniman Museum

— power of the real thing →

Figure 7.2 *Positioning a number of heritage attractions on the plot of real things and real places*

Stonehenge would be found here, as would the street set of top British television soap opera *Coronation Street* in Manchester, which now attracts more visitors than Stonehenge. Slightly to the right of this would be a castle or other historic building which has some, if limited, collections, such as Castle Rushen on the Isle of Man. Diagonally below the castle would be a battlefield site, with a strong sense of place but little or no physical remains, and no collections, such as Bosworth. To the right of this would be found most site museums, such as Jorvik Viking Centre in York, the original time-car ride through a Viking village, where there are associated collections; and Plimoth Plantation in Massachusetts, the reconstruction of the Pilgrim Village, which also has some collections.

In the very top right-hand corner would be a historic house or other building with outstanding collections of real things in their original setting, such as most stately homes, the ultimate being perhaps Buckingham Palace. The problem with many of these historic houses is that the collections have often been brought in to refurbish a house which had become empty, and thus few actually come into this category. For those historic houses where the collection has been recently brought in from elsewhere, the building falls into the top left quadrant, the collection into the bottom right. To the left of these historic houses with excellent collections are the 'time capsules', more ordinary homes which still have their original collections, such as the Tenement House in Glasgow, a perfectly preserved home of a middle-class woman, and Mr Straw's House in Worksop, an Edwardian semi-detached house owned by the National Trust.

National museums such as the British Museum or the Canadian Museum of Civilization (CMC) are in the bottom right-hand corner, with, in the case of the former, perhaps unsurpassable collections but totally decontextualized, as an 'international' as much as a 'national' museum, as much of the collections are not British. To the left of this, but within the same box, would be a non-national museum such as the Horniman in London, which has fine collections, but with little or no connection to the museum's locality. Above are museums such as Beamish in England or Old Sturbridge village in New England, which have fine collections in a regional context. To the left of these are typical local museums, which have some sense of place, but weaker collections.

What can we conclude from this? It is not simply a question of reading off that those in the top right-hand corner are the 'best'. Much depends on the quality of interpretation. And the quality of interpretation in historic houses with collections is often very poor. I would stress, however, that historic site collections which combine 'real things' in a 'real place' have far more potential to succeed in bringing the past 'alive', through this double power of the real. Objects in museums lose so much of their power through having been removed from the 'real place'. That the object remains as part of an original collection helps to only a limited extent. Historic sites such as battlefields have the sense of the 'real place', but in lacking 'real things' face challenges in interpretation. Heritage attractions with no power of the real at all face the biggest challenge of all in interpretation.

This point can be reinforced by considering current practice in interpretation in the four quadrants. The quality of interpretation arguably bears an inverse relation to the combined power of the real which the attraction possesses. The greater the power of the real is, the weaker the interpretation tends to be, because it appears that less effort is required to bring the past to life. The interpretation of historic sites with collections is usually the weakest, as in most historic houses, such as National Trust properties. The double power of the real such sites possess leads to an overreliance on the formalist perspective. At the other extreme, interpretation in heritage attractions – such as 'Luxor' – is often very strong, for without any power of the real, the quality of the interpretation is everything. Museums and historic sites generally fall somewhere between these two extremes in terms of the quality of their interpretation, as they each possess a single power of the real, and tend to assume that this is sufficient.

The implication is that in future heritage and museum practice we should look to preserve real things in their real place, given the head start this provides, and that this is the ideal. It would also be enormously beneficial to apply the most advanced techniques of museum and heritage interpretation to historic house collections, which are currently largely so poorly interpreted.

This does not mean that the other three sectors have no future. Looking again at Figure 7.2 I am struck by the fact that those attractions I have enjoyed the most as a visitor, in terms of both entertainment and education, fall in all four quadrants: Castle Rushen and Plimoth Plantation, the Tenement House, Luxor, and Beamish, Old Sturbridge and the Canadian Museum of Civilization. How can this be? Further analysis suggests that a common thread to these heritage experiences can be identified. What they share is a sense of 'real things in a real place', but through artifices, through devices of reconstruction in their interpretation. They successfully *recreate* a sense of real things in a real place, if they do not sufficiently possess this in the first place.

In museum terms, this means reconstructing the real place, by providing room sets or even complete buildings for objects. Curators, as we have seen, often disparage the room sets that are ubiquitous even in the smallest local museums, and the street scenes found in larger museums, such as at York Castle. They seem surprised at their popularity, and tolerate them only because of their public appeal. The model proposed here explains why they work, by providing a sense of a real place, through reconstruction, for the real things. Room sets and street scenes, such as some of those at York Castle, can be rightly criticized by curators for their lack of historical accuracy, but this should not lead to a condemnation of such devices outright. The outstanding new displays at the Canadian Museum of Civilization (CMC) are testament to what can be achieved by museums, through high-quality research, to recreate a 'real place' for real things. For a national (and indeed international) museum, it is clearly very difficult to establish a sense of place for the objects, but the interpretative approach used achieves this brilliantly. In Chapter 3 it was discussed how the CMC had identified weaknesses in both the formalist and analyst approaches. Both are still used in the new CMC displays, 'but not in excess'. Instead, the approach is to recreate a sense of real place for real things:

> The dominant approach has been to liberate artifacts from the artificial frames of display cases, and recontextualise them meaningfully through environmental reconstructions in which numerous objects are seen in their relationships to one another, as well as in the context of use. Eliminating the display case does not by itself solve the problem. The interior architecture of the museum becomes the new wrapping for the exhibit, and thus the medium whose messages may influence, or override, messages from the artefacts. The architecture can be disguised through the 'environmental reconstruction' technique of display – manifested in indoor museums as dioramic, period room, and streetscape exhibits. It allows artifacts to be set in their natural and social contexts.   (MacDonald and Alsford, 1989, pp. 73–4)

This can be seen in the (in my view) magnificent Pacific Coast Native American village in the Grand Hall.

You do not need to have the resources of the CMC to benefit from this approach. The People's Shows displays at Walsall have been much better than those elsewhere, because the interpretation sought where possible to recreate the original setting of each collection. This means, for example, reconstructing a teenager's bedroom with its collection of material relating to the pop star Madonna, so that the visitor gains a strong sense of how the material was arranged in its actual setting.

Site museums such as Beamish and Sturbridge have an advantage over the CMC in that they have real buildings to house their real things, and very often, if not always, the two were collected together. The buildings are no longer in their original place, but by the placing of the buildings together, a sense of real place is again reconstructed. Such museums are as a result hugely popular with the public, to the dismay of some 'analyst' social history curators. Beamish and Sturbridge might perhaps be criticized for failing to look sufficiently at class conflict, ethnic or gender issues, for example. But these are elements in interpretation which could be relatively easily introduced, as Sturbridge, at least, has done in recent years. Any such criticisms cannot take away from the fact that these museums are already enormously successful through their double power of the real, which puts them far ahead in popular appeal of most history museums.

Historic sites can achieve excellence by the opposite route: they have the power of the real place, they need to create the power of the real thing. Castle Rushen is arguably the finest interpretation anywhere of a medieval castle. With few original artefacts, the castle has been brilliantly brought to life through impeccably researched reconstructions in several rooms, from the wall decorations and furniture down to the smallest details of food and smells.

Jorvik and Plimoth Plantation have the power of the real place, but no significant structural remains, and significant if not particularly extensive collections. In both cases the interpretive choice is to present the collections in a traditional museum. The collections are not extensive enough, as at CMC or Beamish, to be powerful if placed in reconstructed settings. Both Jorvik and Plimoth therefore have largely to create the double real power by recreating both real things and their original settings. The key here, as at Castle Rushen, is the quality of the research. The village constructions at Plimoth and Jorvik succeed both curatorially and in their popularity with the public, because, as is pointed out to the visitor, they are based on enormously detailed research. Such is the power of the reconstruction at Plimoth that relatively few visitors appear to bother to view the traditional museum building, where the only real things on site are displayed. A lack of real things and a real setting does not matter at Plimoth, because there is a sense of the real place – the village was here – and the reconstruction is believed to be as authentic as possible.

In this sense there is little difference between the reconstructions at Jorvik and Plimoth and 'Luxor', except that at 'Luxor' there is no additional traditional museum display of real things. Yet 'Luxor' also works because it recreates the real thing and gives a sense of the real place by recreating a setting, as at the CMC.

'Luxor' raises a further key point for the overall analysis. Reconstructions of 'real things' in the 'real place' seem to be accepted by the public if it is known that they cannot be seen, in this form: we cannot see Tutankhamun's tomb at the moment Sir Howard Carter entered it, even if we know that we could travel to Egypt and gain some sense of the real place and see the real things in a museum. But The Oxford Story does not work anything like as well as 'Luxor', because its recreations of both place and things seem to pall compared to the very strong sense of history that is gained simply by wandering through the real colleges of Oxford, as they are today. The Oxford Story would probably be more effective if it was moved to Las Vegas!

Through well researched reconstructions of 'real things' in a 'real place', some museums, historic sites and heritage attractions, such as the CMC, Beamish, Sturbridge, Castle Rushen, Jorvik, Plimoth and 'Luxor', can gain the strength of the double power of the real. People respond to the power of real things in a real place – or an authenticated reconstruction. But quite why should this be? I argued above that successful interpretation of objects relied upon engaging as far as possible all five (six?) senses. Museums and heritage attractions which have or create this double power of real things and real place powerfully engage all the senses. We have a sense of being transported back in time, we are there, in sight, sounds, smells and touch, and sometimes even taste. Where the smells do not naturally come, even through the careful reconstruction, as at Plimoth, they can be added artificially, as at Jorvik.

The power of the real person

Having introduced this concept of the double power of the real – things and place – I will now argue that there is a third power of the real, that of the 'real person'. It is generally recognized these days that interpretation through people, as guides or demonstrators, for example, is stronger than more traditional methods, such as labels. But this is only part of what I mean by the power of the 'real person'. I would argue that we can only fully appreciate and understand material culture when we gain some awareness of its meaning, whether now or in the past, for the people who created or used it. This is nothing like the 'people-centred' approach to interpretation of the analyst social historians. It is a recognition that in focusing on material culture we need to consider a third element: 'real things in their real place as experienced by real people'.

How can we experience 'real people' in relation to real things in a real place? This is possible in exhibitions which explore contemporary culture or history within living memory. The power of the 'real person' is demonstrated in the People's Shows exhibitions, which gain significantly in effectiveness when the collectors are present. Settings for the displays mean that on such occasions there is the triple power of real things in a reconstructed 'real' place with the real person. The People's Shows would therefore be even more powerful if the process was inverted, and the public viewed the exhibitions and met the collectors in the collectors' own homes! After all, isn't this what the aristocracy do in stately homes?

But how can we have the power of the real person when we are dealing with subjects beyond living memory? How can we resurrect the dead? How can we get inside their minds?

Our ancestors have left behind a route into their minds through their material culture – through the things they made and used, and the places they constructed and used. These can be decoded, as we have seen, in a number of ways, to reveal the 'real person'. Alongside this, however, are other sources – written, visual and oral – which even more directly give an insight into some aspects of the lives of our forebears, which are perhaps less well revealed by material culture. These sources – letters, diaries, oral history tapes, portraits, photographs, film and video interviews etc. – also provide major insights into their relationship with material culture, defined as both things and places.

These sources can be activated through a number of interpretive devices to provide a sense of the 'real person'. Some of these are 'real' in the sense that they involve the direct use of primary sources, others rely on reconstruction. Of course, one must be aware that 'primary evidence' needs to be interpreted carefully: it is obviously not simply a direct route to seeing or hearing our forebears. A portrait or photograph, as much as an object, can lie or distort – but so can a letter or diary. Each also varies in the degree to which it engages each of the senses in the visitors' relationship with the 'real person'. We can simply 'hear' them, or 'see' them, or 'hear and see' them. Touch, smell and taste are, one would suggest, out of bounds. These various interpretive approaches are outlined in Figure 7.3.

First, we can 'hear' our forebears by reading their thoughts. This can be directly 'real', by reading, for example, original letters and diaries, or a reconstruction, where we read extracts from these, or from a transcription of an oral history tape, on a text panel. We can directly hear the real person on an oral history tape, or through a reconstruction by an actor. We can only see the real person to varying degrees of accuracy: in two dimensions (original portraits and photographs); in two dimensions but moving (silent films); and in three dimensions (sculpture). Graphics, dummies and holograms offer reconstructed alternatives to these. We can see the bodies of real people in the form of human remains, a highly regrettable and inappropriate form of interpretation in my view. We can see reconstructions of 'real people' through costumed interpreters who remain strictly third person and do not go into character – they therefore only give us the sensation of seeing, not hearing. We can hear and see in a 'real' but two-dimensional sense through video and sound film. We can reconstruct in three dimensions with sound, through dummies with tapes, and provide some movement through computer-operated dummies, or where faces are projected on to them. Virtual reality may be used for this in the future, but at the moment it is stronger in reconstructing a sense of place. Finally, we can hear and see (and touch and smell?) the real person only in displays which focus on history within living memory and contemporary culture. But, for the past, this can be reconstructed through first-person interpretation.

'hear'

real	**read** original letters and diaries	**listen** oral history
reconstruction	letters, diaries and oral history on a text panel	actor's voice

'see'

real	**2-dimensional** portraits and photographs silent film	**3-dimensional** sculpture	**real person** human remains
reconstruction	graphics	dummies holograms	costumed interpreters not in character

'hear and see'

real	**2-dimensional** video, sound film	**3-dimensional**	**real person** real people
reconstruction		dummies and holograms with sound	first person interpretation

Figure 7.3 *The power of the 'real person'*

What can we conclude from this? The real is generally far more effective than its comparable reconstruction. Indeed, most of the reconstructions tend to be very tacky and seemingly inauthentic. The interpretive devices which engage more of the senses, to the right of the chart, are generally also more effective. Human remains are perhaps disturbingly popular with the public. It is more difficult to read diagonally between the real and reconstruction levels: is a piece of spoken oral history more powerful in creating a sense of the real than a dressed dummy; is strictly third-person interpretation better than a speaking moving dummy?

I would argue that only one of the reconstructions is of any significant value and power, and that is first-person interpretation. Again, if this is believed to be authentic by the public, as, for example, at Plimoth Plantation, it is so powerful in recreating 'the real person' as to be perhaps the strongest of all of these interpretive devices. As with the creation of the power of real place and real things at Plimoth, this creation of the real person transcends the limitations that might be expected in reconstruction. Only where it is possible to employ the actual real person is the interpretation stronger.

If we look at this in terms of the attractions discussed so far, in my view the exceptional interpretations, in terms of the power of the 'real person' are those which employ either the 'authentic' real person, as at the CMC, or first-person interpretation, as at Plimoth, or, because it is felt that in certain circumstances the public have misgivings about the first-person approach, those that employ a combination of first person and third person, as at Beamish and Sturbridge. Interpretations which use dummies with tapes, such as Castle Rushen or Jorvik, are, I would argue, much less effective. Indeed, an approach which uses tapes along with actors' voices, as at 'Luxor' or at many English Heritage historic sites, seems far more effective, as the visitor's own imagination is used, as opposed to the artificiality of the dummy figure. At the time of writing it is understood that Jorvik is soon to employ first-person interpretation. Most museums, including analyst social history displays, are weak in the power of the 'real person', because they again rarely rise above the use of dummies and tapes. Most historic site collections, with some notable exceptions (colonial Williamsburg, for example) from the formalist perspective, tend to have displays which lack any sense of the real person, through their object fetishization, despite the presence of a guide or attendant in most rooms of the typical historic house display. Imagine how much more powerful the Tenement House or Mr Straw's House would be if first-person interpretation was used, and Miss Toward or Mr Straw were there to greet you.

The CMC is a particularly interesting example in terms of how it uses and recreates the 'power of the real person'. Taped guides, third- and first-person approaches and theatrical presentations are used to recreate this power, in combination with real things: 'demonstration of an object's use, or re-enactment of a cultural ritual, reveals more than seeing the relevant objects sitting in a display case'. A richly 'peopled' interpretation of the culture of past and present societies, and the role of material culture within this, is developed using the 'environmental reconstructions', the simulations of the 'real place', as 'stage-sets for the programmable interpretation'. For example, 'Effort has been made to engage the services of natives as actors, artisans, singers, musicians, dancers and story-tellers ... to ensure that exhibits in the Grand Hall ... are enriched by a full range of interpretive activities such as totem pole carving, demonstrations of food preparation and fishing apparatus, enactments of myths, and performances of cultural rituals' (MacDonald and Alsford, 1989, pp. 144–6). At the CMC, the triple notion of 'real things' in a 'real place' interpreted by 'real people' is richly realized.

The CMC also highlights a final point with regard to the power of the 'real person': that there is perhaps an even more powerful stage where the visitors themselves 'become' the real person. 'At times visitors will be invited to don a reproduction of a period costume – to put themselves in the shoes of people in the past – and play a role in an unfolding drama. This type of involvement can provide an emotionally charged experience which ... challenges one's culturally biased assumptions' (MacDonald and Alsford, 1989, p. 146). At Plimoth the visitor experiences 'real' things in a 'real' place, and meets 'real' people, who interpret their world for you. A deeper level of interpretation would be, as at the CMC, for the visitors themselves to become historical characters – do-it-yourself first-person interpretation. This currently happens widely outside museums, in the hugely popular phenomena of historical re-enactments, including but by no means exclusively battles. Again, unfortunately, some museum professionals tend to look down on this kind of activity as somehow eccentric or inauthentic. Yet it seems to me to offer enormously valuable opportunities for museums in interpretation, if effective partnerships are developed. People involved in these activities, which can range from the English or American Civil Wars to an obsession with the style of the 1960s, are often extremely knowledgeable about the times and its material culture. They are very often collectors. Dressing up and 'becoming' a historical character is seen as a logical extension of much collection activity, and is a major popular phenomenon. Research in this area would be of value. The portrayal of mythical, literary, film or television characters and events in this way, such as the cults of Robin Hood, *Star Trek* or *Doctor Who*, is of no lesser importance in this respect, for it reflects popular cultural phenomena. Why do thousands of people spend their weekends at conventions dressed as Friar Tuck, Mr Spock or Atlanta Shore from Gerry Anderson's *Stingray*? While some museums have begun to appreciate the appeal of historical re-enactments as popular public events, and of involving the visitor in more direct experience of the 'real person' through dressing up and taking on a character, this remains largely unexplored, though it has begun to be used highly successfully with children. The visitor can become the 'real person' who interprets 'real things' in a 'real place'.

The triple power of the real

The implications of all of this are, I would argue, that the most effective heritage interpretations are those which either intrinsically possess this 'triple power' of the 'real', or, as at Plimoth, successfully recreate it from fragmentary evidence. Figure 7.4 indicates rather schematically how the examples I have used compare in terms of my triple notion of the real.

Formalist and analyst museum displays, scoring only one out of three, lag far behind in effectiveness. The traditional museum is one among many approaches, and very often far from the most effective. Those museums that have so far failed to do so, unlike Plimoth, Beamish or the CMC, must recognize what can be learnt from those heritage attractions, historic site collections and historic sites which possess or reconstruct this triple power. These other sectors can in turn learn from the museums and other attractions which have harnessed this triple power. How much more powerful would Stonehenge be if there were first-person interpreters on site using material culture? How much better would the *Coronation Street* tour be if the actors were present and you could enter the homes, which at present are merely a facade? Bosworth must come alive on days when re-enactments take place. The Tenement House and Mr Straw's House merely need the presence of their owners. Historic houses,

	real things	real place	real person
Stonehenge	no	yes	no
Coronation Street	no	yes	no
Bosworth Battlefield	no*	yes	no*
The Oxford Story	no	reconstructed	reconstructed
Luxor	reconstructed	reconstructed	reconstructed
Castle Rushen	reconstructed	yes	reconstructed
Jorvik	yes/reconstructed	yes/reconstructed	reconstructed
Plimoth Plantation	yes/reconstructed	yes/reconstructed	reconstructed
Tenement House/ Mr Straw's House	yes	yes	no
Buckingham Palace	yes	yes	no
Beamish/ Old Sturbridge	yes	yes/reconstructed	reconstructed
Typical local museum	yes	no	no
Horniman Museum	yes	no	no
British Museum	yes	no	no
Canadian Museum of Civilization (CMC)	yes	reconstructed	reconstructed

*Reconstructed on re-enactment days, and to a degree in the visitor centre.

Figure 7.4 *How the heritage attractions, including museums from the plot in Figure 7.2, compare in terms of the 'triple power' of the real*

including Buckingham Palace, would similarly benefit from the reconstruction of the real person, including the servants. Local or national
museums have a lot more to do to gain the triple power, but the CMC has
demonstrated what can be done.

What evidence is there to back this hypothesis that heritage attractions
(including museums) which possess the triple power of the real, even if
this is reconstructed, are the most effective form of heritage interpretation? One can point to the popular appeal of all those attractions and
museums that have been argued to possess this triple power, but further
research into visitor perceptions is required. Existing studies provide some
supporting evidence. Some of the findings of Merriman's survey support
the hypothesis of the power of the real place. Seventy per cent of respondents
agreed or strongly agreed that castles and historic houses 'bring the past
to life better than museums', with only 15 per cent disagreeing. Of those
in the sample who did visit both castles and historic houses, and museums, a staggering 79 per cent agreed with the statement. In answer to the
question, 'If you wanted to find out about local history or some old local
place, what would be the most enjoyable way of doing it?', the top
answer was 'visit the local area or site by yourself' (20 per cent), followed
by 'having a guided tour of the local area or site' (19 per cent), followed
by watching a television programme, reading a book, listening to an
expert and, sixth, 'visiting a museum' (just 7 per cent) (Merriman, 1991,
pp. 69, 120). The Susie Fisher Report for Croydon Museum, which
employed qualitative focus group techniques, found support for the
power of the real place in terms of multi-sensory reconstructions:

> People talk of the recreation of Trafalgar at Madame Tussauds where they were deaf-
> ened by gunfire. This has a deep effect because suddenly you begin to understand
> what it must have been like for the sailors and the gunners. ... Real objects lying life-
> less amount to a wasted opportunity. Many would rather have reproductions which
> they are allowed to play with, than the real thing in a glass case, which is meaning-
> less. Young people also enjoy the fun of the sounds, tastes, smells and textures which
> dramatise the events. ... Once they started musing about an ideal museum, the idea
> which came naturally to mind was to have a working pub from 100 years ago where
> they could actually get a drink.

In terms of the 'real' person, 'Young people are very keen on using an ani-
mateur in costume. This benign person would enact scenes, use artefacts
and allow them to touch and do'. When people were asked which museums
were already doing a good job, the suggestions made were museums
which relate to the notion of the triple power of the (reconstructed) real –
Jorvik, the Imperial War Museum with its Blitz experience, MOMI – but
also heritage attractions which attempted the same, such as the London
Dungeon, Madame Tussauds and Rock Circus (Fisher, 1990, pp. 32–3).

The territory lying between museums and heritage theme parks or sites
is therefore suggested as a fruitful one for museums to occupy more fully,
if they wish to be more appealing to the public. No doubt some people in
museums view this with horror. Museums will stop being museums. But

does this matter? What is important is that the past and present (and future?) are explored in a way that is appealing to the public. If the best means to do this is through the realization of the triple power of the real, by reconstruction if necessary, then so be it. Museums which adapt to this will survive, even if they can no longer be considered museums. The museum is dead. Long live heritage provision with 'real' things in 'real' places and 'real' people.

If such museums become more like theme parks, this does not mean they will become theme parks, just that they will have learned what can usefully be learned from them. By the same token, theme parks are becoming more like museums, but are not seeking to become museums. There is common ground, but the ultimate objectives are clearly very different (MacDonald and Alsford, 1995). But museums do have much to learn from theme parks and a range of other approaches to the past. The establishment of the Canadian Museum of Civilization indicates this most clearly, in that in formulating a model for the museum, the staff

> looked around the world for the best and the most innovative, not only in museums, but in a range of cultural, educational, and recreational institutions ... if there is one trend which seems most overpowering in the museum world ... it is the development of the theme park ... the latter have moved in the direction of greater historical content, formal exhibits, 'living history' experiences, and collection building. It is now becoming hard to determine, in a few cases, whether they are theme parks, expositions, cultural centres or open-air museums, so many are the shared features and so blurred the boundaries between those institutions.
>
> (MacDonald and Alsford, 1989, pp. 45, 51)

The ultimate example is Disney, which at its Epcot centre has established national pavilions for a range of countries which display collections loaned from some of the most prestigious museums in the world, including the Louvre, the Hermitage and the CMC, and as it expands it will soon 'be a museum experience second only to New York, London and Paris' (MacDonald, 1988, p. 28). These museums gain money and exposure to the 25 million visitors each year. George MacDonald, the founding director of the CMC, considers that it is not just in terms of customer care that museums can learn a great deal from the likes of Disney: 'Theme Parks tend to have high presentation standards but low standards when it comes to information content; as a generalisation, one could suggest the reverse to be true of museums' (MacDonald, 1992, p. 173; see also MacDonald and Alsford, 1995). The interpretation at Epcot is based on something akin to the triple notion of the real: real treasures from around the world, in very well researched reproductions of the real place, even if these are disguised false-front movie sets, and with real people in the guise of top-quality performers of music and dance and other cultural activities from each country. Even the food is authentic. MacDonald concludes: 'At Epcot you are never out of touch with "a real person" of that particular culture even in the movie theatre, restaurant or market area. Once you have crossed the threshold into a national pavilion, everyone you see and interact with is the "real thing"' (MacDonald, 1988, p. 29). As well as displaying the collections more effectively, one might also suggest that within a certain ideological approach, Epcot even does more for multicultural awareness and understanding than many museums.

The CMC has taken what can be learned from Disney, in terms of customer care *and* interpretation, to heart. If other museums do not, how will they fare against public perceptions which are increasingly based on visits to sites such as Epcot rather than museums? 'The image of museum directors as the high priests of abandoned cathedrals of abandoned culture haunts us all, yet we have done little to address it' (MacDonald, 1988, p. 31). Museums like the British Museum should be warned.

Which real things, real places, real people?

If I have sketched this notion of what form the most effective heritage provision could take in future, in terms of interpretation, this does not answer the question of which aspects of our heritage are worth preserving or interpreting. Which 'real' things in which 'real' places through which 'real' people out of all of those possible should current and future heritage provision explore? While the ideal form is real things in a real place interpreted by real people, Plimoth suggests that all three elements can be highly authentically recreated from fragmentary evidence. The choice of which aspects of the past to explore is therefore wide, and as our understanding and techniques develop, will grow even wider; more will become possible, ultimately almost unlimited. So what should we choose? Who will decide?

It is a paradox that in the private sector the needs and interests of the public are fully addressed through marketing research, yet in the public sector this is rarely undertaken. Private sector heritage developments, including independent museums, reflect what the public wish to see far better than those in the public sector. It is necessary to add the rider that the private sector reflects the aspirations of that section of the public, the vast majority, who can afford and are willing to pay an admission charge. Private sector developments have shown, therefore, that the public do wish for a wide range of aspects of popular culture largely ignored by museums to be reflected, as we saw in Chapters 5 and 6. The kinds of attractions which are being developed to meet this market further support the notion of the power of the real place, as at *Coronation Street*, Elvis Presley's birthplace or his home at Gracelands, Paul McCartney's teenage home or tours of football stadia. They also support the notion that this can be successfully reconstructed, if the public believe that this has been authentically done, as in the Cavern Club in Liverpool, where The Beatles first shot to stardom, which was demolished but later rebuilt on the original site. This is a powerful change in the market for heritage which cannot be underestimated. In the public museum sector, the low status of marketing means that less attention is paid to the needs and wishes of those such museums purport to serve.

It is crucial also to recognize the continued appeal of displays of high culture, though this needs to be qualified. The most popular are often historic houses and sites, which already possess a double power of the real. These also increasingly find it necessary to reflect the lives of the servant class, as in the *Upstairs Downstairs* approach at many National Trust properties. But a move to reflect popular culture does not mean that what was traditionally high culture should be marginalized. I have argued that the horizontal and vertical axes of the plot should be removed, to reveal *all* material culture as the subject matter of museums, or perhaps, I should now add, heritage attractions. While this opens up a huge new territory for museums, it does not mean that the existing territory should be ignored. There has perhaps been an inevitable overreaction in opening up the hidden history of disadvantaged groups, to marginalize the history of the advantaged. The one cannot be understood without the other; they are causally linked. I would agree, therefore, with a reviewer who suggests that Kavanagh's notable study, *History Curatorship*, is 'dangerously limited' in focusing on museums which reflect only the poor, and not the affluent: 'There is almost no mention of museums such as ... the Victoria and Albert, the royal palaces, the country houses. ... However focused on the "high-born", these historical institutions ... must be accounted for' (Swank, 1992, p. 73; Kavanagh, 1990).

High culture should not be marginalized but reinterpreted. The polysemantic quality of this needs to be revealed. As we saw in Chapter 3, it can be understood as the product of the labour of the working class. How was it then appropriated? Did this represent a fair return for the labour it entailed? If the high culture material in such institutions was subjected to the kind of exposition indicated by the model of artefact analysis, radically different interpretations could be developed. This would be particularly revealing for items which have been appropriated in other ways, such as through war and plunder. If this serves only to reignite debates about cultural restitution, then it will have usefully brought this into the public domain, for wider and more democratic discussion. This kind of process might also raise other issues of public access to collections, such as how 'Tory MP Winston Churchill avoids tax by promising to let the public view his heirlooms, but getting in proves almost impossible' (Editorial, *Sunday Mirror*, 9 June 1996). A reinterpretation of the material in the elite museums and collections would also reveal that much of it is ordinary and everyday, and that only its age makes us treat it like treasure. Think, for example, of those playing balls from ancient Egypt in the British Museum. I look forward to seeing them juxtaposed alongside the balls from 1966 and 1996.

Market forces and cuts in funding are pushing public museums in new directions. Utilization of the triple power of the real will need to be an important part of the survival strategy for any public museum. But if the British Museum has the resources to mimic the Canadian Museum of Civilization, what of the local museum, particularly if it is not also a historic site? It is still possible, I would argue, imaginatively and cheaply to recon-struct the power of the real person and the real place to an extent, but there is only so much you can do on a shoestring. Ultimately many smaller public museums face a very uncertain future.

There is, of course, the National Lottery, which many local councillors see as the potential saviour of their museums. The danger is that funding is gained for new capital projects without adequate revenue funding. But the key problem with the National Lottery's funding of museums is that it has made the decision making about our heritage even less democratic, by effectively privatizing major developments in the public museum sector. Elected councillors may back a project, but only appointed trustees will decide if it succeeds. The kinds of projects so far granted substantial sums have heightened a concern that the Lottery money will only go to high culture, as in the £55 million for the Royal Opera House, £30 million for Sadler's Wells ballet company and £50 million for the Tate Gallery. It is not surprising that the Lottery has been accused of taking from the poor to subsidize the culture of the rich. Where money has gone to relatively socially deprived areas, often the projects look to be far removed from the needs or interests of ordinary local people, even in terms of museum pro-vision. The City of Salford received £64 million in February 1996, the largest Lottery award to go outside London, towards a £127 million cul-tural complex named after the artist L. S. Lowry, including a gallery to house the city council's collection of 350 Lowry paintings. Prominent art critics commented: 'It is just plain barking lunacy. There is a terrible sameness to all Lowry's work'; and 'if I say Matisse to you, I would put Lowry a thousand miles away. But if you talk about regional, quirky, slightly folksy, misogynistic art, he is obviously eminent' (*Guardian*, 23 February 1996, p. 5).

Such decision making needs to be democratized. Indeed, a wide range of decision making in publicly funded museums should be opened up. It is the public's money! When the V&A bought the statue of the Three Graces, were you or I consulted as taxpayers? Given the choice of buying the ball from the 1966 World Cup Final or one of the toes of one of the Graces, which do you think a majority of the English public would have chosen? Come to think of it, have we ever been asked whether we would like to fund the V&A?

Strategies for the museum sector as a whole need to be based on a far more realistic appraisal of the resources that will be available. If extra funding does not become available, or is even cut, despite your best efforts, what will you do? What such an analysis reveals for museums as a whole is that resources are spread too thinly. There are simply too many museums chasing financial resources, which, owing to political and eco-nomic constraints, are not growing at the same pace as the ever-increasing number of museums. The end result is that the individual museums lack the 'critical mass' to succeed (McDaniel, 1984). The MGC, presumably not wanting to alienate existing museums, has fudged the issue: 'There is a limit to how many museums can be sustained, and that limit may not be far off. Our priority must be to look after and improve what we already have' (MGC, 1994, p. 8). In my view, too many smaller independent and local authority museums in Britain are simply untenable, and should be humanely put down rather than face a slow and lingering death: 'Short of outright insolvency the museum field seems to have few ways to identify those institutions whose chronic inability to achieve any demonstrably beneficial outcome cannot possibly justify the ongoing expense of their maintenance' (Weil, 1995, p. 36). If governing bodies cannot or will not fund them adequately, closure is the best option in everyone's interests. A leaner, fitter museum sector, which places more emphasis on quality than quantity, is a far better strategy. The poor quality of so many current museums goes a long way to explaining the public perception of museums as 'Dingy places with different kinds of bits'. 'Small ill-funded museums do not attract visitors; rather they disenchant visitors and drive them away from even those sites that deserve public visitation and support' (McDaniel, 1984, p. 34).

The museums which would be left, bolstered by staff and other resources, in formulating their strategy would need to look in far more detail at the external forces in the environment around them. The views of visitors, non-visitors and other stakeholders need to be explored much more fully, even though the findings may be extremely uncomfortable. The absurd paradox is that for too long the strategies of museums have been formulated without due regard to the views of those for whom they exist, and who provide the funding. Marketing, therefore, must play a key role in strategic formulation. It is the real key to the democratization of museums.

An analysis of the external environment must also consider competitors and allies. As was discussed in Chapter 2, museums need to be more realistic about what they are in competition with, by carefully considering 'critical resources' and only entering races they can win. Obversely, too often potential allies are seen as competitors. Other museums should be seen as allies. The potential for joint marketing initiatives between museums is enormous. A more streamlined, quality museum sector could directly copy the marketing success of the National Trust as English Heritage has done, and combine in a membership scheme. This would raise the public profile of museums individually and as a whole, and raise considerable revenue. The natural next step in marketing terms is to turn the National Trust and English Heritage into allies rather than competitors, through a further joint heritage marketing initiative.

Museums must seek partnerships to survive. One route is with each other. Certainly the local public museums are too isolated at present. County or even regional services would be preferable. But the logic of the argument of this chapter suggests that another strategy should be simultaneously employed, moving towards integrated local or regional heritage services, overcoming, in Sola's phrase, the nonsense of division between movable and immovable heritage. Sola therefore argues that there should be an amalgamated profession of heritage care, which contains within it specialists in, for example, museum work or archives. He argues that museum workers have been too arrogant in their search for a distinct identity, placing museums at the centre of heritage, marking out a unique territory, rather than recognizing it as just one aspect (Sola, 1991, 1992a, b). This is not to deny museums a unique role but to recast it, and to question the need for a separate identity as an institution. Gee has concurred that smaller museums in particular, in an effort to ensure their survival in difficult times, need to stress not their unique function, but what they share with others involved in heritage preservation in the broadest sense (Gee, 1994). The integrated and highly successful approach to heritage on the Isle of Man is an example of what might be achieved (Wright, 1993, p. 23).

It has been suggested that the idea of a national museum service should be debated (Editorial, *Museums Journal*, October 1991, p. 7). We need to go much further than this. The ideal would be a National Heritage Service, integrating all the public museums, including the nationals and historic sites, and working in partnership as far as possible with the independent museums and the National Trust. Partnerships with non-heritage organizations also need to be sought. Indeed, this is already happening, in the sense that almost all the major museum developments in Britain in the 1990s have been partnerships with the private sector, with the museum often just part of a larger leisure attraction. If the British Museum will get into bed with Disney ...

'Change is not what it used to be'

'Change is not what it used to be' (Handy, 1990, p. 4). Even those who have accepted some, if not all (this would be impossible), of the arguments I have made in this book might object at this point: 'This is all very well, but we have tried and tested ways of doing things. Museums on the whole are reasonably successful. There is a need for change, but this can only happen gradually, otherwise there is a danger of losing what we already have. Resources are limited, we have to work with what we have. In the real world, your proposals are little more than dreams, fantasies. They are too radical to be implemented, even if we wished to.'

But there are other voices in my head (which may confirm suspicions some readers may have developed) who are not imaginary, most notably Charles Handy, who are telling me radically different things, about what non-profit organizations such as museums must do to survive in a rapidly changing world, an age of unreason, a time 'for thinking the unlikely and doing the unreasonable' (Handy, 1990, p. 4). On the contrary, I do not think that what I have said is probably radical enough, particularly in terms of the future of museums as organizations. The era of the museum, and even the need for some of its functions, may be ending. But the need to provide opportunities for the public exploration of the meaning of our material world lives on.

Coda

When you read this book, it did set you thinking, it did make you see your work slightly differently, you were meaning to use the ideas it helped you to generate to influence your work, but somewhere along the line ... A week passes, and then another and the weeks turn into months, the months turn into years ...

If this happens, I have failed. This has not, of course, been a manual for museum staff of what to do or not to do. Even if this were possible, I would view it as arrogant of me to be so prescriptive. Yet it is my desire that this book will have an impact on your work. Realistically, you and I know that this has to be here and now, as you read this, or it is likely to be never. If you have enjoyed reading this book, and have found that it does usefully stimulate debate about the future role of museums, this is my last chance to influence you to use the ideas to initiate some of the changes in museums that you, to some extent at least, have agreed are necessary, if not indeed imperative. I would like you to at least think of one thing you will do differently at work tomorrow as a result of reading this book. But, please, don't let it end there. Whether this book has any significant impact depends entirely on you ...

References

All titles are published in London and the United Kingdom unless otherwise stated.

Ambrose, T., 1993, *Managing New Museums*, Scottish Museums Council/HMSO, Edinburgh.

Ambrose, T. and Paine, C., 1993, *Museum Basics*, Routledge.

Ambrosen, T., 1989, *The Illustrated Footballer*, Breedon Books, Derby.

American Association of Museums (AAM), 1984, *Museums for a New Century*, AAM, Washington, DC.

American Association of Museums (AAM), 1992, *Excellence and Equity: Education and the Public Dimension of Museums*, AAM, Washington, DC.

Ames, K., 1989, 'Meaning in artifacts: hall furnishings in Victorian America', in Schlereth, T., (ed.), 1989a: 206–21.

Ames, K., 1992, 'Finding common threads: an afterword', in Ames, K., Franco, B. and Frye, L., (eds), 1992: 313–24.

Ames, K., 1994, 'Book review: *Museums, Objects and Collections: A Cultural Study*', *Curator*, 37(4): 283–5.

Ames, K., Franco, B. and Frye, L., (eds), 1992, *Ideas and Images: Developing Interpretive History Exhibits,* American Association for State and Local History, Nashville, Tennessee.

Anderson, P., 1980, *Arguments within English Marxism*, Verso.

Anderson, D., 1992, 'Museums at a time of change', in International Council of Museums (ICOM), *Marketing the Arts*, Watermark Press: 159–66.

Appadurai, A., 1994, 'Commodities and the politics of value', in Pearce, S., (ed.), 1994b: 76–91.

Audit Commission, 1991, *The Road to Wigan Pier?* Managing Local Authority Museums and Art Galleries, HMSO.

Baldwin, K., 1995, *This Supporting Life: How to Be a Real Football Fan*, Hodder Headline.

Bale, J., 1991, 'Playing at home: British football and a sense of place', in Williams, J. and Wagg, S., (eds), *British Football and Social Change*, Leicester University Press, Leicester: 130–44.

Barthes, R., 1973, *Mythologies*, Paladin Books.

Beevers, L., Moffat, S., Clark, H., and Griffiths, S., 1988, *Memories and Things: Linking Museums and Libraries with Older People,* Workers Education Association, Edinburgh.

Belcher, M., 1991, *Exhibitions in Museums*, Leicester University Press, Leicester.

Bennett, T., 1986, 'The politics of the "popular" and popular culture', in Bennett, T., Mercer, C. and Woollacott, J., (eds), *Popular Culture and Social Relations*, Open University, Milton Keynes.

Bennett, T., 1988, 'Museums and "the people"', in Lumley, R., (ed.), *The Museum Time Machine*, Routledge: 65–88.

Birmingham Museum and Art Gallery, 1993, *The Art, Craft and Lifestyle of the Custom Bike Movement*, Birmingham Museum and Art Gallery, Birmingham.

Bigsby, C., (ed.), 1976, *Approaches to Popular Culture*, Edward Arnold.

Borg, A., 1991, 'Confronting disposal', *Museums Journal*, September: 29–31.

Bott, V., 1988, *Labour History in Museums*, Society for the Study of Labour History, Social History Curators Group, Manchester.

Bott, V., 1990, 'Beyond the museum', *Museums Journal*, February: 28–30.

Brown, I., 1993, 'The New England cemetery as a cultural landscape', in Lubar, S. and Kingery, D., (eds), 1993: 140–59.

Bryson, B., 1994, *The Lost Continent: Travels in Small Town America*, Abacus.

Bulmer, L. and Merrills, R., 1992, *"Dicks Out!" The Unique Guide to British Football Songs*, Chatsby Publishing, Tunbridge Wells.

Bunch, L., 1995, 'Fighting the good fight: museums in an age of uncertainty', *Museum News*, March/April: 32–5, 58–62.

Carey, F., (ed.), 1991, *Collecting the 20th Century*, British Museum Press.

Chapin, D. and Klein, S., 1992, 'The epistemic museum', *Museum News*, July/August: 60–1, 76.

Clark, H., 1988, 'Community involvement in the People's Story', *Scottish Museum News*, Autumn: 4–6.

Clarke, J. and Critcher, C., 1986, '1966 and all that: England's World Cup Victory', in Tomlinson, A. and Whannel, G., (eds), *Off the Ball: The Football World Cup*, Pluto Press.

Cohen, L., 1989, 'Embellishing a life of labor: an interpretation of the material culture of American working-class homes, 1885–1915', in Schlereth, T., (ed.), 1989a: 289–305.

Copp, C., 1994, 'Researching popular culture: a case study – boxing Harborough', *Social History in Museums: Journal of the Social History Curators Group*, 21: 53–6.

Corn, J., 1989, 'Tools, technologies and contexts: interpreting the history of American technologies', in Leon, W. and Rosenzweig, R., (eds), *History Museums in the United States*, University of Chicago Press, Chicago: 237–61.

Cornwall, P., 1996, 'Europe's finest', *When Saturday Comes*, June: 18.

Corrin, L., 1993, 'Mining the museum: an installation confronting history', *Curator*, 36(4): 302–13.

Cosgrove, S., 1989, 'The zoot suit and style warfare', in McRobbie, A., *Zoot Suits and Second-Hand Dresses: An Anthology of Fashion and Music*, Macmillan.

Crew, S. and Sims, J., 1991, 'Locating authenticity; fragments of a dialogue', in Karp, I. and Lavine, S.: 159–74.

Davies, S., 1985, 'Collecting and recalling the twentieth century', *Museums Journal*, 85(1): 27–9.

Davies, S., 1988, '"School-days: an exhibition on schools and schooling in Hull": a review', *Social History Curators Group News*, 18: 4–5.

Davies, S., 1993, 'Social history in museums: the academic context', in Fleming, D., Paine, C. and Rhodes, J., (eds): 3–12.

Davies, S., 1994a, *By Popular Demand*, Museums and Galleries Commission (MGC).

Davies, S., 1994b, 'A sense of purpose: rethinking museum values and strategies', in Kavanagh, G., (ed.), 1994: 33–40.

Davies, S., 1994c, 'Back to Basics 2', *Museums Journal*, September: 20–2.

Davis, K. and Gibb, J., 1988, 'Unpuzzling the past: critical thinking in history museums', *Museums Studies Journal*, Spring/Summer: 41–5.

de Bono, E., 1992, *Serious Creativity*, HarperCollins.

Deetz, J., 1977, *In Small Things Forgotten: The Archaeology of Early American Life*, Anchor Books, New York.

Deetz, J. and Dethlefsen, E., 1994, 'Death's head, cherub, urn and willow', in Pearce, S., (ed.), 1994b.

Dickenson, V., 1994, 'The economics of museum admission charges', in Moore, K., (ed.), 1994a.

Digger, J., 1994, 'The People's Show: one strategy towards the democratic museum', *Social History in Museums: Journal of the Social History Curators Group*, 21: 40–3.

Digger, 1995, 'The People's Shows at Walsall: collections by local people' (unpublished MA thesis, University of Leicester).

Doxtator, D., 1992, *Fluffs and Feathers: An Exhibit on the Symbols of Indianness*, Woodland Cultural Centre, Brantford, Ontario, Canada.

Doyle, A. Conan, 1981, 'The blue carbuncle', in Doyle, A. Conan, *The Adventures of Sherlock Holmes*, Penguin, Harmondsworth: 144–64.

Doyle, R., 1994, 'Republic is a beautiful word: Republic of Ireland, 1990', in Hornby, N., (ed.), *My Favourite Year: A Collection of New Football Writing*, Gollancz/Witherby.

Durbin, G., Morris, S. and Wilkinson, S., 1990, *A Teacher's Guide To Learning From Objects*, English Heritage.

Ellison, M., 1994, 'Home run hit for art market', *Guardian*, 28 July: 3.

Elsner, J. and Cardinal, R., 1994, 'An interview with Robert Opie', in Elsner, J. and Cardinal, R., (eds), *The Cultures of Collecting*, Reaktion Books: 25–48.

Ettema, M., 1987, 'History museums and the culture of materialism', in Blatti, J., (ed.), *Past Meets Present: Essays about Historic Interpretation and Public Audiences*, Smithsonian Institution Press, Washington DC: 62–85.

Fardell, R., 1995, 'The People's Show Festival at Harborough Museum', *Museological Review*, 1(2): 72–6.

Feaver, W., 1994, 'High on the energy of street fashion', *Observer Review*, 27 November: 12.

Fisher, S., 1990, *Bringing History and the Arts to a New Audience: Qualitative Research for the London Borough of Croydon*, Susie Fisher Group.

Fishwick, M. and Browne, R., 1970, *Icons of Popular Culture*, Bowling Green University Popular Press, Bowling Green, Ohio.

Fishwick, N., 1989, *English Football and Society: 1910–1950*, Manchester University Press, Manchester.

Fiske, J., 1989a, *Reading the Popular*, Unwin Hyman.

Fiske, J., 1989b, *Understanding Popular Culture*, Unwin Hyman.

Fleming, D., 1987, 'You really can't do that! problems of interpretation in social history', *Social History in Museums: Journal of the Social History Curators Group*, 15: 3–4.

Fleming, 1992, 'Cain's people: approaching the urban environment', *Social History in Museums: Journal of the Social History Curators Group*, 19: 37–44.

Fleming, D., 1993, 'Introduction', in Fleming, D., Paine, C. and Rhodes, J., (eds): 1.

Fleming, D., Paine, C. and Rhodes, J., (eds), 1993, *Social History in Museums: A Handbook For Professionals*, HMSO.

Francis, R., 1994, 'The People's Show: a critical analysis', *Social History in Museums: Journal of the Social History Curators Group*, 21: 44–8.

Freedland, J., 1995, 'Truly, badly, cheaply', *Guardian*, 16 October: 8–9.

Freedland, J., 1996, 'A tacky bow to the king of kitsch', *Guardian*, 15 January: 2.

Friedel, R., 1993, 'Some matters of substance', in Lubar, S. and Kingery, D., (eds): 41–50.

Frostick, E., 1990, *The Story of Hull and its People*, Hull City Museums and Art Galleries and Hutton Press, Hull.

Frostick, E., 1992, 'The Story of Hull and its People! a measure of success?', *Social History in Museums: Journal of the Social History Curators Group*, 19: 45–53.

Garfield, D., 1993, 'Making the museum mine: an interview with Fred Wilson', *Museum News*, May/June: 46–9, 90.

Gascoigne, B., 1986, 'Foreword', in Johnston, S. and Beddow, T., *Collecting: The Passionate Pastime*, Viking Penguin, Harmondsworth.

Gee, K., 1993, 'The heritage web: structures and relationships' (unpublished discussion paper).

Gee, K., 1994, 'Debating the future: the heritage web', *South Eastern Museum News*, Summer: 8–9.

Gelly, D., 1994, 'What Charlie didn't blow', *Observer Review*: 5.

Gilborn, C., 1989, 'Pop pedagogy: looking at the Coke bottle', in Schlereth, T., (ed.), *Material Culture Studies in America*, American Association for State and Local History, Nashville, Tennessee: 183–91.

Goode, G., 1994, 'The principles of museum administration', in Kavanagh, G., (ed.): 47–50.

Goodwin, M., 1990, 'Objects, belief and power in mid-Victorian England: the origins of the Victoria and Albert Museum', in Pearce, S., (ed.), *Objects of Knowledge,* vol. 1, New Research in Museum Studies, Athlone Press.

Hale, W., 1996, 'Balls!', *Four Four Two*, April, 92–4.

Hall, J., 1994, 'The Arsenal Story: comment', in Wade, M., (ed.), *Museums in Britain*, McMillan Group, Macclesfield: 45.

Handy, C., 1990, *The Age of Unreason*, Arrow Books.

Harland, L., 1993, 'The object is dead, long live the object', *Social History Curators Group News*, 33: 6.

Harrison, J., 1993, 'Ideas of museums in the 1990s', *Museum Management and Curatorship*, 13: 160–76.

Hartfield, R., 1994, 'Challenging the context: perception, polity and power', *Curator*, 37(1): 46–62.

Hattenstone, S., 1995, 'Collector's item', *Guardian*, 23 October: 10–11.

Hatton, A., 1994, 'Museum planning and museum plans', in Moore, K., (ed.), 1994a.

Hawes, E., 1986, 'Artifacts, myths and identity in American history museums', *Museology and Identity: International Committee for Museums (ICOFOM), Series* 10: 135–9.

Haynes, R., 1994, *The Football Imagination: The Rise of Football Fanzine Culture*, Arena, Aldershot.

Hebdige, D., 1979, *Subculture: The Meaning of Style*, Methuen.

Hebdige, 1988, *Hiding in the Light: On Images and Things*, Routledge.

Hesseltine, B., 1989, 'The challenge of the artifact', in Schlereth, T., (ed.), 1989a: 93–100.

Hooper-Greenhill, E., 1991, *Museum and Gallery Education*, Leicester University Press, Leicester.

Hooper-Greenhill, E., 1992, *Museums and the Shaping of Knowledge*, Routledge.

Hooper-Greenhill, E., 1994, *Museums and their Visitors*, Routledge.

Hornby, N., 1992, *Fever Pitch*, Gollancz.

Hornby, N., 1994, 'The Arsenal story', in Wade, M., (ed.), *Museums in Britain*, McMillan Group, Macclesfield: 43–4.

Hull, K., Callaghan, S. and Walker, G., 1994, 'Freeing the spirit is the object', *Museums Journal*, August: 25–7.

Jary, D., Horne, J. and Bucke, T., 'Football "fanzines" and football culture: a case of successful "cultural contestation"', *Sociological Review*, 39(3): 581–8.

Jenkinson, P., 1989, 'Material culture, people's history, and populism: where do we go from here?', in Pearce, S., (ed.), *Museum Studies in Material Culture*, Leicester University Press, Leicester.

Jenkinson, P., 1994, 'Museum futures', in Kavanagh, G., (ed.): 51–4.

Johnson, P. and Thomas, B., 1991, 'Museums and the local economy', in Kavanagh, G., (ed.), *The Museums Profession: Internal and External Relations*, Leicester University Press, Leicester: 99–123.

Johnson, P. and Thomas, B., 1992, *Tourism, Museums and the Local Economy*, Elgar, Aldershot.

Johnstone, C., 1994, 'Balancing the magic of real things', *Social History Curators Group News*, 34: 3.

Jones, C., 1995, 'Rock miners seek slice of the auction', *Guardian*, 19 August: 31.

Kaplin, F., (ed.), 1994, *Museums and the Making of 'Ourselves': The Role of Objects in National Identity*, Leicester University Press, Leicester..

Karp, I., 1991, 'Culture and representation', in Karp, I. and Lavine, S.: 11–24.

Karp, I. and Lavine, S., 1991, *Exhibiting Cultures*, Smithsonian Institution Press, Washington DC.

Karp, I. and Lavine, S., 1993, 'Communities and museums', *Museum News*, May/June: 44–5, 69, 79–84.

Karp, I., Kreamer, C., and Lavine, S., 1992, *Museums and Communities*, Smithsonian Institution Press, Washington DC.

Kavanagh, G., 1989, 'Objects as evidence, or not?', in Pearce, S., (ed.), *Museum Studies in Material Culture*, Leicester University Press, Leicester: 125–37.

Kavanagh, G., 1990, *History Curatorship*, Leicester University Press, Leicester.

Kavanagh, G., 1993a, 'History in museums in Britain: a brief survey of trends and ideas', in Fleming, D., Paine, C. and Rhodes, J., (eds): 13–24.

Kavanagh, G., 1993b, 'The future of museum social history collecting', *Social History in Museums: Journal of the Social History Curators Group*, 20: 61–5.

Kavanagh, G., (ed.), 1994, *Museum Provision and Professionalism*, Routledge.

Kelly, F., 1994, 'If only I'd kept my ... ', *Today*, 6 August: 7.

Kennedy, M., 1996, 'Constable makes room for plates and firescreens', *Guardian*, 13 February: 7.

Kettle, M., 1996, 'Time to topple the twin towers', *Guardian*, 27 April: 23.

King, E., 1988a, *The People's Palace and Glasgow Green*, Richard Drew, Glasgow.

King, E., 1988b, 'Labour history at the People's Palace', in Bott, V., 1988, *Labour History in Museums*, Society for the Study of Labour History, Manchester: 11–16.

Knell, S. and Moore, K., forthcoming, *Carry on Collecting? Towards a Strategy for the Future of Collecting*.

Knowles, L., 1993, 'Museum of Liverpool Life', *Social History Curators Group News*, 32: 8–9.

Kulik, G. and Sims, J., 1989, 'Clarion call for criticism', *Museum News*, November/December: 52–6.

Laing, D., 'The grain of punk: an analysis of the lyrics', in McRobbie, A., 1989, *Zoot Suits and Second-Hand Dresses: An Anthology of Fashion and Music*, Macmillan.

Lee, V., 1995, 'Rolling back (some of) the years', *Guardian*, 1 September: 10.

Leon, W., 1987, 'A broader vision: exhibits that change the way that visitors look at the past', in Blatti, J., (ed.), *Past Meets Present: Essays about Historic Interpretation and Public Audiences*, Smithsonian Institution Press, Washington DC: 133–52.

Leon, W. and Rosenzweig, R., (eds), 1989, *History Museums in the United States*, University of Chicago Press, Chicago.

Lever, J., 1983, *Soccer Madness*, University of Chicago Press, Chicago.

Lewis, M., 1981, *Collecting for Fun and Profit*, Proteus Books.

London Museums Consultative Committee, 1991, *'Dingy Places with Different Kinds of Bits': An Attitudes Survey of London Museums amongst Non-visitors*, London Museums Service.

Lovatt, J., 1995, 'A People's Show *means* a People's Show', *Museological Review*, 1(2): 66–71.

Lowenthal, D., 1992, 'From patronage to populism', *Museums Journal*, March: 24–7.

Lubar, S., 1993, 'Machine politics: the political construction of technological artifacts', in Lubar, S. and Kingery, D., (eds): 197–214.

Lubar, S. and Kingery, D., (eds), 1993, *History From Things: Essays On Material Culture*, Smithsonian Institution Press, Washington DC.

McDaniel, D., 1984, 'Stop museum proliferation!', *History News*, March: 33–4.

McDaniel, G., 1982, *Hearth and Home: Preserving a People's Culture*, Temple University Press, Philadelphia.

MacDonald, G., 1988, 'Epcot Centre in museological perspective', *Muse*, 6(1): 27–37.

MacDonald, G., 1992, 'Change and challenge: museums in the information society', in Karp, I., Kreamer, C. and Lavine, S., *Museums and Communities*, Smithsonian Institution Press, Washington DC: 158–81.

MacDonald, G. and Alsford, S., 1989, *A Museum for the Global Village: The Canadian Museum of Civilization*, Canadian Museum of Civilization, Hull, Quebec.

MacDonald, G. and Alsford, S., 1995, 'Museums and theme parks: worlds in collision?', *Museum Management and Curatorship*, 14(2): 129–47.

Macquet, J., 1993, 'Objects as instruments, objects as signs', in Lubar, S. and Kingery, D., (eds): 30–40.

McRobbie, A., 1989, *Zoot Suits and Second-Hand Dresses: An Anthology of Fashion and Music*, Macmillan.

McRobbie, A., 1991, *Feminism and Youth Culture: From 'Jackie' to 'Just Seventeen'*, Macmillan.

Malbert, R., *et al.*, 1996, 'Artists as curators', *Museums Journal*, May: 25–34.

Mansfield, N., 1986, 'George Edwards and the Farmworkers Union and Norfolk and the Great War: oral history in Norfolk rural life museum', *Oral History*, 14(2): 51–8.

Marsh, G., 1984, 'Twentieth century collecting in social history', *Social History Curators Group News*, 7: 3–4.

Martin, P., 1994, 'The origins and relevance of popular collecting', *Museological Review*, 1(1): 42–5.

Martin, P., 1995, '"I've got one just like that!" collectors, museums and the community', *Museological Review*, 1(2): 86–93.

Mason, R., 1994, 'Steam buffs rail against Cossons attack', *Museums Journal*, January: 14.

Mayo, E., 1982, 'Contemporary collecting', *History News*, 37(10): 8–11.

Meltzer, D., 1981, 'Ideology and material culture', in Gould, R. and Schiffer, M., (eds), *Modern Material Culture: the Archaeology of Us*, Academic Press, New York.

Merriman, N., 1989, 'The social basis of museum and heritage visiting', in Pearce, S., (ed.), *Museum Studies in Material Culture*, Leicester University Press, Leicester: 153–71.

Merriman, N., 1991, *Beyond the Glass Case: The Past, the Heritage and the Public in Britain,* Leicester University Press, Leicester.

Middleton., V., 1990, *New Visions for Independent Museums in the UK,* Association of Independent Museums (AIM), West Sussex.

Miller, D., (ed.), 1995, *Acknowledging Consumption: A Review of New Studies*, Routledge.

Mills, E., 1995, 'People in grass houses mustn't get stoned', *Observer Review*, 5 November: 9.

Moore, K., 1993, 'Open house, open mind', *Museums Journal*, March: 19.

Moore, K., (ed.), 1994a, *Museum Management*, Leicester Readers in Museum Studies, Routledge.

Moore, K., 1994b, 'Labour history in museums: development and direction', in Pearce, S., (ed.), *Museums and the Appropriation of Culture,* vol. 4, New Research in Museum Studies, Athlone Press.

Moore, K. and Tucker, D., 1994, 'Back to basics? social history in museums', *Museums Journal*, July: 22.

Morris, D., 1981, *The Soccer Tribe*, Jonathan Cape.

Museum Management and Curatorship, 1994, Editorial, 'On babies and bath-water', 13: 123–9.

Museums Association (MA), 1991, *A National Strategy for Museums*, MA, 1991.

Museums and Galleries Commission (MGC), 1992, *Museums Matter*, MGC.

Museums and Galleries Commission (MGC), 1994, *'Towards a Government Policy for Museums': The MGC's Policy Statement and The MGC's Response to the DNH Policy Review*, MGC.

Myerscough, J., 1988, *The Economic Importance of the Arts in Britain*, Policy Studies Institute.

Nisbet, C., 1993, 'Leisure on display: an examination of current collecting and recording of music and entertainment material in museums, focusing on its use in contemporary displays' (unpublished MA thesis, University of Leicester).

Nisbet, C., 1994, 'Subject: objects', *Social History Curators Group News*, 36: 6–9.

Ormrod, D., 1994, 'Historians, objects and evidence ... what objects?', *Social History in Museums: Journal of the Social History Curators Group*, 21: 11–16.

Orna, E., *et al.*, 1993, 'Interaction: liberation or exploitation?', *Museums Journal*, February: 27–32.

Orwell, G., 1982, 'England your England', in Orwell, G., *The Lion and the Unicorn*, Penguin, Harmondsworth: 35–70.

Pavlidou, T., 1995, 'Marketing in the museum context' (unpublished MA thesis, University of Leicester).

Pearce, S., 1990, *'Objects as meaning, or narrating the past'*, in Pearce, S., (ed.), *Objects of Knowledge*, vol. 1, New Research in Museum Studies, Athlone Press.

Pearce, S., 1992, *Museums, Objects and Collections: A Cultural Study*, Leicester University Press, Leicester.

Pearce, S., 1993a, 'Artefacts as the social anthropologist sees them', in Fleming, D., Paine, C. and Rhodes, J., (eds), 1993, *Social History in Museums: A Handbook For Professionals*, HMSO: 65–72.

Pearce, S., 1993b, 'Making up is hard to do', *Museums Journal*, December: 25–7.

Pearce, S., 1994a, 'Thinking about things', in Pearce, S., (ed.), 1994b: 125–32.

Pearce, S., (ed.), 1994b, *Interpreting Objects and Collections*, Leicester Readers in Museum Studies, Routledge.

Pearce, S., 1995, *On Collecting: An Investigation into Collecting in the European Tradition*, Routledge.

Pearson, H., 1996, 'Book of love', *When Saturday Comes*, July: 6–7.

Pes, J., 1993, 'Up the Arsenal', *Social History Curators Group News*, 33: 9–11.

Porter, G., 1988, 'Putting your house in order: representations of women and domestic life', in Lumley, R., (ed.), *The Museum Time Machine*, Routledge: 102–27.

Porter, G., 1991, 'Partial truths', in Kavanagh, G., (ed.), *Museum Languages: Objects and Texts*, Leicester University Press, Leicester: 103–17.

Porter, R., 1992, 'Social history: current trends', *Social History in Museums: Journal of the Social History Curators Group*, 19: 5–13.

Prown, J., 1993, 'The truth of material culture: history or fiction?', in Lubar, S. and Kingery, D., (eds), 1993: 1–19.

Putnam, T. and Newton, C., (eds), 1990, *Household Choices*, Futures Publications.

Redhead, S., 1991, 'An era of the end, or the end of an era? Football and youth culture in Britain', in Williams, J. and Wagg, S., (eds), *British Football and Social Change*, Leicester University Press, Leicester: 145–59.

Resnicow, D., 1994, 'What is Watkins really asking?', *Curator*, 37(3), 150–1.

Rhodes, J., 1993, 'Methods of study: introduction' in Fleming, D., Paine, C. and Rhodes, J., (eds): 101–3.

Robbins, M., 1971, 'The neighborhood and the museum', *Curator*, 14(1): 63–8.

Roberts, L., 1994, 'Rebuttal to "Are museums still necessary?"', *Curator*, 37(3): 152–5.

Rollin, 1966, *England's World Cup Triumph*, Davies Books.

Ross, C., 1993, 'Great idea, even better execution?', *Social History in Museums: Journal of the Social History Curators Group*, 20: 42–6.

Ross, C., 1994, 'Watching the curators', *Social History in Museums: Journal of the Social History Curators Group*, 21: 17–22.

Rubinstein, H., 1990, 'Welcoming workers', *Museum News*, November/December: 39–42.

Russell, D., 1990, 'What is popular culture?', *Social History in Museums: Journal of the Social History Curators Group*, 17: 5–10.

Schlereth, T., 1980, 'American material culture technique: historical museum exhibit review', in Schlereth, T., (ed.), *Artifacts and the American Past*, American Association for State and Local History, Nashville, Tennessee: 233–7.

Schlereth, T., (ed.), 1989a, *Material Culture Studies in America,* American Association for State and Local History, Nashville, Tennessee.

Schlereth, T., 1989b, 'Material culture studies in America, 1876–1976', in Schlereth, T., (ed.), 1989a.

Schlereth, T., 1989c, 'Museum exhibition reviews: introduction', *Journal of American History*, 76 (1): 192–5.

Schlereth, T., 1989d, 'History museums and material culture', in Leon, W. and Rosenzweig, R., (eds), 1989, *History Museums in the United States*, University of Chicago Press, Chicago: 294–320.

Schroeder, F., (ed.), 1981, *Twentieth-Century Popular Culture in Museums and Libraries*, Bowling Green University Popular Press, Bowling Green, Ohio.

Schuster, J., 1995, 'The public interest in the art museum's public', in Pearce, S., (ed.), *Art in Museums*, vol. 5, New Research in Museum Studies, Athlone Press.

Seddon, P., (ed.), 1995, *A Football Compendium: A Comprehensive Guide to the Literature of Association Football*, British Library.

Shaw, J., 1985, 'Museums: an obsolete medium?', *Museum Professionals Group News*, 21: 1–4.

Shiach, M., 1989, *Discourse on Popular Culture: Class, Gender and History in Cultural Analysis, 1730 to the Present*, Blackwell, Oxford.

Smith, G., 1994, 'In off the post: Chelsea 1973/4' in Hornby, N., (ed.), *My Favourite Year: A Collection of New Football Writing*, Gollancz/Witherby.

Smith, G. and Sherwood, A., 1995, 'Secrets of a woman's bedroom', *FHM: For Him Magazine*, January/February: 70–3.

Sola, T., 1991, 'Museums and curatorship: the role of theory', in Kavanagh, G., (ed.), *The Museums Profession: Internal and External Relations*, Leicester University Press, Leicester: 125–35.

Sola, T., 1992a, 'Museum professionals: the endangered species', in Boylan, P., (ed.), *Museums 2000*, Routledge: 101–13.

Sola, T., 1992b, 'The future of museums and the role of museology', *Museum Management and Curatorship*, 11: 393–400.

Sotto, E., 1994, *When Teaching Becomes Learning: A Theory and Practice of Teaching*, Cassell.

Stam, D., 1993, 'The informed muse: the implications of 'The New Museology' for museum practice', *Museum Management and Curatorship*, 12: 267–83.

Strinati, D., 1995, *An Introduction to Theories of Popular Culture*, Routledge.

Sturgis, M., 1992, 'Rich legacy for the 70s generation', *Independent on Sunday*, 29 November: 30.

Sudjic, D., 1996, 'The spiralling galleries', *Guardian*, 16 February: 5.

Suggitt, M., 1989, 'Reading the illegible', *Social History in Museums: Journal of the Social History Curators Group*, 17: 3–4.

Suggitt, M., 1990, 'Emissaries from the toy cupboard', *Museums Journal*, December: 30–3.

Suggitt, M., 1994a, 'Desperately seeking synthesis', *Social History in Museums: Journal of the Social History Curators Group*, 21: 5-10.

Suggitt, M., 1994b, 'Doctors in taste', *Social History in Museums: Journal of the Social History Curators Group*, 21: 26–31.

Sullivan, R., 1993, 'Lessons for the ruling class', *Museum News*, May/June: 54–5, 70–1.

Swank, S., 1992, 'Muddling in a bygone era', *Museum News*, July/August: 70–3.

Sykes, H., 1993, 'The representation of cultural diversity in history museums' (unpublished MA thesis, University of Leicester).

Taylor, R., 1992, *Football and its Fans*, Leicester University Press, Leicester.

Thompson, E.P., 1963, *The Making of the English Working Class*, Penguin, Harmondsworth.

Ticher, M., 1996, 'Review: *The Football Imagination*', *When Saturday Comes*, May: 22.

Tressell, R., 1965, *The Ragged Trousered Philanthropists*, Panther.

Trustram, M., 1990, 'The National Museum of Labour History', *Social History in Museums: Journal of the Social History Curators Group*, 18: 6–9.

Trustram, M., 1992, 'A miner celebration', *Museums Journal*, May: 25–6.

Trustram, M., 1993, 'The Museum of Liverpool Life', *Social History Curators Group News*, 31: 4–5.

Tucker, D., 1993, 'A traditional view or a radical re-think?', *Social History Curators Group News*, 32: 6–8.

Tucker, D., 1994, 'Response to Helen White', *Social History Curators Group News*, 34: 3–4.

Turner, G., 1990, *British Cultural Studies: An Introduction*, Unwin Hyman.

van Lakerfeld, C., 1994, 'Sensitivities on display: dealing with controversial subjects in a museological context', *Social History in Museums: Journal of the Social History Curators Group*, 21: 32–5.

Wallace, M., 1995, 'Changing media, changing messages', in Hooper-Greenhill, E., (ed.), *Museum, Media, Message*, Routledge: 107–23.

Walter, T., 1991, 'The mourning after Hillsborough', *Sociological Review*, 39(3): 599–626.

Watkins, C., 1994, 'Are museums still necessary?', *Curator*, 37(1): 25–35.

Washburn, W., 1968, 'Are museums necessary?', *Museum News*, October: 9–10.

Weil, S., 1983, *Beauty and the Beasts: On Museums, Art, the Law, and the Market*, Smithsonian Institution Press, Washington DC.

Weil, S., 1990, *Rethinking the Museum and Other Meditations*, Smithsonian Institution Press, Washington DC.

Weil, S., 1995, *A Cabinet of Curiosities: Inquiries into Museums and their Prospects*, Smithsonian Institution Press, Washington DC.

West, B., 1988, 'The making of the English working past: a critical view of the Ironbridge Gorge Museum', in Lumley, R., (ed.), *The Museum Time Machine*, Routledge: 36–62.

When Saturday Comes, Editorial 'War of words' 1996, June: 4–5.

White, H., 1993, 'Reply to David Tucker', *Social History Curators Group News*, 33: 3–4.

Whittaker, J., 1994, 'Editorial', *Social History in Museums: Journal of the Social History Curators Group*, 21: 3–4.

Wicken, O., 1992, 'Scarf ace', *When Saturday Comes*, November: 23.

Wilkinson, P., 1989a, 'That's Entertainment: popular culture in Hull', *Social History in Museums: Journal of the Social History Curators Group*, 17: 35 40.

Wilkinson, P., 1989b, *That's Entertainment!*, Hull City Museums and Art Galleries, Hull.

Williams, R., 1988, *Keywords*, Fontana.

168

References

Willis, P., 1990, *Common Culture: Symbolic Work at Play in the Everyday Cultures of the Young*, Open University Press, Milton Keynes.

Wilson, D., 1989, *The British Museum: Purpose and Politics*, British Museum Publications.

Wilson, D., 1992, 'National museums', in Thompson, J., (ed.), *Manual of Curatorship*, Museums Association/Butterworth: 81–5.

Windsor, J., 1992, 'The junk they serve up with food', *Independent*, 5 September: 37.

Windsor, J., 1994, 'Identity parades', in Elsner, J. and Cardinal, R., (eds), *The Cultures of Collecting*, Reaktion Books: 49–67.

Wolf, T., 1990, *Managing a Nonprofit Organization*, Prentice Hall, New York.

Wolverhampton Art Gallery and Museum, 1992, *Thunderbirds are Go! The Worlds of Gerry Anderson*, Wolverhampton Art Gallery and Museum, Wolverhampton.

Woroncow, B., 1989, 'Breaking down the barriers: approaches to interdisciplinary displays', *Museum Professionals Group Transactions*, 24: 11–14.

Wright, N., 1993, 'All together now', *Museums Journal*, February: 23.

Name index

Subject index